בס״ד

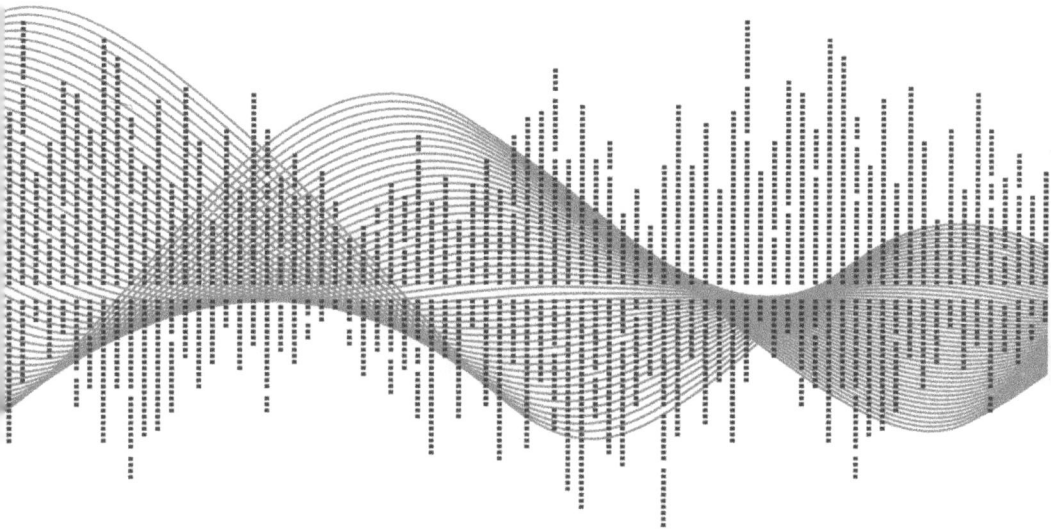

SOUND AND
VIBRATION

TUNING INTO THE ECHOES OF CREATION

RAV DOVBER PINSON

RAV DOVBER PINSON

SOUND
&
VIBRATION

TUNING INTO THE
ECHOES OF CREATION

THE JEWISH MEDITATION SERIES

THE EXPERIENCE & PRACTICE OF KABBALAH

IYYUN PUBLISHING

IN DEDICATION TO

משה אהרן שיחי'

MOZES STASZEWSKI

A
salomon foundation
PROJECT

IN LOVING MEMORY

·········· SARA BAS SARA ··········

SHIRLEY FRYSH

שרה בת שרה ע״ה

MAY HER MEMORY BE A BLESSING

CHESTON & LARA MIZEL

LOS ANGELES, CALIFORNIA

TABLE OF CONTENTS

PART ONE

PART TWO

PRACTICES

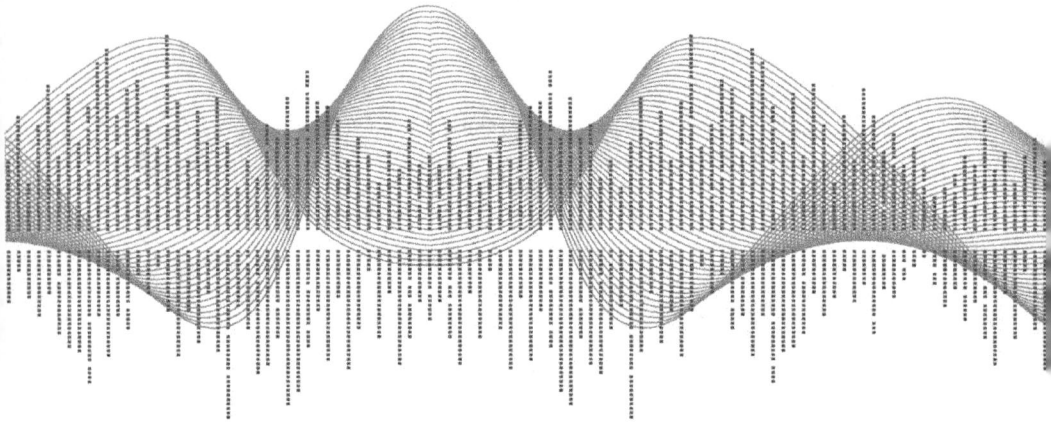

The practices in this book, as well as in our previous books, Breathing & Quieting the Mind and Visualization & Imagery, are very subtle and deep.

In order for them to be truly transformative and beneficial, they should be approached through *Kedushah* / holiness and *Teharah* / purity, and a total commitment to the way of *Torah* and *Mitzvos*.

Before attempting these practices, we would recommend you prepare yourself by reciting a few chapters of *Tehilim* / Psalms, immersing yourself in a *Mikvah*, giving *Tzedakah* / charity, and so forth.

OPENING

....

THE POWER
OF SOUND

TO BE HUMAN IS TO COMMUNICATE, CONVERSE AND DIALOGUE. AN ESSENTIAL DISTINCTION BETWEEN HUMAN AND ANIMAL IS THE MASTERY OF COMPLEX AND CONCEPTUAL LANGUAGE. Of course, animals 'speak' to each other through various sounds and gestures, but it is the human being, referred to by the Sages as a *M'daber* / speaker, who epitomizes the power and precision of speech. And yet, we cannot say what we have not heard. We can only give voice to the sounds, words and concepts with which we are familiar.

The defining feature of what distinguishes us as human is therefore founded primarily upon our ability to listen [Maharal, *Chidushei Agados*, Kidushin, 22a]. By listening, we learn to speak, and then to engage in dialogue. The ear is the first fully operating sensory organ in a fetus; within the first four months of pregnancy, a baby has already developed functioning ears. As such, long before children can speak, they are able to recognize the various sounds they hear, starting with the soothing prenatal sound of their mother's voice.

The distinctly human ability to have meaningful dialogue is initially learned and practiced in utero. Between mother and child, a call-and-response pattern is gradually established whereby the fetus begins to expect and wait for the sound of its mother, then hears her voice, and is soothed. Similarly, at a certain point the fetus will also begin to communicate certain rudimentary needs and emotions, through various kicks and burps. Once this begins, the mother, too, will wait expectantly for the next pre-linguistic communique. This interplay of expression and acknowledgment is a precursor to more complex forms of dialogue that will develop as the child masters language. The fact that our sense of hearing is the first sense to develop shows the fundamental role of sound in human experience.

Our relationship with sound post-utero is also unique and a bit different than our relationship with the other senses such as smell and taste. For instance, we can passively take in different smells and tastes, but we cannot actively and consciously manufacture them. However, we can passively hear sounds and actively create sounds on cue. The underlying spiritual reason for this is, on a fundamental level, we *are* sound, movement and vibration.

SOUND AS A BRIDGE
BETWEEN SELF & WORLD

Rhythm affects us very deeply because our entire being is alive with pulses, heartbeats, breath cycles and brain waves, and the dynamic nature of matter itself on an atomic level. On a physical level, we are literally vibrating at every moment. Our souls, as well, are in a constant state of rhythmic 'running and returning'. We rhythm; we are sound.

From this perspective, everything that exists is sound, as everything has a unique vibration. On a macro and micro physical level, everything that moves has an easily identifiable pulse and pattern. The entire planet, and everything in it, is vibrating at different rates — every stone, every leaf, every drop of water, every animal and every person. Every atom has a nucleus that is surrounded by electrons, which are spinning at a speed of 600 miles per second. This means that even things that don't seem to be alive are in motion and vibration, however imperceptibly.

Motion creates frequencies. A frequency is the speed at which that particular material vibrates. Wherever there is vibration and frequency, there is sound. All of Creation is therefore producing sound, whether audible or inaudible. Sound waves move at about 770 miles per hour, almost a million times slower than the speed of light. The frequency of vibration that most humans are able to audibly detect is 20 hertz to 20,000 hertz, although sounds are best heard in the range of 1,000 hertz to 5,000 hertz, and voiced speech of a typical adult human being is between 85 to 255 hertz. Although human beings do not hear frequencies that are lower or higher than these, it does not mean they do not exist. We have developed instruments that detect frequencies and tones that are far beyond our capacity to hear, such as the frequency of an electron revolving around its nucleus.

On a deeper level, everything in the world is created and sustained by Divine sound and resonance. The physical vibrations and movements of this world reflect spiritual movements and vibrations emanating from within the 'stillness' and Oneness of the *Ohr Ein Sof* / Infinite Light out into the world. All of Creation is therefore quite literally an echo of the Song of the Creator.

We are created by means of sound, and can create sound — because we *are* sound. With the tool of sound, we can let go of our egoistic dependencies and defense mechanisms, and merge our vibration into the cosmic sonic stream. We can tune ourselves to resonate along with Creation in perfect time and harmony, and to absorb through our ears and even skin the sounds and vibrations of the world into our own frequency.

We can use sound to focus and enhance mental activity or to quiet the mind, to release positive emotions or defuse negative experiences, to induce sleep or to rouse ourselves from sleep. We can listen to sound, play with sound, manipulate it according to our design, and even unify with sound and 'ride' it into an experience of merging with the Source of All Sound.

Throughout this text, we will delve much deeper into the subtleties of the ideas introduced above. What does it really mean that we are sound, and that the entire world is filled with sound? How can our 'microcosmic' sound-body resonate with the cosmic Source of All Sound? How can we navigate the challenges inherent in the fact that we become 'entrained' to our surroundings by means of the sounds we hear? What are the guiding principles and best practices for incorporating sound into our path of personal and spiritual development? All this and much more will be covered in the following pages. Before we begin, let us establish a frame of reference for this volume as a whole.

FINDING YOUR UNIQUE PATH

No two people are alike. Knowing your distinct and unique self is the first and most important step in any type of meaningful, developmental or transcendental experience. For *you* to experience the experience, you must know *who* and *what* you are. For instance, some people are more visually-oriented and some are more auditory. Is it easier for you to learn through visual means or auditory means? This self-knowledge will help you on your path, for there are paths that emphasize imagery, and paths that emphasize sound. A person who is naturally inclined towards visual stimuli may struggle with relating or surrendering to the power of sound. So, too, one who is more sensitive to sound may have trouble with visualization.

It is important, before embarking upon any particular path of learning or practice, to reflect upon your own deep structures in order to acknowledge any sensory biases or unconscious preferences you may have at the outset. This will enable you to have compassion on yourself during any difficulties over the course of your learning, and to push yourself to grow beyond your comfort zones.

In previous texts, we explored basic breathing techniques (*Breathing & Quieting the Mind*) and visualization practices (*Visualization and Imagery: Harness the Power of the Mind's Eye*). In the present text, we will expand upon the transformative power and spiritual potential of sound and vibration. Sound has a great effect upon us. Our sense of hearing quite literally provides us with our sense of balance in this world.

Our inner ear is responsible for maintaining our physical equilibrium; it takes the sensory information received through the various organs of the body and integrates this information, informing the body where it is in relationship to the earth and gravity. A person who has an earache can have trouble walking a straight line. But the power of hearing and sound goes far beyond the physiological functions, as mysterious and mind-boggling as they are in and of themselves. Sound can also influence and impact us on the deepest and highest levels of our being, balancing our higher and lower selves into perfect harmony. Sound even has the capacity to initiate utterly transcendental experiences which have the power to take us well beyond the rigid definitions and divisions of the self, and connect us, in harmony, to the Source.

In the following chapters, the basic power of sound and various spiritual practices that utilize sound will be explored. These practices range from the very practical and ethical to the more mystical and transcendental.

The ethical path of self-development, which encourages refining the expression of one's *Midos* / character traits in relation to others, is the way we expand and grow 'horizontally'. Through this path, we can begin to include and embrace more of ourselves. By extension, we become more embracing and less judgmental of others.

However, the path of *Sheleimus* / wholeness is both horizontal and vertical. To activate our full physical, emotional, mental and spiritual potential, we need to expand into a 'width' of being, and also to climb higher. We need to ensure that our *Midos* / character traits are in order, that we are *Mentchen* / wholesome, ethical human beings — having horizontal 'breadth' — before attempting to climb higher on the narrow spiritual ladder. After we explore the ethical practices that utilize sound, we will also delve into rarified mental practices that allow us to access spiritual and mystical experiences available through sound.

We will touch upon the practice of chanting, repetitive *Nigunim* / melodies and music in general. The Biblical prophets harnessed music and rhythm to induce and inspire prophetic consciousness. When the prophet *Shmuel* / Samuel sent king *Shaul* / Saul off to prophesize, he told him: "As you approach the town, you will meet a procession of prophets coming down from the high place with lyres, timbrels, pipes and harps being played before them, and they will be prophesying. The Spirit of Hashem will come powerfully upon you, and you will prophesy with them, and you will be changed into a different person" [*Shmuel* 1, 10:5-6]. Elisha, a later prophet, says: "Now play for me the instruments of music... and when the musician will play... the hand of Hashem will be affixed upon me" [*Melachim* 2, 3:15].

Music has the power to transform the prophet's ordinary consciousness into more imaginal and expansive states [Rambam, *Hilchos Yesodei HaTorah* 7:4. Rabbi Yitzchak Armah, *Akeidas Yitzchak*, Shemos, 35]. In the language of contemporary scientific theory, the auditory stimuli of music activate the brain's limbic system, triggering a release of pain-killing endorphins. This induces a quieting of the anxious rational mind. As the state of tranquility and transcendence deepen, their soul untangles from their body. When the music ceases, the prophet is left in a deep state of *Deveikus* / cleaving and unification with the Source of Life. We will explore these ideas in greater detail later on.

Methods of sacred chanting which include breath control provide us with another spiritual path of sound. Developed by the 13th Century Spanish Kabbalist, Rabbi Avraham Abulafia, and based on esoteric teachings of the Sefer Yetzirah and early German Kabbalists, this genre of practices makes up a particularly advanced and complex pedagogy to achieve ecstatic and prophecy-like states of consciousness.

R. Abulafia teaches a system where one chants various letters with specific respiratory patterns while making head movements corresponding to the vowel being chanted, until one reaches a higher state of consciousness.

This particular practice deserves its own treatment and will be further expanded, G-d willing, in a future text in which we will explore other advanced practices and exercises where our ambition is nothing less than total *Deveikus /* experiential unity with the Divine.

Again, there are people who are sensitive to sight who do not perceive the subtleties of sound, and there are others who are not connected to visualization but are highly responsive to sound and vibration. The previous text in this series, *Visualization and Imagery*, is meant for the visually-inclined meditator, or for one who wants to develop their visual capacity. The current text is written for those who already have a connection to sound, or want to deepen their connection to its power.

We should note that most people are sufficiently skilled at both faculties and can gain much by developing proficiency in harnessing them together, in a fusion of senses. This can be called 'activating all aspects of the tree', employing the roots, shoots, trunk, branches, leaves, fruits and seeds of sense perception, sequentially as well as in unison.

In order for a visual or auditory practice to create a significant shift in consciousness, we need to engage the others senses, too, as fully as we can. Using the example of visualization, not only should we conjure up an image of what we are trying to achieve, but we should also strive to imagine hearing, smelling, tasting and touching it as well. Ideally, every practice should be a full-body immersive experience, as it is most impactful to involve the whole self and all bodily faculties and powers. When we are listening to, or generating, contemplative sound, we should also visualize an image, if possible, and fuse our power of imagination, along with all the rest of our senses, with the experience the sound is evoking.

It is good to keep in mind that no two people experience the Divine in the same way. Some people can find G-d sitting at the beach at sunset, while for others that experience does nothing. Some people find G-d through textual contemplation. Some people find G-d in love. Some people find G-d in silence, and some in prayer. The first question one should ask in the quest to find and connect to G-d should be: "How do I find and connect to myself? What makes me feel most alive? What helps me feel most connected and inspired? Is it vivid visualization? Or do sound, music and vibration speak to me more clearly?" Once you reflect upon and acknowledge your preferences and nature, you will be better equipped to cultivate an experience of connection to your soul, and ultimately to your Source.

And now, before venturing any further into the actual sound-based practices, it is necessary to say a few words about the power of sound in general, as well as about the art of truly listening and being open to hear the Sound of the Creator within Creation. This will establish a common conceptual foundation to help contextualize any further practices and experiences that will be discussed.

///////////////////////////////////////

CHAPTER 1

···

HEARING THE INNER SOUND OF CREATION

THE WORLD WAS CREATED WITH THE ASARA MA'AMOROS / TEN UTTERANCES, WHICH LITERALLY MEANS TEN DIVINE SOUNDS OR VIBRATIONS.

As the Sages mention, of course Hashem could have created the world in a *Ma'amar Echad* / single Divine utterance, and yet Hashem chose to speak the world of multiplicity into being through a series of multiple 'sayings' [*Pirkei Avos*, 5:1].

The Torah describes Creation as a process of Ten Divine Utterances, which give rise to the world as we know it. It is through these primary and primordial utterances that Creation first emerges and is ultimately manifest. "G-d said: 'Let there be light', and there was light" [*Bereishis*, 1:3]. Each time there was a Divine saying, a new dimension of Creation came into being. From this deceptively simple statement describing Hashem's creative process, we learn that speech, and by extension, that sound, too, are essentially creative.

In the beginning of the Torah, which describes the Genesis of Creation, the phrase, "and G-d said…" is mentioned only nine times. What about the tenth utterance? The Sages point out that there is a 'hidden' tenth utterance. This is the first word in the Torah, *Bereishis*, meaning "With (or, In) the Beginning" — as the Sages say, "Bereishis is also a Ma'amar" [*Rosh Hashanah*, 32a. "This is the hidden utterance;" *Maharsha*, ad loc.]. In other words, the Ma'amar Echad is thus the word *Bereishis* itself. [According to the *Zohar* 3, 11b and *Pirkei d'Rebbe Eliezer*, "Let there be Light" is considered the Ma'amar Echad, the *Klali* / comprehensive light or utterance that contains all of manifest, revealed reality.]

Everything — all of history and all of Creation — was essentially created in raw potential with the *Ma'amar Echad* / the first or unified utterance [Rashi, *ad loc.*]. Everything initially existed as one unified whole within this Ma'amar Echad. And then, gradually, through the process of the other nine utterances, manifest reality became increasingly individuated and atomized — from lights, stars, plants and animals, to humans, and so forth.

Every utterance thus has a minimum of two stages. First, it begins as a unified, undifferentiated *Kol* / voice or sound coming from deep within, from the lungs, so-to-speak. This is the level of the 'utterance' prior to articulation or specific meaning. As this primordial sound passes through the throat and then to the tongue, palate, teeth and lips, a distinct *Dibbur* / word, is formed. The Ma'amar Echad is the all-inclusive Kol that precedes the individual Dibbur. It is the primordial sound that comes before speech.

Speech uses the building blocks of letters. Letters create words, and words create reality. In this way, the Sages are revealing to us that hidden deep within the 'nine utterances', giving rise to the multiplicity of created reality, is the Ma'amar Echad, the One Sound that contains and conceals all of reality as one unified whole.

The phrase *Bereishis Bara Elokim, Es…* literally translates as, "In (or, With) the Beginning, G-d created the…" [*Bereishis*, 1:1]. Here, the word *Es* is interpreted in its most basic grammatical sense, as the modifier of the proper noun that follows it; in this case, it is "…(*Es*) the Heavens and (*Es*) the Earth". There are, of course, alternative interpretations.

Bereishis Bara Elokim Es..., can also be translated as, "With *Chochmah* / wisdom [*Targum Yonason* translates the word *Reishis* as wisdom], G-d created *E-S*..." In this *lettriste* translation, the word *E-S* is not interpreted as a grammatical modifier that is linguistically dependent on the noun which follows it, but as a word in its own right. To complicate, or poeticize, matters further, the word *E-S* is also understood here as an acronym made up of the first and last letters of the Hebrew alphabet, meaning 'from Alef to Tav'. According to this interpretation, the first creation, even before the creation of the Heavens and the Earth, was that of the 22 letters of the Aleph-Beis. Preceding everything else were the primary building blocks or vibrations of speech, communication and creativity.

Another allusion to the preliminary creation of the 22 letters is found hidden within the same first verse of the Torah. There are seven words in the full verse. Numerically, the sum of all the first letters of these seven words is 22. The world is rooted in the 22 letters, which in turn is rooted in the *Ma'amar Echad* / the One Sound of all Creation.

From a different perspective, there are six Hebrew letters in addition to the basic 22. These are the five letters in the Aleph-Beis which change graphically at the end of a word [*MaNTzePaCh* or Mem, Nun, Tzadik, Peh and Chaf], and one letter called 'the missing letter' [*Sefer haTemuna*, quoted by the Radbaz, *Magen Dovid*, Os Shin] — identified by some as a 'hid-

den Aleph' [See: *Siddur Admur haZaken*, Kavanos Tekias Shofar].
The Hebrew word *Ko'ach* / power or potential equals 28,
alluding to the generative power and creative potentiality of
these 28 letters. This idea is also alluded to in the first verse
of the Torah, as it is comprised of 28 letters.

The world of multiplicity begins with sound and then
speech, which is the first expression and externalization
of the way the world exists in potential, in the 'thought'
of Hashem. The second word of the Torah, *Bara*, normally
translated as 'created', comes from the word *Bar* / outside or
external. Therefore, we can read the first verse as, 'In the beginning, G-d *externalized...*' This existential externalization
process begins with a swelling of sound and spiritual vibration, which gives rise to the initial formation of letters, and
finally the words that give birth to all energy and matter.

The grand metaphor for the emergence of Creation is
speech. In other words: the fruit of Creation manifests out
of its root in Divine speech.

Let us understand this a little bit deeper from a different angle. "Hashem looked into the Torah and created the world"
[*Medrash Rabbah*, Bereishis, 1:1]. Here again, we see that letters
are the fundamental building blocks of Creation. Additionally, "With 32 mystical paths of Wisdom, Hashem, the
G-d of Israel, the Living G-d...engraved and created His
universe... [These 32 paths are the] Ten Sefiros and the 22

Foundation Letters" [*Sefer Yetzirah*, 1:1-2]. If we are able to understand the spiritual mechanics of the letters — their power, structure and depth — we would then attain enhanced creative powers. It is for this reason that the main architect of the *Mishkan* / Tent of Meeting in the Desert was Betzalel, whose name literally means, '*in the shadow of G-d*'. Betzalel was chosen for this most cosmic of creative projects specifically because, "Betzalel knew the combinations of letters that the Creator used to create the world" [*Berachos*, 55a]. This knowledge gave Betzalel the wisdom and insight necessary to construct a finite container that could paradoxically conceal and reveal the Infinite Presence of Hashem.

THE SOUND OF THE LETTERS

There are 22 letters in the Aleph Beis. Each letter can be analyzed and understood from a myriad of perspectives including its geometric shape, its numerical value, the meaning of its name, or its position within the sequence of the 22 letters, to name a few.

Take the letter Aleph for example. Its general shape is a point above and a point below with a diagonal line in between connecting them. Numerically, Aleph equals 1, as well as 1,000 (*Eleph*), thus it represents the paradox of ultimate unity within multiplicity. The word 'Aleph' comes from the same root as the word *Aluf* / Master or *Alephcha* / teach.

Aleph, a silent letter, is also the first letter of the Aleph Beis, showing that it is the quiet cornerstone of Creation.

In our context, we are primarily interested in the sounds of the letters when they are expressed and vocalized. Regarding the Aleph, our question then becomes: How does the letter Aleph sound when it is vocalized, and what might we learn from that? [See Ramak, *Ohr Yakar*, Shelach.]

Before a letter is sounded, all that exists is its shape. This is the letter on the page or the scroll. Once a letter is sounded, it takes on completely different dimensions. The letter in vibration leaps beyond the script into the realm of time, communication and comprehension. Vocalizing any of the 22 letters inscribes their shape upon the parchment of time. The 22 letters of the Aleph Beis are a perfect illustration of this dynamic unity that exists between shape/space and sound/time, everywhere in Creation.

Using sophisticated instruments that transform sound waves into images, a scientific study demonstrated that the vocalization of most of the letters of the Aleph Beis can generate a wave pattern very similar to the graphic shape of the letter. When a person vocalized the letter Beis, for example, the sound created an image resembling the shape of a Beis. This discovery is perhaps related to a rabbinic teaching regarding *Matan Torah* / the Giving of the Torah at Mount Sinai. During Matan Torah, when the deepest sound frequencies of Creation were revealed, it says that, "The entire nation *saw the sounds*" [*Shemos*, 10:15]. This could mean (according to Rabbi Akiva) that the Israelites saw what is ordinarily heard, and they heard what is normally seen" [*Rashi*, from the *Mechilta* at loc. *Targum Yonoson Ben Uziel*].

What does it mean that they "saw what is ordinarily heard"? How can sound itself be 'seen'? On one level this could imply synesthesia, the blurring or translation of the senses from one to another, so that one sees the energy or even the meaning of a spoken word. However, this idea could also be understood on a natural level, similar to the way in which one's spoken words create a visible effect in the air when it is cold outside [R. Bachya Ibn Pakudah, *Toras haNefesh* 3. R. Menachem *Recanti*, Parshas Vayera. R. David Ben Zimra, *Magen Dovid*, Os Tes. R. Meir Ben Gabbai, *Tolaas Yaakov*, Sod Tefilah Meumad]. This could mean that at the giving of the Torah, a thick, dark cloud descended upon Mount Sinai and it caused the words of Revelation to be 'seen' within the clouds. The Divine sounds of revelation that were, according to some commentators, perhaps spoken through the lips of Moshe, generated a tapestry of visible sound waves seen by the Israelites [*Amud haAvodah* (Kasuv), Kuntreisim L'Chochmas Emes].

'Seeing the sounds' could also be understood to mean that the sounds of the 'Divine Utterances' of the Ten Commandments became the actual engravings in the *Luchos / Tablets*. [See *Ohr Hachayim*, Shemos, 20:1. Devarim, 4:12. *Zohar* 2,

83a]. In this sense, the spoken letters and words of Torah expressed themselves in a visually relatable and materially impactful way, engraving their vibrations into stone for a more potent effect.

THE 22 LETTERS / VIBRATIONS

Sefer Yetzirah, an ancient and mysterious book of early Kabbalah, breaks down the 22 letters into three groups: a) three 'mother' letters, b) seven 'double' letters, and c) twelve 'simple' letters.

The three Mother Letters are Aleph (א) Mem (מ) and Shin (ש). These are the primary sounds of Creation:

א — Aleph is the vocal space that is created before the sounding of a vowel, for example the quiet opening of the throat necessary to initiate an 'ah' sound. Aleph is *the silent beginning of all sound.*

מ — Mem is sounded as the mouth is closed (the *mmm* sound). Mem is *the 'end' of all sound.*

ש — Shin (the *shhh* sound) is the consonant most humans use to create quiet. [See *Rashi*, Bamidbar, 13:30.] It is thus *the synthesis of sound and silence.*

Our world was created with the letter Hei [*Menachos*, 29b]. Hei is the simple sound of *Hevel* / breath, , and thus the beginning of the movement of Divine speech and creation.

["The annunciation of the Hei is merely a type of, breath" *Tanya*, Igeres HaTeshuvah, 4]. It is associated with the sound of a person deeply sighing from tiredness [*Amud Ha'avodah*, Kuntreisim l'Chochmas Emes]. Aleph, on the other hand, is understood as the sound of *speech* — as in *Amar* / said. This is where *Kol* / voice begins to become *Dibbur* / speech. The Hei of breath and the Aleph of speech go hand in hand; breath is the root of speech [*Sefer haMa'amarim*, Tav-Reish-Tzadik-Tes, *Karov Hashem*], speech is the fruit of breath. Sequentially, first there is the movement of breath, then the vibrations of voice, and then the intention of speech.

The *Ah* of Aleph is a *Kol Pashut* / a simple, wholesome sound . In a sense, it is the intermediary between breath and actual language [*Siddur Admur HaZaken*, Kavanos haMikvah, p. 314]. An older Medrash teaches that the three letters of the word Aleph (Aleph, Lamed, Pei) make up an acronym for the phrase *Eftecha Lashon Peh* / I will open the language of my mouth. [*Osyos d'Rebbe Akiva*, Aleph]. In other words, the Aleph opens up the possibility for language, thus silently creating the beginning of speech.

Every sound begins in the open space of the Aleph. As the Baal Shem Tov teaches: "There is no word, big or small, that does not contain an Aleph" [*Degel Machena Ephrayim*, Likutim]. Aleph is the root of the letters of Creation [Leshem, *Hakdamos v'Shearim*, Sha'ar Hapone Kadim, 6].

As we mentioned, Shin is the universal sound used to create quiet, which synthesizes sound and silence. Without the letter Shin, the two Mother Letters, Aleph and Mem together, representing the beginning and end of sound, form the sound *A-m*. This sound is associated with the *Koach* / power of *Tum'ah* / the impure, stuck or blocked energy of the world of separation and duality. [See Yerushalmi, *Sanhedrin*, 6:6, regarding the sound of *A-m* and witchcraft.] Duality and opposites are part of the natural world, where things appear pitted against each other. This is the Aleph and the Mem without the Shin. With the letter Shin included, the synthesizing third letter in the equation, that unites sound (Aleph) and silence (Mem), the combination is one of *Kedusha* / holiness and unity. We could say it 'silences' the sound of *Tum'ah*.

LETTERS & ELEMENTS

The letter Aleph is connected with the element of *Avir* / air or wind, which corresponds to the middle column of *Sephiros* / attributes, and thus balances opposites. Mem is associated with the element of *Mayim* / water, which corresponds to the right column attribute of boundless giving. Shin is aligned with the element of *Aish* / fire, the left column attribute of defined boundaries. The element of Earth is connected to all three Mother Letters, as earth is subtly included within the other three elements.

SEVEN DOUBLE LETTERS

Beis, Gimel, Dalet, Chaf, Pei, Reish and Tav (ב,ג,ד,כ,פ,ר,ת), are the seven Double Letters. The reason these are called Double Letters is that they each have both a harsh and soft pronunciation.*

The first three letters, Beis, Gimel and Dalet, together spell the word *Beged* / garment. The other four letters are Chaf, Pei, Reish and Tav. These letters together spell the words *Kapores* / covering, or *Paroches* / curtain; both of which are items in the Temple that served as a partition, covering and separating what is within the Ark or between the Holy and the Holy of Holies.

---

* The letter Beis can be voiced as either Beis in the hard pronunciation, or as Veis in the softer variation. The letter Gimel can either be *Gimel* with a hard 'G', or in the soft pronunciation *Jimel*, as some Yemenites pronounce it. The same is true with the letter Dalet, which can be pronounced with the hard sound of *Dalet*, or the softer sound of *Tha-led*, as many Sefardim do. Parenthetically, our Sages teach that when saying the Shema, one should extend the word *Echad* / one at the end. If the sound of the Daled at the end of *Echad* is only pronounced harshly as Daled, it is difficult or perhaps impossible to extend the 'D' sound [and thus it should be done in one's thoughts [*Shulchan Aruch haRav*, Orach Chayim, 61:7]; yet, the softer 'Th' sound is much easier to elongate and makes much more sense in this context. Chaf is pronounced as either *Kaf* or *Chaf*. Pei is either *Pei* or *Fei*. Reish can also be pronounced two ways, as an 'R', the way most of the world pronounces it, or as a rolled 'R' (such as in Arabic and Spanish) as done by certain Yemenite Jews. Finally, Tav is either *Tav* or *Sav*.

Something that serves as a medium between two elements needs to contain both aspects, so that it can build a bridge and create the unity. Garments, the Kapores, and the Paroches are all items which serve as partitions between two different areas or entities. A partition is at once a separator and an interface that joins and unites different spaces. These Double Letters each allude to this dual function of separating and uniting.

These seven Double Letters also represent the primary spiritual vibrations and energies of the Seven observable planets. Beis is connected with Saturn, Gimel to Jupiter, Dalet to Mars, Chaf to the Sun, Pei to Venus, Reish to Mercury, and Tav with the Moon. The other, more distant planets, which are not visible to the naked eye, such as Uranus, Pluto and Neptune, were considered by the ancients to have little astrological influence.

The seven observable planets are connected with the seven days of the week. In the English language we have a linguistic remnant of the ancient Greek system: Sunday is connected with the sun ('Sun-day'), Monday is connected with the moon ('Moon-day'), and Saturday is connected with Saturn ('Saturn-day'). This is based on the idea that the sun is 'dominant' during the first hour on Sunday. During the first hour of Monday, the moon is dominant, and during the first hour of Saturday, Saturn is dominant. In other languages, such as French, the other days of the week are also named after the planets: Tuesday is called *Mardi*, from the planet Mars; Wednesday is *Mercredi* referring to Mercury; Thursday is called *Jeudi*, from the planet Jupiter; and Friday is called *Vendredi* from Venus.

Sefer Yetzirah offers an alternate correlation of planets to the days of the week [4, Mishnah 8-14]: Sunday/Moon; Monday/Mars; Tuesday/Sun; Wednesday/Venus; Thursday/Mercury; Friday/Saturn; Shabbos/Jupiter.

THE TWELVE SIMPLE LETTERS

After the three Mother Letters and the seven Double Letters, the remaining twelve letters — Hei, Vav, Zayin, Ches, Tes, Yud, Lamed, Nun, Samach, Ayin, Tzadik, Kuf (ה,ו,ז,ח,ט,י,ל,נ,ס,ע,צ,ק) — are called the 'Simple Letters'. Just as the seven Double Letters are connected to the seven days of the week, the twelve Simple Letters are connected with the twelve months of the year, one letter per month. The months correspond to the letters in the order that they appear in the Aleph Beis. Hei, the first 'simple' letter of the Aleph Beis is connected to Nisan, the first month of the year; Vav, the second Simple Letter, is connected to Iyyar, the second month of the year; Zayin, the third Simple Letter, is connected to Sivan, the third month, and so on.

POINT OF THE LETTERS

As suggested, every letter is a distinct building block or conduit of Divine life-force, which combines with others to vibrate and animate a specific reality or life form. The letters are the means through which Divine Creativity animates, sustains and regenerates Creation.

If the sound 'Ah' of Aleph, for example, creates an energetic opening, then, when the letter Aleph is joined to the letters Vav and Reish, the word *Ohr* / light is formed, and actual light is brought into being. The spiritual sound wave created by the combination of these three letters is the meta-linguistic source of light. When Hashem said "Let there be light", and revealed the word *Ohr*, light was immediately present.

As depicted in the Torah, speech is the grand metaphor and medium for Hashem's creative process. This quasi-magical understanding of the power of language is echoed in a colloquial saying that is actually an old Aramaic formula: *Ab'ra k'Dab'ra* / I will create as I speak. Speech is a movement from the inside-out, from unity to duality. When we speak and communicate our feelings to another we are taking something from inside us, and through speech, revealing it to an 'other', outside of ourselves. Speech externalizes our internal experiences and impressions. Communication builds a bridge between ourselves and the world, inevitably altering both in the process of poesis.

Deeper than the world of Speech is the world of Thought, and deeper than thought is only Oneness.

Before Creation is spoken into being, within the *Ohr Ein Sof* / the Infinite Light of One, a thought arises to create an other outside of Oneself. Within this rarified world of thought before speech there is a detailed conceptual structure of what this other will look like and how it will function. This cosmic process of Hashem's Creation can be understood in human terms when considering that we too get initial ideas and inspirations that we then develop internally before bringing them more fully into being through our words and actions.

First, there is the inner movement within the Mind of the Creator, giving rise to a desire and will to create an other within the stillness, the infinite, unbroken unity of the Ein Sof. This *conception* of Creation is still within the reality of Unity at this point, as it is a movement within the mind, as it were, of the Creator.

To create physical reality, a spiritual vibration or metaphysical sound is uttered, giving rise to a defined physical vibration and flow of energy, which gradually condenses and is then solidified as actual matter. Hashem said, "Let the earth sprout vegetation…", and it was so.

The Torah recounts only ten Divine Utterances creating the entire world (lights, spheres, vegetation, fish and birds, etc.).

And yet, there is an almost infinite variety in manifest reality. Even two rain-drops are distinct from each other. These Ten Utterances are therefore best understood as the root expressions of the Divine creativity, and the Ma'amar Echad as the root of the root. Through the creative act of *Tzirufim* / letter permutations, all of the unique, creative 'words' emanate, as they form, enliven and sustain all phenomena.

This complex idea is summarized quite succinctly in the words of *The Tanya* when considering the creation of a stone, which is not mentioned specifically in the Ten Divine Utterances: "Now, although the word *Ehven* (אבן) / stone is not mentioned in the Ten Utterances recorded in the Torah (how, then, can we say that letters of the Ten Utterances are the life-force present within a stone?), nevertheless, the stone is animated through the Ten Utterances by means of letter permutations and substitutions…so that ultimately the specific combination of letters [that forms] the word אבן descends from the Ten Utterances… And so it is with all created things in the world" [*Sha'ar haYichud ve-haEmunah*, 1].

Everything in this world has a distinct vibration and frequency; every phenomenon that we can observe in the world is a manifestation of its corresponding spiritual vibrations. The Hebrew word for 'thing' is *De'var*, which also means 'word' or utterance. Every 'thing' is thus essentially a physical manifestation of a unique Divine word. Things are *Devarim* / words that are based on *Tzirufim* / combinations of letters and sounds.

The Divine act of birthing Creation into existence is continuous. At every moment there is a new Creation. At every instant, all Divine word-vibrations are re-expressed as the world we experience in the 'now'. Divine speech is the real-time metaphysical vibration that triggers a series of materialization-processes which transform *word* to *world*.

HOLY LANGUAGE

Lashon haKodesh / the holy language is the root-system and medium that carries the Divine energy into Creation. Just as the word and reality of *Ohr* / light is created through the sound and sequence of the letters Aleph, Vav and Reish. The word 'table' (*Shulchan* in Lashon haKodesh) is comprised of the letters Shin, Lamed, Ches, Nun. The letters are the spiritual DNA that configure and express the physical manifestations in the world. The same dynamic is true for every phenomenon.

During the Medieval Period, there was a great debate between the Rambam (Rabbi Moshe ben Maimon, 1335-1204) and the Ramban (Rabbi Moshe ben Nachman, 1194-1270) regarding why Biblical Hebrew is called *Lashon haKodesh* / the holy tongue.

According to the Rambam, there is no intrinsic sanctity or holiness to Lashon haKodesh. Rather, its *Kedushah* / sanctity comes from its complete lack of vulgar and coarse language. In Biblical Hebrew, there are no specific words that specifically describe male or female private parts, nor are there literal words used to describe the act of physical intimacy, or any other physical emission or excretion. All the terms and words the Torah uses for such things are euphemisms [*Morah Nevuchim*, 3:8].

The Ramban, however, argues [*Shemos*, 30:13] that according to the view expressed by the Rambam, Biblical Hebrew should have been called a 'modest language' not a 'holy language'. And so, the Ramban contends that Hebrew is a 'holy' language because it was and is the medium used by the Creator to create the world and communicate with Creation. It is the language of Creation, liberation and revelation, of Torah, justice and prophecy.

We can view Lashon haKodesh as the root spiritual vibration of the universe and the primary sound of the natural world. As the original and primordial language of Creation, it is also necessarily the root language of the creations. It is the essence and foundation of all languages, and it is the universal language that unlocks the gates of the spiritual worlds.

It is worth pointing out that the notion of a universal language may be related to the contemporary theory of 'universal grammar'. Universal grammar posits that all human languages share common properties. This could well be attributed to our idea that all the world's languages share a root in Lashon haKodesh.

The following is an illustration of this primacy and universality. Rabbi Yaakov Emden (1697-1776) once posited that a child born in the wild would speak — on some level — the natural language, Lashon haKodesh [R. Yaakov Emden, *Migdal Oz*, Beis Midos, Aliyas haLashon, 2]. Similarly, our Sages tell us [*Pirkei d'Rebbe Eliezer*, Chap. 26], that when Avraham was born he was hidden underground for thirteen years, and when he emerged, he was speaking Lashon haKodesh. This is perhaps a source for the teaching of Rabbi Emden.

THE ONE INTO THE SEVENTY LANGUAGES

In the beginning of human civilization, "The whole earth was of one language, and a common purpose" [*Bereishis*, 11:1]. What was this one language? Lashon haKodesh [*Rashi* ad loc]. The statements 'one language' and 'a common purpose' are inherently interlinked. Humanity had a single language *because* they were expressing and living a common purpose. As our Sages interpreted, "They spoke the language of the One of the world" [Yerushalmi *Megillah* 1:9]. As they were a unified people, with one cause, they spoke the language of Unity, of the One, Lashon haKodesh. "Lashon Kodesh is *one*" [*Zohar* 2, p. 206a].

There are 70 archetypal nations of the world. Correspondingly, there are 70 archetypal languages. Every nation is deeply influenced by and connected to their own indigenous language [Maharal, *Gur Aryeh*, Devarim 1:23]. There is a unique consciousness, soul and musicality to every nation. Each people's language expresses these distinctive attributes — from the vocal tonalities they make and words they use, to the curse words they employ and the humor they enjoy. There is a deep relationship between each of the 70 archetypal nations and their particular ways of expressing themselves in their native modes of communication.

Klal Yisrael / the Collective People of Israel is called a *Goy Echad baAretz* [*Shmuel* 2, 7:23]. This phrase can be translated in different ways: "a singular nation in the land", "the one nation within the world", or "a nation of Oneness within the world". In each case, the emphasis is on the relationship of this nation to Oneness. The 'singular *Goy*' [as opposed to *Goyim*, which refers to the many nations of the world] expresses and uses the primordial language of the One, Lashon haKodesh.

The Torah is transcribed in Lashon haKodesh. Because of this, Lashon haKodesh is the *Klal* / the general principle, the unified tongue, and all the other languages are the *Peratim* / the details, derivatives or manifestations. As the root and source of language, the Torah contains the seeds of the other 70 languages. Aspects and traces of each derivative *Perat* can be found within the Torah, including 'foreign' words and phrases such as *Yagar Sahadusa* [*Bereishis*, 3:47]. Thus the phrase Shiv'im LeShonos / seventy languages, has the numerical value of the words Tziruf haOysyos / the combinations of the letters [R. Avraham Abulafia, *Imrei Shefer*, p.

185], as all the seventy languages are reflections and variations of the initial sounds of the universe, the language of Lashon haKodesh.

Lashon haKodesh reflects the *Panim* / face of reality and projects the *P'nimius* / inner reality of the Creator within Creation. All of the 70 derivative languages express only the *Achorayim* / back side of reality. [See Arizal, discussing the language of Aramaic, which resembles Biblical Hebrew in *Eitz Chayim*, Sha'ar haKadish, 4]. Perhaps this is what the Raavad (1125-1198) hints to when he writes that all other languages are a *Pirush* / commentary on Lashon haKodesh [Raavad, on the Rambam, *Hilchos Krias Shema*, 2:10]. Besides the literal meaning, that translation is always just a commentary of the original, perhaps he is also saying that Lashon haKodesh is expressing the thing itself, whereas other languages are expressing a Pirush on the idea of that thing.

In a state of cosmic *Geulah* / redemption, when everything in the world is in perfect harmony, the Panim and the Achorayim, the Klal and the Peratim, will all be integrated and unified. The seventy languages and the One language, the many nations and the One people, will all be revealed as an organic whole. In a state of exile, separation and misalignment, however, these 70 languages and nations are disconnected from their root, from the One Language and One people. Even now, all peoples and all languages are essentially linked, it is only that the essence has not yet been fully revealed.

In Lashon haKodesh, a table is called a *Shulchan* because its letters, Shin, Lamed, Ches, Nun, are the 'DNA' that animates, and sustains the table. There is an inherent connection between the letters and sound-sequence of the word *Shulchan* and an actual table. Not only is there a connection, but the word/sound/letters of *Shulchan* are the spiritual root vibrations from which an actual table arises and is sustained. In the words of *The Tanya*: "The names (of all creatures) in Lashon haKodesh are the very letters of speech which descend, degree by degree, from the Ten Utterances recorded in the Torah, by means of substitutions and transpositions of letters…until they reach a particular created thing and become invested in it, thereby giving it life" [*Sha'ar haYichud ve-haEmunah*, 1].

There is a tremendous amount of creative potential within Lashon haKodesh, but what about all other languages? How do their words and sounds connect to Creation and relate to reality? The English word 'table' is not even similar to the word *Shulchan*. They resonate with completely different sounds and frequencies. The reason a table is called 'table' and not 'chair' is, in a sense, arbitrary. In English, there seems to be no inherent correspondence between the word 'table' and an actual table. Rather, there is an unconscious, collective *consensus* among all English speaking people to refer to something that looks like a table as a 'table'. [See: The *Ran*, Nedarim, 2a]. From a deeper perspective , even the word 'table' in English, or in any language, is energetically connected to the physical table for the people who see it that way. [See *Likutei Sichos*, 26. p, 308, note 1].

The letter sequence and sounds of the word *Shulchan* are what connect both the conceptual table and the actual table to the very same 'essence' and 'source'. This is the *Panim* / the inner face of the table that is expressed in Lashon haKodesh. The English word and sound 'table' is related to the *Achorayim* of the actual table. While in exile, and as a result of the *Sheviras haKelim* / Shattering of the Vessels, English speaking people relate to the concept and object of a table by means of the word 'table'.

This understanding of the ultimate root connection and redemptive potential of all human languages helps us understand why many *Mekubalim* / Kabbalists chose to employ Greek, Arabic, Aramaic or their own native tongue, in their esoteric studies and writings. They would look for *Gematriyos* / numerical values, and various other linguistic hints and allusions hidden within the structures of these languages just as they would with Hebrew, in order to access and arrive at deeper wellsprings of meaning [*Chayei Olam Habah*, (Abulafia) p. 148. Or in Yiddish, *Bnei Yissachar*, Tishrei, Ma'amar 2:21. See also: *Regel Yeshara*, Oven (from the Sefer *Dan Yadin*. *Emek HaMelech*, 20:4). *Pri Ha'aretz*, Vayigash. *She'eirus Yisrael*, Sha'ar 1:2. *Divrei Torah* (Munkatch), Mahadura 2:7. Rebbe Rayatz, *Sefer HaSichos*, Tav/Shin/Hei, p. 8].

From this deeper perspective it is not arbitrariness or mere unconscious consensus that a table is referred to as a table and not a chair. Rather, there is a real resonance and relationship. However, it is still an indirect relationship, via the 'back' of the spiritual reality of the table.

Every people, every nation, and in fact every individual person sees and experiences reality in their own distinct way. The manner in which objects and subjects are referred to and named reflects the manner in which these objects and subjects are experienced and appreciated. We can glean deeper meanings and gather many holy sparks from the languages people speak and the words people use, even though the process will be indirect.

The emergence of all worlds and all realities — inner and outer, 'face' and 'back', redemption and exile — is made possible by the seemingly infinite permutations of the original Ten Utterances. All of the particular sounds, vibrations, letters, words and languages of the world are rooted within Lashon haKodesh. The myriad of possible permutations and re-combinations of the 22 letters is what gives birth to all the languages of the world.

There will come a time when the world will reach redemption, perfection and harmony. Eventually, the world will be healed from its state of brokenness and exile, and will be whole and harmonious once again. A time will come when the inside and the outside, the 'front' and the 'back', the spiritual and the physical, the soul and the body will be unified and revealed as one. All languages, sounds and expressions will have done *Teshuvah* / realignment and returned to their root in the One Language. The sound of Lashon haKodesh in the future will be enhanced by the accumulation and ingathering of all the languages of the entire world, reunited and unified, singing and declaring the Oneness of Hashem.

"*Az* / then I will cause the nations (to speak) a pure language, that they may all call upon the name of Hashem, to serve Him with one consent" [*Tzephaniyah*, 3:9], says the *Navi* / Prophet. This means that in the times of Moshiach, in a redeemed and perfected world of unity, all Peratim will be re-connected and returned home into the Klal. All the scattered and broken sounds of the universe will be unified into the one great sound of a healed humanity, declaring *Hashem Echad* / Hashem is Oneness. Following the Tower of *Bavel* / Babel there was a splintering of the One language into many languages. There will come a time when everything and all will return to the One [*Yalkut Shimoni*, Tzephaniyah, 3:567].

"Hashem exiled Israel among the nations in order that converts will be added onto them" [*Pesachim*, 87b]. This teaching is referring to more than just the literal adding of converts, as important as that is. On a deeper level, it is implying that all the sparks of Divinity, no matter in what vessel they now reside, that have been exiled and scattered to the four corners of the world at any point throughout history will ultimately be reintegrated back into holiness [Shaloh, *Torah Ohr*, Matos-Maasei. *Resisei Layla*, 57].

The inner purpose of our collective exile is to gather the fallen sparks that lay dormant or hidden within all objects, subjects, peoples and languages. When, for example, a person living in Chile studies Torah in Spanish because that is his native tongue, he is revealing and elevating the fallen sparks within that remote corner of the world and within that distinct Chilean dialect.

Today, you can experience a glimmer of this unified, redeemed reality when you quiet down enough to hear the still, small voice of Torah, of revelation, of the Creator's 'voice' within all Creation. In deep calm, you can hear the sounds of Creation singing the Creator's praise. At the same time, you can sense the Creator's 'song', revealed through all the sounds of Creation. When we are able to hear the tune of the Creator within every sound and vibration, we are living the 'song of Moshiach'.

On the surface, the prophet's vision is of the future: "*Az* / then I will cause the nations (to speak) a pure language..." The word *Az* is an ambiguous word, however, and it can refer to both a future 'then', and also past 'then', as in *"Az*

Yashir Moshe / then Moshe sang a song" [*Shemos*, 15:1]. On an inner level, this is because the word *Az* is comprised of the letters Aleph and Zayin. Alef represents the One beyond time, and Zayin is the numeral seven, representing the natural cycle of time [Maharal, *Gur Aryeh*, ibid.]. *Az* thus means 'the One riding upon the seven', representing a timeless reality manifest within time. Furthermore, the numerical value of *Az* is 8 (1+7=8), hinting at timelessness, a step beyond the natural cycle of seven. As such, *Az* can refer to both the past and the future simultaneously, because it is connected to and beyond both.

When the prophet says, "*Az* / Then I will cause the nations (to speak) a pure language", it is a hint that it *will* be this way because it *was* this way in the beginning of Creation. In the future, all will return to expressing pure Oneness similar to the beginning, when all spoke the Language of One, when all languages were unified in a singular purpose.

/////////////////////////////////

CHAPTER 2

....

THE SONG OF
CREATION

THE META-ROOT AND SKELETON KEY OF CREATION, THE TORAH, IS ONE BEAUTIFUL SONG.* The entire world, too, is filled with music and mellifluous sounds, from the heavenly spheres above to the warbling waters below, from the dancing particles within to the ruffling sounds of the

---

* The Torah itself is called a *Shirah* / song in Devarim, 31:19. Although on the surface this pasuk seems to refer to only one specific part of the Torah (i.e., the song of Moshe), nonetheless, it is from this verse that we know that there is a Mitzvah to write the entire Torah [*Sanhedrin*, 21b]. The rabbi's reasoning is that since one is not permitted to write only a portion of the Torah, this Mitzvah of writing the Shirah mentioned in Devarim implies the entire Torah, thus equating the Torah itself with Song. [See *Sha'agas Aryeh*, 34. *Maharatz Chayos*, Nedarim, 38a. Note, *Maharsha*, ad loc. *Tehilim*, 119:54. *Reishis Chochmah*, Sha'ar haAhavah, 10. See also: *Degel Machana Ephrayim*, Yisro. *Eitz Ephrayim*, Anaf, Ohr Ein Sof]. King David was punished for calling the Torah a *Zimrah* / melody. [*Sotah*, 35a. Note, *Rabbi Akiva Eiger*, ad loc. *Eiruvin*, 18b] Perhaps *Shirah* is different from *Zimrah*, as *Shirah* represents a *Shir* / circle, Infinity, whereas *Zimrah* means to cut away, as in, the purpose of the Torah would be as a medium for something else.

wind brushing against the leaves, everything and everywhere is filled and teeming with life, sound and movement.

Let's begin with the sky above us: "If not for the noise created from the bustle of Rome, man would hear the sound (from the movement) of the sun" [*Yumah*, 20b]. What is this mysterious sound of the sun? According to the Zohar [2, 196a]: "Rabbi Eliezer said, 'If the hearts of human beings were not closed off, and if their mind's eyes were not shut, they would not be able to stand, for they would melt from the sweet sounds of the orbiting sun, who travels and sings the praise of the Holy One.'"

Whatever moves creates waves of sound, and therefore generates some form of music. This is not just the sun — all the heavenly spheres are producing their own 'music', their own song, generated naturally by their movements. [See *Medrash Rabbah*, Bereishis, 6:12. *Medrash Tehillim*, 33:1. Rambam, *Moreh Nevuchim*, 2:8. *Even Ezra*, Iyov, 38:7. *Ya'aros Devash 2. Divrei Yisroel*, Ma'amar Echad M'Remazei Chanukah].

The vibrations created by these heavenly bodies are subtle, but quite powerful. A great 16th Century Tzefas Kabbalist writes of a person who traveled to India and returned deaf from the sounds generated by the motion of heavenly bodies [*Reishis Chochmah*, Sha'ar haAhavah 10]. Although not normally detectable, in heightened states of awareness even the faintest sounds can reverberate like a clap of thunder.

Besides the 'singing' celestial spheres, our Sages teach that the leaves and grass sing Hashem's praise through the *Tenuah* / movement and the rustling caused by the wind. Our Sages also speak about the song of the corn. [see *Rosh Hashanah*, 8a. They 'appear' to be singing. *Rashi*, ad loc. Or, the ears of corn may actually be in harmony creating a type of song (albeit, via a natural phenomenon), which the wise of the world can discern. *Rabbeinu Bachya*, Bereishis, 43:33].

Additionally, our Sages speak of certain elevated human beings who were able to discern the *Sichas Chayos* / the speech of animals, *Sichas Ofos* / the speech of birds, and even the *Sichas Dekalim* / the speech of palm trees. [See *Baba Basra*, 134a. *Sukkah*, 28a. *Gittin*, 45a]. "When a fruit tree is cut down, its cry travels from one end of the world to the next" [*Pirkei d'Rebbe Eliezer*, 34:19]. Moreover, trees are constantly whispering to each other and also conversing with us if we would but listen [*Medrash Rabba*, Bereishis, 13:2].

Perhaps this is also connected to what we know today about 'the secret life of trees', namely that all trees in proximity actually communicate with each other. If there is a parasite in one tree, for example, that tree will signal to the trees around her that there is a parasite looming, and the other trees will then release a toxic vapor that scares away the parasite. Besides trees, birds and animals, the mountains also "speak" and the valleys "sing". These environmental dialects are also heard by those with open hearts, minds and ears [Meseches *Sefarim*, Chap. 16]. Indeed, everything in Creation has its own language [Maharam miPanu, *Assara Ma'amoros*, Ma'amar Chikur Din, 2:22].

As everything moves, including stones, everything is emitting sounds, vibrations and music. The sounds produced by the tree 'treeing' and the lion 'lioning' make up their languages and means of expression. Certainly, it is easier to appreciate the 'language' of creatures that have perceivable vocal communication. But this is also spiritually and poetically true of all nature, even the seemingly silent stones. Everything is singing its own song, and there are some very sensitive souls who are attuned to the world's whisper.

PEREK SHIRAH / CHAPTER OF SONG

There is an ancient text called the *Perek Shirah* / the Chapter of Song, which teaches the various songs of Creation. [*Perek Shirah* was first properly published with a commentary by Rabbi Moshe Metrani in his book *Beis Elokim*]. The text itself is based on the fundamental idea that all of Creation is constantly singing praises to Hashem. The text lists dozens of different plants, animals, elements and entities, along with the lyrics to the particular song sung by each, which, for the most part, are Biblical verses.*

---

* There are three fundamental ways the songs in Perek Shira have been interpreted: a) The song is sung by each entity's angel, as the Sages teach, "Every blade of grass has an angel that encourages it to grow." b) The songs of Creation are actually sung by human beings. That is, when we

The point, however, is not that a roaring lion is literally saying the verse in *Perek Shirah*, "Hashem shall go out as a warrior, He will arouse zeal, He will cry, even roar, and He will triumph over His enemies" [*Yeshayahu*, 42:13]. Rather, the lion speaks to us in its own language, and the roar reminds us of Hashem's power.

Ultimately, *Perek Shirah* is concerned with what we as humans hear when nature speaks. The lion knows what he is saying; the eagle does not need a book to tell her how or what to sing as she soars through the open skies.

Perek Shirah is written for humans and is meant to provide us with a creative and holy way to connect to and understand the deeper significance of the sounds of nature.

The lion, just by being a lion, roars when hungry and growls when fending off an attacker. This is natural. It is up to us to be open and awake enough to sense Hashem's supernatural power within the roar of the lion. The elephant is not *verbally* saying, "How Great are Your works" [*Tehilim*, 92:6]. But just by being an elephant, it is expressing this sentiment to Hashem. We just need to sensitize ourselves to hear this inner message, this sacred song.

---

sing these sacred verses we are giving voice to the specific aspects of Creation to whom they are attributed. c) The plants, animals, rivers, and stars sing the songs themselves. Perhaps this means how we hear them.

When King David completed composing what is perhaps the greatest book of poetry and praise of all time, the book of *Tehilim* / Psalms, he turned to Hashem and boasted: "Is there any creature in your entire universe who sings your praises more than I?" At that moment, a toad leapt from the waters, landed upon a rock in front of David and croaked, "I sing more praises in one day than you can sing in a lifetime" [Medrash, *Yalkut Shimoni*, Tehilim, 150:6].

All of nature is moving and stirring with life, and movement creates sound. Even the inanimate world is swarming with vibrating particles. In Hebrew, inanimate objects are called *Domem* / silent only because their sounds, movements and way of being, expressing and praising, are very quiet. As it says in the Zohar, "All that Hashem has created sings His praise" [*Zohar* 1, p. 123a. *Zohar* 2, p. 196a]. This is because all of Reality is alive. Stones and minerals, which we usually think of as inanimate, normally move very slightly or slowly, but they have a flow of life-force from the Creator like everything else. Even a stone, a *Domem* / silent object, speaks in truth [*Chababuk*, 2:11. *Ta'anis*, 11a], and sings Hashem's praise. In every pebble and speck of dust and every tectonic plate, in every frozen mountaintop and surge of magma beneath the ground, there stirs a spark of the Creator which animates and gives it life — and voice.

Simply by being, a stone quietly expresses 'stone-ness', thereby expressing the will and desire of the Creator for it to be a stone. A stone yearns to be what it was created to be, and thus to be part of the universal movement of returning to and remaining connected to the Source of Existence.

Every being and object sings its own tune and expresses itself in its own distinct way, filling the world with music. Every blossoming flower contributes to the symphony of Creation, which is none other than Hashem's glory. Rabbi Yonason Eybeschitz, the famed mystic and Talmudic genius (1690-1764) writes that all plant life sings melodies while sprouting and flowering [*Tifferes Yonasan*, Bereishis, 2:5. See also: *Shemiras haDa'as*, Imrei Tal, Ma'amar Nigun, p. 25]. Indeed, every blade of grass has a distinct song with which it sings, and every shepherd has a unique melody that he learns from the grasses in the places where he pastures. As the grass is just 'grassing', without any ulterior motives or intentions for reward, the melodies that the shepherd gathers from the meadows are pure and untainted by ego. His melodies are in harmony with nature [*Likutei Moharan*, 2:63].

Everything in this world has a tune, a song, a way of expressing and being itself. The mountains and valleys, the trees and plants, the animals and grasses, all are singing their unique song. The ultimate song of Creation is the song of yearning to return to Hashem, the Source of All Life. This is the song of *Teshukah* and *Ga'aguim* / yearning and longing that each *Alul* / effect feels towards their *Ilah* / cause. The song of yearning is inspired by the aspiration of each individual spark to return to the Source of Light.

All of Reality is alive. There is nothing inanimate or lifeless, although some things may appear that way to the human eye. In Hebrew, stones and minerals, which we usually think of as inanimate objects, are called *Domem* / silent
because their movements are very slight or slow, and their
song is very quiet. However, in every speck of dust or kernel
of grain there exists a spark of the Creator which animates
and gives it life.

Empirically, we can detect life and movement even on a
subatomic level, where all the particles interact and are being created and destroyed continuously. Once these particles are created, they do not remain static and silent, but
continuously move in rhythmic movements. Sound is produced by a wave with a certain frequency, thus with each
movement new sound waves are generated, thus every particle in a sense is singing.

In the great symphony of Creation, each creature expresses
another mood or octave of the Creator's praise. Everything
in the world has a particular form of *Sichah* / speech and
Shirah / song. Poetically, birds and trees are often singled
out because they more clearly produce audible, even musical,
sounds. However, just by being, all of Creation is singing.

Even a stone, a Domem, speaks in truth [*Chababuk*, 2:11.

Ta'anis, 11a] and sings Hashem's praise. As the tree 'trees' and the tiger 'tigers', the mountains 'mountain' and stones 'stone'. A stone simply being and expressing 'stone-ness' is silently expressing the will and desire of the Creator to be a stone — yearning to be, yearning to return and remain connected to its Source of life.

Being itself is a song, the song of Hashem's desire that each particular thing continue to exist.

The moment a creation stops 'singing' and expressing its being, as it were, it will cease to function or be itself. There is a charming Medrash [*Tanchumah*, Acharei, 9] that teaches that when Yehoshua / Joshua wished to stop the sun from setting, he said, "Sun at Giv'on, be quiet!"[*Yehoshua*, 10:12]. He did not tell it to 'stop appearing to move', he only told it to "be quiet." The moment the sun became quiet and stopped singing its 'sun' song, it ceased functioning as a sun, and thus stopped in its path through the sky [*Reishis Chochmah*, Sha'ar haAhavah 10].

Each and every creation sings Hashem's praise [*Zohar* 2, p. 196a] and does so simply by expressing and being themselves. The moment they stop expressing themselves, the moment there is no vitality, vibration or energy, they cease operating. Yehoshua was saying to the sun: 'stop expressing yourself', for he knew that the moment it stopped singing, it would cease to function. The life of any creation is its song, and its song is its life. All movement is due to song [Alter Rebbe, *Likutei Torah*, VeZos haBerachah], and all movement is song. The very moment that a creation's song ceases, it stops being what it is.

The songs of the Creator cause each thing to exist, and the song of each creature expresses its 'commitment' to existence. If we become sensitive, attentive and present enough, we can learn to listen to the songs of Hashem's praise within each existing thing. We will hear within the sound of a dog barking the song of existence sung to the Source of Existence. We need to learn to stop, be present, and truly listen.

Just as we should learn to sense the Divine Presence within the colors, forms and textures of Creation, as explored in the book *Visualization and Imagery*, we should train ourselves to hear the Divine Song within the sounds of nature. When we see the color red, for example, we should instinctively sense the *Gevurah* / strength and power of Hashem. When we see white we should automatically sense Hashem's *Chesed* / loving-kindness. And we can have the same approach to the sounds we experience. Essentially, this is what *Perek Shirah* is helping us to do — to make specific meaningful associations within the sounds of Hashem's Creation. In this way, everything we see and hear becomes another opportunity to sense, feel, see and hear Hashem's presence in our lives.

Every sound in the universe — even silence, in fact — is singing Hashem's praise and revealing another aspect of Hashem's glory. The more sensitive we become, the more we can actually hear it. Yet, for all the beauty and harmony in the natural world, the human being alone is vested with free-choice and has the ability to tamper with the tonalities and sounds of Creation. Through our creative prowess and pension for self-centered negative manipulation, we can, at times, send the sounds of Creation into *Galus* / exile. We can cause a particular creation to sing melodies that are alien to its indigenous nature, so to speak. Our task then becomes to 'return' the scattered sounds of the universe back to their Source.

As explored earlier, in the time of *Geulah* / Redemption there will be an integration of all languages and expressions, into *Lashon haKodesh*, the One Holy Tongue. Similarly, our task leading up to that eschatological climax is to pick up the pieces and gather the shards of shattered sounds and images and return them to their true Unified Source.

We find the kernel of this idea expressed beautifully by a student of the Baal Shem Tov, Rabbi Nachum of Chernobyl (1730-1787):

> "There is no creation without a life force of 'letters' (i.e., sounds and vibrations) which animates it and gives it life. For this reason, everything within the universe has a 'language' of its own, for example, the

chirping of birds or the rustling of trees. However, this language (in the other non-human forms of life) is only called 'chirping' (not speech or dialogue) because the 'letters' have descended to the lowest levels (in exile) and as such, those creatures expressing these letters (sounds) do not have complete nor proper 'speech'.... And yet, through his own speech uttered in the service of Hashem, a person elevates each and every creation and perfects it (returns it to its intended internal vibration)" [*Me'or Einayim*, "Likutim", Tehilim].

Our first spiritual assignment in this book is to sensitize ourselves to hear the sound of each creation as it expresses its own uniqueness and sings its particular melody in nature's great symphony of praise to the Creator. You may want to make journal entries exploring your challenges and successes in this practice. Once we are able to hear the sounds of nature in such a way, we then must gather in those sounds, along with all the broken and alienated sounds of the world, and raise them up to be healed, to be whole and holy once again.

CHAPTER 3

//

THE POWER OF HEARING

THE TWO HIGHER SENSES: SEEING AND HEARING

AMONG THE FIVE SENSES WE POSSESS, IT APPEARS THAT THE AUDITORY AND THE OPTICAL SENSES ARE THE MOST IMPORTANT AND VITAL TO US [*Maharsha, Nedarim*, 32b]. Yet, there is an interesting debate among the ancient wise men of the world as to which of these two is the most important — hearing or seeing. In ancient Greece this was a debate between Plato and his student Aristotle. [See: Rabbi Yehudah Abarbanel, *Vikuach Al Ahavah*, p. 41-42].

The Rishonim — the Rabbis and scholars from the 10th to 16th Century — also debated this question. All agreed that among the five senses the most integral and highest of them are the optical and auditory faculties. The question among them was, which of these two is the very highest?

Rabbi Avraham Ibn Ezra (Spain, 1089-1167) in his commentary [*Shemos* 3:6, 20:1], along with Rabbi Levi ben Gershon (the Ralbag, France, 1288-1344) and many others, argue for the supremacy of 'sight' and insist that it is the most refined sense. [See *Reishis Chochmah*, Sha'ar haYirah 8. The Maharal, *Derech Hachayim*, 2:9. *Sefer Habris* 1, Ma'amar 17:5].

Rabbi Moshe ben Nachman (the Ramban, Spain / Israel, 1194-c.1270) [*Emunah U'bitachon*, 18], along with his in-law Rabbeinu Yonah of Gerona (1200-1263) [*Sha'arei Teshuvah*, Sha'ar 2:12], Rabbeinu Bachya ben Asher (Spain, 1340-1255) [*Kad Kemach*, Zenus Halev V'Ha'ayin, 7. Rabbeinu *Bachya*, Shemos, 3:7. See also *Rikanti*, Bereishis, 29:32], and later, the Spanish Tzadik, Rabbi Yoseph Yavetz [in his commentary on *Avos* 6:2], argue that 'hearing' is the highest and deepest sense.

Looking more closely at the context of this debate, it is interesting to note the personalities of the rabbis involved. It becomes evident that this is an argument between the *Chokrim* / 'philosophers' and anti-philosophers or *Mekubalim* / mystics. On one side of the debate, the Even Ezra and the Ralbag were known as philosophers. On the other side were mystics and opponents of philosophy; the Ramban was a Mekubal, as was Rabbeinu Bachya, and Rabbeinu Yonah was a known opponent to the study of philosophy. Rabbeinu Yonah was in fact one of the foremost original opponents to the philosophical work, *Guide to the Perplexed*. Rabbi Yoseph Yavetz wrote an entire text arguing against the study of philosophy, entitled *Ohr haChayim*.

The philosophers argue that 'seeing is believing'. In other words, what you see with the naked eye is what is most real. The eye perceives physical things, therefore the physical is the most real and important paradigm. The mystics contest this approach and insist that hearing is the most essential sense because the ear perceives what is beyond the physical and immediate reality.

Rabbi Avraham, the son of the Rambam, a profound mystic and spiritual teacher (Egypt, 1186-1237), writes: "Although the sense of sight is the most refined, according to the opinion of the philosophers, still, the pleasure that the soul receives from hearing, and the awakening it arouses because of this, is undeniable and clear. This sense serves the human spirit itself, and is very beneficial. It is especially required for the learning of wisdom and faith. It would be enough to remember that hearing is one of the great awakeners for the service of the heart" [*HaMaspik l'Ovdei Hashem*, 12].

Seeing is connected with physicality. What is present in the immediate vicinity is what can be observed with the eye.

But we can hear what is off in the distance, both literally and metaphorically. Hearing opens us up to the world beyond the immediate and tangible. For this reason, if a person harms another and makes them deaf, the financial punishment is substantially greater than when harm is done to any other organ. [See *Baba Kama*, 85b. Rashi. Rambam, *Hilchos Chovel uMazik* 2:12. *Choshen Mishpat*, 420:25].

HEARING VS. SEEING:
TORAH AND WESTERN CIVILIZATION

The word *Shema* is a very prevalent word in the written Torah. In the book of Devarim alone, the word appears some 92 times. *Shema* means to hear, to listen, to pay attention, to internalize, to understand, and to be sensitive to what is beyond us. In the Gemara, the main oral aspect of the Torah, when someone wants to introduce an idea he might say, *Ta Shema* / Come and hear. After proving a point he might say, *Ka Mashma Lan* / This comes to teaches us, or *Shema Minah* / We infer from this.... All these phrases are rooted in the word *Shema*, listening and understanding. [See *Pesachim*, 41a]. And yet, in the Zohar [and in the Talmud Yerushalmi], which is a *Moshiach* or messianic text, the common phraseology is *Ta Chazi* / Come and see, intimating an expansive, prophetic quality of vision.

This is in contrast to the perspective of the ancient Greeks (and for that matter, most of modern Western Civilization) who worshipped only what can be seen, such as art, sport, sculpture, architecture, theatre, etc. The Torah teaches and inspires us to 'listen' for and ultimately hear the Transcendent One who is beyond all form or image. [Philosophers function primarily in the world of sight, where there was a metaphysical *Shevira* / breaking on a root level. The *Mekubalim* / Kabbalists operate primarily in the world of hearing and sound. See *Derech Pikudecha* (Dinov), Mitzvah 13].

Even within our everyday language we can observe this stark contrast of worldviews. In modern English, for example, an idea is called an 'in-sight'. We say things like, 'I see what you are saying', to express our comprehension. The word 'idea' itself comes from a Latin root related to the word 'video'. All these metaphors emphasize the act of seeing. The Torah counterbalances this visual bias. When the Torah wants to describe a person thinking to himself the Torah says, "He said in his heart...." [Note, however the *Baal haTurim* on Bamidbar, 22:2]. This is a metaphor of speech and hearing used to describe the intellective experience.

The fundamental difference between 'seeing' and 'hearing' is that seeing is predominantly focused on physical reality, whereas hearing can be more sensitive to the invisible movements of the spiritual realm. When you see something there is still some 'separation' between you and what you see. There is a necessary level of detachment — or so it seems — between the observer and the observed. Hearing, on the other hand, is internal and intimate. In the language of the Chasidic teachers, hearing "enters *into* the ear". There is an intimacy in hearing that is not usually experienced with seeing. With hearing there is no separation. When we declare "*Shema Yisrael*... Hashem is One", this intellectual concept enters into our core and becomes accessible, intimate knowledge.

TO BE ENSLAVED TO WHAT YOU SEE
VS. HEARING BEYOND THE IMMEDIATE

On a deep level, one way to understand the difference between a free person and one who is enslaved is that a free person can 'hear' or connect intimately to what is beyond his immediate space and time, while a slave is totally dependent on what he sees in front of him, in the moment.

To understand the above statement let us delve into the first teachings the Torah offers following the Giving of the Torah at Mount Sinai. The Giving of the Torah was the culmination of the Exodus from Egypt, and the final step in attaining true freedom. Our leaving Egypt freed us from the bondage of Egyptian slavery, and shook off the shackles of externally-imposed servitude. But this elimination of the negative was only the first step. To truly be free, it was not enough to be physically free from the oppressor; we needed to be free in our minds as well. We need to be free 'from' constricting limitations, but we also need to be free 'to' choose how we are going to live our lives. The receiving of the Torah was the moment we chose to live a higher, more spiritual life. In an existential response to that revelatory moment we exclaimed, *Na'aseh veNishmah* / We will do and we will listen. We can comprehend from this instance how closely intertwined Torah and the sense of hearing truly are. Full reception of Torah requires both a doing and an understanding which are achieved through a self-reflective process of deep listening.

Puzzlingly, immediately following the account of the Giving of the Torah, where we were finally free, the very next portion is focused on laws regarding slaves and serfs within ancient Israelite society. Why, from this highest point of freedom, do we move directly into the concept of slavery?

To provide some context, this is the opening statement of the Torah portion immediately following the revelation at Mount Sinai: "These are the laws which you shall set before them: If you buy an *Eved Ivri* / a Hebrew indentured servant..."[*Shemos*, 21:1-2].

The obvious question is: why are Hebrew slaves called *Ivri*, and not the usual title, *Bnei Yisrael* / Children of Israel? The statement could have read: "If you acquire a servant from among Bnei Yisrael".

Ivri is not a common title for a Jewish person. In fact, *Ivri* is never employed for a member of *Klal Yisrael* / the Community of Israel after leaving Egypt and receiving the To-rah. [Because of this, the Even Ezra (on *Shemos*, 21:2) brings down a disputed opinion that *Ivri* may actually refer to a descendent of one of the other children of Avraham.] We find the phrase *Elokei haIvrim* / G-d of the Hebrews used when Klal Yisrael was still enslaved in Egypt, but there is no reference to *Ivrim* after going out of Egypt. [Despite our Sages teaching that Klal Yisrael is called *Ivrim* because they "passed through the sea". *Medrash Rabbah*, Shemos, 3:7] In general, it appears from these verses that the name *Ivri* in the Torah refers to an individual from the People of Israel who is a slave. [Although this is later in TaNaCh, not in the Torah itself. The descriptive *Ivri* is used outside the context of slavery; for example, Yonah 1:9. Although, perhaps, Yo-nah was speaking this way to the sailors, who 'knew' *Elokei ha'Ivrim*, see *Pirkei d'Rebbe Eliezer*, Chap. 10]. This is, then, question one: why is an Israelite slave called *Ivri*? Grammatically, there is another problem.

Seemingly, the text should have said: "If you buy an *Ivri l'Eved* / a Hebrew *as* a slave...." When the verse says, *Eved Ivri* / slave-Hebrew, it is an ambiguous phrase. As Rashi notes, are we talking about a Hebrew slave or a slave that was previously *owned by* a Hebrew?

Beyond the ambiguity, let us assume that the term means a Hebrew slave. Still, grammatically, it should have said *Ivri l'Eved* / Hebrew for a slave, not *Eved Ivri* / slave-Hebrew, which hints at a possibility that one has purchased a He-brew person who was already psychologically a slave.

Further on, regarding a gentile slave, the Torah teaches, "If [a slavemaster] hits the eye of his slave...to freedom he shall send him...and if he takes out the tooth of his slave... to freedom he shall send him" [*Shemos*, 21:26]. The owner is forced to set his slave free if he injures his eye or knocks out his tooth.

Why does the Torah only mention the eye and tooth in this discussion? What is unique about an injury to a slave's eye or tooth? In truth, according to our Sages, the gentile slave is to be freed if the master injures any one of his *Roshei Eivarim* / main bodily organs [*Kidushin*, 24a, *Rashi*, ad loc.]. So, why does the Torah use these body parts specifically as examples of a more general principle? There is in fact a technical halachic reason why these two body parts are singled out [as Rashi explains], but our question is more philosophical.

THE CURSE OF SLAVERY

The Medrash explains [*Medrash Rabbah*, 36:8] that the whole idea of slavery was introduced to humanity following the episode when Cham saw his father Noach passed out naked after a night of heavy drinking. As it says, "And Cham, the father of Canaan, *saw* the nakedness of his father, and *told* his two brothers outside" [*Bereishis*, 9:22]. When Noach awoke from his drunken stupor and discovered what his youngest son had done to him, he said: "Cursed be Canaan; a servant of servants shall he be unto his brothers." [See *Ibid*,

24-25. He cursed Cham's 'fourth' son (*Sanhedrin*, 70a), as he was not able to curse Cham himself: *Tosefos*, ad loc.] Since 'seeing' and 'telling' are the roots of the curse, "as he saw…and told", when a slave's master damages his eyes or his teeth (mouth) he becomes freed from the predicament of slavery [*Rabbeinu Bachya*, Parshas Mishpatim].

Beyond the simple reading of this Medrash, there is something much deeper going on. The Medrash is suggesting to us that there is some intrinsic bond between seeing, speaking and slavery. What is this connection?

The Chasidic Rebbes teach [e.g., *P'nei Menachem*, Mishpatim, p.121] that if you want to live like a free and holy person, you need to be especially careful about your *Ta'avas Achilah* / eating habits, represented by the 'tooth', and be scrupulous with *Shemiras Einayim* / protecting your eyes from seeing negative, unholy or disruptive images.

Let us deepen the concept. It is known that the 'punishments' of the Torah are based on a system of cause and effect, as the Shaloh haKodesh writes. This means that they are objectively correlative to one's subjective actions. If a child does not put the milk back into the refrigerator, for example, and because of this his parents withhold his allowance, this punishment is not 'cause and effect' in the manner we are describing. There is no intrinsic relationship between putting back the milk and receiving an allowance. But, if the milk spoiled because he did not put it back, and therefore there is no fresh milk for the family to drink the next morning, this would be more of a cause and effect form of 'retribution'. Noach did not curse Cham to be poor, blind or crippled. Rather, he cursed him that his descendants will be slaves to their brothers. So then, what is the intrinsic cause and effect connection between this form of 'punishment' and the act of seeing his father's nakedness and telling his brothers about it?

The reason Noach curses Cham with slavery to his brothers is because that is who Cham already was. Someone who 'sees and speaks' is already a slave to his environment and others' opinions. If what you see on the outside determines how you feel inside, then you are a slave to your surroundings. And if you 'need' to tell others what you see and know, then once again you are enslaved to their validation and acceptance of your experience. If you see something, experience something or learn something, and you must tell another person what you saw, experienced or learned for it to be true in your eyes, you are mentally enslaved to others. And so, when Noach recognized this weakness in Cham he said: just as you are already acting as if you were a slave to your brothers, you will end up becoming literally enslaved to them. You will ultimately become the person who you are behaving as.

When Cham "sees" his father's nakedness he straightaway goes to tell his brothers. He is easily impressed and immediately needs to impress others. His father's curse to be a slave to his brothers was therefore directly related to what he had done: *VaYar VaYagid* / he saw and spoke. The curse itself was merely revealing a dynamic of slavery that was already present.

The freeing of a gentile slave due to the damage done to his eyes or mouth is now a little more understandable. As he no longer has the *Kelim* / vessels or instruments that condition him to an internal life of slavery, he is no longer subject to that role.

Now let us return to the case of the Eved Ivri. To refresh our memory, the questions that we previously asked were: 1) why refer to him as *Ivri*, an unusual and seemingly derogatory term, and 2) why is he called *Eved Ivri* / a slave that is a Hebrew, and not an *Ivri l'Eved* / a Hebrew for a slave, a more conventional phrase?

Indeed, *Ivri* is a term used for the people in Egypt who were living as slaves. That is precisely why the Torah uses this term here, to hint at the slave mentality of this individual person who has legally become a slave. [Perhaps the words *Eved* and *Ivri* share a common root, as both words begin with an Ayin-Beis]. He is therefore called *Eved Ivri* / slave a Hebrew, even before he becomes an actual slave. He is already living with a slave mentality. The only reason he becomes an actual slave, by selling himself into slavery, is because in his mind and heart he already is a slave.

The Eved Ivri is a slave in his consciousness, even before he sells himself. The way he thinks and lives his life is *as if* he were already enslaved. The process of becoming an actual slave is merely a manifestation of his internal reality. He was an *Eved* / slave to his lower self even "before" he actually became a slave to someone else. This is the archetype of the *Ivri*, which is how we were referred to in Egypt.

When we left Egypt we became *Bnei Yisrael*. The word *Yisrael* comes from the root *Sar* / prince or master [*Rashi*, Bereishis, 35:9]. Our Sages tell us that "we were not called *Bnei Yisrael* until Sinai" [*Chulin*, 101b]. The person who becomes an actual slave is someone who is not living from a place of their own power and dignity as one of Hashem's People, and as such is not referred to as *Bnei Yisrael*.

A free person is one whose life is not negatively entangled with or totally dependent on other people. To live as a master is to be the cause of your life, not the effect. You choose your path. You decide how you are going to live. 'Free' means not being dependent on outside influences [*Gevuras Hashem*, 51]. To live freely is to live your life outward from your deepest insides.

The definition of a slave is someone whose life is contingent upon and fused with his master: "Everything an Eved acquires, he acquires it for his master" [*Pesachim*, 88b]. A free person, on the other hand, is independent and autonomous.

Unfortunately, on a deep level, most people are slaves. They 'need' other people for validation, and in this way, they are 'enslaved' to them. They have given up their power of self-determination and identification, and must rely on the world outside of themselves to tell them who they are and how they should behave.

Living with a slave mentality is to continually be *impressed* by others and to live with a need to *impress* others. 'Seeing' is needing to be impressed; 'telling' is needing to impress. Seeing means absorbing truth only from the outside. A person 'looks' outward, sees what others have and do, and then thinks he needs to have and do the same. In such a case, who decides what he wants or needs? Others. In this state, you are dependent on others. You are psychologically and socially enslaved.

Why do some people have the 'need' to tell other people all about their lives and share every experience that they encounter? It is because of a lack of self-confidence and a need to find validity from others. Similar to the slavery of sight, this is another form of slavery characterized by speech, by 'telling'.

HEARING IS BEING FREE

Hearing is essentially beyond seeing. True hearing opens us up to more than what is immediately present. Hearing gives us access to the realm of the transcendent. This is real freedom.

There is, however, a paradigm of 'false hearing', enslavement in relation to hearing. In the case of an Eved Ivri, if after a certain period of time he decides by his own free will to remain a slave, the master must pierce their ear. "If the slave says, 'I love my master, my wife, and my children. I will not go free', his master shall bring him to the judges, and he shall then bring him to his doorpost, and his master shall bore his ear" [*Shemos*, 21:5-6]. Why? "The ear that heard (the words), 'For the children of Israel are now slaves *to Me*' [*Vayikra*, 25:55], and then went and acquired another master for himself, this ear shall be bored" [*Kedushin*, 22b]. Since it was the ear that heard at the Giving of the Torah that we belong to Hashem alone and not to any mortal man, that ear shall be pierced if its owner chooses to enslave himself to a master other than Hashem.

There is a clear, symbolic correlation between an ear that hears and an ear that is not truly listening. The entire idea of freedom — which is the essence of Matan Torah — is connected to the ear and the sense of hearing.*

* The Torah's revelation of the concept *Anochi Hashem* / I am Hashem..., and the concept of "...Who brought you out of Egypt and slavery", are especially connected to hearing. The *Tikkunei Zohar* (130a) teaches that

True hearing has a strong spiritual component corresponding to the ability to sense beyond the immediate, to intimate and infer that which is beyond. The eye can only see that which is in its immediate vicinity, but the ear can hear from a long way off.

We need to close these lids when we know we should not be ingesting negative imagery or harmful foods. Similarly, we need to know when to stop talking or projecting outward when it does not serve us or others. This is the inner purpose for these lids.

The nose is a channel for both inhaling and exhaling. Therefore, even though it does not have lids, it is functionally similar to the eyes and the mouth which are interfaces for inward and outward transmissions. The ear, on the other hand, is totally unique, in that it has no lids [although it does have a natural covering: *Kesuvos*, 5b] and it only receives, and doesn't transmit. The ear is exclusively dedicated to taking in sound.

---

the shape of the ear is similar to the letter Aleph. The Aleph is intrinsically connected to the revelation of *Anochi Hashem* / I am G-d.

The human ear is created for a specific purpose: it "serves to receive, alone" [Maharal, *Be'er Hagolah*, Be'er 3]. Various orifices in the body have lids and coverings, such as the eyes and mouth, and some do not, such as the nose and ears. The eyes and mouth have lids because they both receive (e.g. foods or sights) and express or project (e.g. speak or visualize, as we explore in the book, *Visualization and Imagery*).

At least twice every day we proclaim *Shema Yisrael…Hashem Echad* / Hear Israel… G-d is One. We do not say '*See* Israel,' because the way the world is today we cannot yet 'see' that Hashem is One. It is not the 'immediate' and obvious reality. However, we can listen deeply and 'hear' the distant rumblings of the ever-approaching reality of Oneness, as it gradually reveals itself.

Deriving one's sense of self and reality only by what can be observed by the naked eye is to live as if in slavery, where life is defined and dictated solely by appearances and what can be immediately seen. When functioning from this state of mind, humans are like all other animals. It takes a refined and developed sense of hearing and deep understanding to be truly human. Only human beings have the ability to truly listen, reason and dialogue. Only humans can learn to transcend themselves. But this takes a certain degree of active reflection. The understanding gained through reflection is akin to listening.

'Doing' is another function of a slave. A slave must 'do' exactly what his master instructs him to do, and he must do it well. A slave can say *Na'aseh* / I will do, but cannot say *Nishma* / I will listen. A slave can successfully do as he or she is told, but does not have the ability to listen to their heart, consider alternative courses of action, or reflect on their actions after the fact. They are therefore incapable of truly "understanding" the deeper purpose of their own actions. They do not have the capacity to make their own free-will decisions.

When a slave tells his master "I love my life, I will not go free," he is declaring that he does not wish to "hear". He wants to continue to live in the place of 'seeing' and 'doing', but not have to grow into the place of *Nishma* — hearing, intimating, inferring, and dialoguing.

By saying, "I like my life as a slave", he is denying the whole project of leaving Egypt and receiving the Torah. The whole point of Matan Torah is that we were able to hear *Anochi Hashem* / I am Hashem, and thus to perceive the Oneness (the Aleph) of Hashem, in order to fully understand our eternal bound with the One. By him declaring, "I prefer my life as a slave", he is closing himself off from the level of deep hearing and from the freedom we achieved by leaving Egypt, and as such his ear needs to be 'opened' by boring it with a sharp instrument.

This helps us understand a specific detail regarding the idol worship of the Golden Calf. When the people came to Aharon complaining and asking him to create an idol for them, Aaron said to them, "Take off the golden earrings which are in the ears of your wives, of your sons and your daughters, and bring them to me" [*Shemos*, 32:2]. "Golden earrings" is a subtle reference to the pierced ears of willfully enslaved Israelites. Aaron is intimating to them that making an idol means giving up the ability to truly hear and listen to the Voice of the One. Idol worship by definition is focused on a visible 'image', while Matan Torah freed us from the world of image obsession, and connected us with The Imageless Infinite Creator.

Let us truly listen....

CHAPTER 4

....

HEARING THE ONE
IN THE MANY

HASHEM TOOK US OUT OF EGYPT—A WORLDVIEW IMMERSED IN ICONS, IDOL WORSHIP AND FIXATION ON THE NATURAL WORLD—and then revealed the Torah to us at Sinai. This gave us the spiritual potential to hear the Oneness of Hashem within all the multiplicity and fullness of Creation.

The first word of the revelation at Sinai, *Anochi*, begins with an Aleph, which is also the number one. This Oneness is the essence of revelation. [See: *Osyos d'Rebbe Akiva*, in the beginning].

All of Creation is rooted in the Ten *Ma'amaros* / Utterances of Genesis, as explored earlier. The meta-root of these ten generative utterances are the Ten *Dibros* / normally translated as the Ten Commandments, spoken at Sinai. A *Ma'amar* is the external sound and vocalization of the more internal sound of a *Dibbur* [*Sefas Emes,* Matos, "Tav / Reish / Nun / Aleph"]. This could imply that Ma'amaros are more functional, as in the act of creation, and Dibburim are more revelational, as the act of giving the Torah.

In common human speech, this difference would be between functional requests and revelatory statements. For instance, a Ma'amar would be, 'Please pour me a cup of water. I am thirsty.' A Dibbur would be, 'I am thirsty for more interpersonal connection in my life.' On a deeper level, however, every Ma'amar is revealing a Dibbur. For instance, the deeper reason the person is asking you to pour a cup of water, may be to create connection and relationship. This is the case with regards to the Divine Ma'amaros and Dibburim. The inner essence of the Ten Ma'amaros are the Ten Dibros. The deeper reality of Creation is Revelation.

In the language of our Sages, "Hashem looked into the Torah and created the world." In the language of the later Mekubalim, "The world is a *Roshem* / imprint of the Torah, and the Torah is a Roshem of *Elokus* / Divinity." [See *Shaloh,* Shavuos, Perek Torah Ohr, 34. *Asara Ma'amaros,* Yonas Elam, Ch. 1]. The inner reality of the world is the Torah and the inner reality of the Torah is the Creator.

Just as the *Ma'amar Echad* / the One Utterance could have created the entire world in one unified form, reflecting the root of all reality, the same is true for the Ten Dibros. The meta-root of all the commandments in the Torah are the first two of the Ten Dibros: "I am Hashem, Your G-d" is the source of all positive Mitzvos. "Do not have any other gods" is the root of all negative Mitzvos. "When they heard *Anochi Hashem*, the Torah became ingrained into their hearts, and when they heard 'Do not have any other gods,' their *Yetzer Hara* / evil egoic inclination (the root of all negativity) was uprooted from their hearts" [*Medrash Rabbah*, Shir haShirim, 1:15]. These are the only two Dibros that the Israelites actually heard and understood directly from Hashem [Rashi on Shemos], and they are the basic foundation of all the Mitzvos. [See *Tanya*, Chap. 20. *Pirush haGra*, Shir haShirim, 1:2].

Anochi Hashem / I am Hashem, the first *Dibbur* / Commandment, is the ultimate deepest root of all the Ten Commandments and by extension the entire Torah. *Achas Dibber Elokim* / One Hashem spoke. [See *Tehilim*, 62:12. The first two of the Ten Commandments, the root of all positive and negative commands, were heard as one utterance: *Tanchumah*, Vayelech, 2]. The Zohar says [*Tikkunei Zohar*, Tikkun 22, p. 64a], "This refers to the *Dibbur Echad* / the 'One Saying' which includes the ten sayings." This first Dibbur, the Dibbur Echad, includes all the other nine commandments, as well as all 613 Commandments of the Torah, including all the details of the Torah clarified through the Oral Tradition.

Ever since then our mission and task is to recognize the root of the Ten Dibros within all the myriad sounds of the world, within the Ten Utterances, and then even deeper to recognize the First Dibbur at the root of the Ten, and at the deepest level to recognize the Aleph, which is 'one', as the root of the First Dibbur. Indeed, this is what really happened at Sinai, in the words of Reb Naftali of Ropshitz, "From all four corners of the world they heard the same voice — the sound of the Living G-d," and thus they all screamed, "I am Hashem, your G-d!" [See *Zera Kodesh*, Shavuos, p.41].

To hear the *Anochi Hashem*, the Oneness of Hashem pervading all Creation, is our highest task. As receivers of the Torah, this is our calling — to uncover and connect to the Aleph, the root vibration that ties together the vast multitude of sounds, vibrations and energies animating Creation. A teaching found in the early Kabbalistic writings implies that each letter is essentially another variation of the letter Aleph. Rabbi Hai Gaon (939-1038) writes that "Two Alephs are called a Beis" [*Likutim meRav Hai Goan, Os 4:1*]. In other words, every letter is a compounded Aleph. Later on, this idea was stated more clearly by the Baal Shem Tov who explicitly teaches that the letter Beis (2) is actually two

Alephs, and Gimel (3) is three Alephs. In essence, everything is really an expression of the One Aleph. [See *Toldos
Yaakov Yoseph*, in the end. See *Ner Yisrael* (Maggid of Koznitz) on Rav
Hai Gaon, *ad loc.*] Everything begins with Aleph, as the source
of the word *Anochi* (the Divine 'I') is Aleph.

The word *Aleph* means 'to learn' or teach [*Shabbos*, 104a], as
in *A'alefcha Chochmah* / I will teach you wisdom [*Iyov* 33:33].
The letters that comprise the spelling of the letter Aleph are
the letters that spell the word *Peleh* / wonder. The beginning of all wisdom teachings, the root of all true learning
is the state of wonder, the opening to mystery and knowledge of what is beyond oneself. Indeed, the sound of Aleph,
the *Ah!* sound of wonder, is the origin of all sounds. [See
Amud haAvodah, Kuntreisim leChochmas Emes, p. 328]. All sounds,
including the 22 letters of the Aleph Beis, begin with an
opening sound, the Aleph, and then it morphs into various
other sounds.

The Aleph of *Anochi* is first refracted into the Ten Dibros,
then into the Ten Utterances, and then through billions and
trillions of letter and sound combinations, into all forms
of matter and language. Our Tikkun is to find the Aleph
within everything, the One within the many.

This is the deeper reading of the teaching by the Chasidic
Rebbe, Reb Mendel of Rimanov (1745-1815), who teaches
that, "at Mount Sinai the only sound people heard was the

Aleph of the word Anochi." [See *Zera Kodesh*, Shavuos, p.40. "Aleph is the main (idea) of the Ten Dibros." *Sefer HaBahir*, 79] The essence and foundation of the revelation at Mount Sinai, is *Anochi Hashem*, and the essence of *Anochi* is the Aleph, the One.

The highest human achievement is to, like Moshe, actually become the instrument through which the Aleph of the Creator is revealed within Creation. Practically speaking, this is achieved when a person's life is a *Kiddush Hashem* / a sanctification of G-d's name, in which every moment he is expressing the unity of Hashem, the Aleph.

THE GREAT PRINCIPLE

The Aleph is the *Kelal* / the great principle of reality, the Oneness of Hashem that becomes manifest in the multiplicity of Creation.

Regarding Mount Sinai, the Torah says that "the entire nation saw the sounds" [*Shemos*, 10:15]. According to Rabbi Akiva, "They saw what is ordinarily heard and they heard what is normally seen" [*Mechilta, Rashi, ad loc*]. In hearing, we receive information gradually through bits of data, first a letter, then a word, then a sentence until we get the full picture. In fact, the word *Shema* can mean 'to bring together', as in the verse, *va-YiShama Shaul* / and Saul heard [*Shmuel* I, 15:4], which means here that he called the people together

[*Radak*, ibid], and made the matter known. Hearing is bringing together separate letters and words into a cohesive sentence.

In seeing, we receive the entire image in one shot.[See *Rosh Hashanah*, 18a] Hearing operates by moving from the *Peratim* / details to the *Kelal* / generality, bit by bit until a full sentence is received. Seeing operates by moving from the Kelal to the Perat; we first get a glimpse of the entire image and then gradually break it down or decipher it piece by piece.

To put it simply, when you see something, you first get a glance of the the entire picture, and then you zoom in and notice all the details of the picture. Hearing functions in the opposite manner. You hear speech detail by detail, word by word, and then you finally have a sentence or a full idea. In the path of sound, the movement is from the Peratim to the Kelal.

This indeed was the *Chidush* / novelty of Sinai; they saw what they would normally hear. In other words, they received the Kelal before the Perat, even though it was an auditory expression [i.e., Divine speech]. They right away understood the *Anochi*, the Aleph, the Ma'amar Echad, the Dibbur Echad, which includes all the Peratim. They got the whole point with the opening Divine reverberation, with the Aleph of Anochi.

They stood at Sinai in a condition of *Echad* / unity, as it says: *KeIsh Echad B'lev Echad* / like one person with one heart, and heard the entire Torah as *Echad* / one principle, from Hashem Echad. The Revelation resonated with the One-ness of Hashem as expressed in the oneness of the Torah, and by extension this revealed the unity within Creation.

The sound of the Aleph is the root of *Anochi*, which is the root of the Ten Dibros, which is the root of the Ten Utter-ances reverberating throughout all of Creation at all times. The volume of this original sound was turned up for all future generations at Mount Sinai.

Ever since this revelation, our task is to recreate that experi-ence and connect the multiplicity of sounds and frequencies of 'speech' to the voice of the One. Regarding this gathering of all the sounds back into the One Sound, the celebrated Chasidic Rebbe, the Apter Rav (1748-1825), records in his book entitled *Ohev Yisrael*:

"The words that man creates are (a result of taking undiffer-entiated sound and then) filtering it through letters (mean-ing) and the five 'potentials' of the mouth (lips, throat, teeth, palate and tongue). Through the annunciation of the words, the sounds become distinguished (separated). However, when (the words) are still connected with the one sound (before they are differentiated through the five potentials of the mouth), they are still unified and complete. And the main objective of our inner work...is to unify and connect our 'speech' to the (one) 'sound'...And our main work is to truly listen, to gather...to unify and connect the speech with the sound in the secret of 'One', as it was at the Giving of the Torah" [*Ohev Yisrael*, Parshas Beshalach, p. 92].

Sinai gave us the power to retrieve every sound in the universe and return it to its root in the Aleph. Not only to conceptually and theoretically return every sound to its origin, but to actually hear the *Kol Hashem* / sound of Divine revelation and the *Kol haTorah* / sound of Divine instruction, in everything we hear and sense.

While teaching Torah within the pit of hell, in the Warsaw Ghetto, after his wife, son and so many of his loved ones had already been killed, Rabbi Klunimus Kalmish Schapiro, the Peasetzner Rebbe (1889-1943), presented a profound extrapolation of this idea. In response to the extreme situation he and so many others were in, he explained that we need to train ourselves to hear the voice of Hashem even within the sounds of hell.

To quote:

"All the Ten Dibros originate from the Dibbur Echad (*Anochi Hashem* — and even deeper, the Aleph of *Anochi*) just as the Ten Utterances come from the Ma'amar Echad, *Bereishis*, as everything (all potential life as pure, non-individuated substance) was created on the first day [*Rashi, Bereishis*, 1:1]. And when we go even deeper, then these and these, the

Ten Utterances and the Ten Dibros, are *one sound* — because Hashem and His words (expressions) are One. Just as Hashem is One, so are His words. And the person who elevates himself and unifies with the unity of the voice of Hashem in the Torah *will then hear from the entire world the sound of the Torah* — from the chirping of birds, the bellowing of cows and from the sounds and noise of people; from everyone he will hear the "sound of Hashem" of Torah…. As a result, all evil is elevated to good. And thus, *all the evil words and evil expressions that emanate from the lips of the haters of Israel* (i.e., in his times, the diabolical Nazis, may their names be erased), *are transformed into the sound of Torah.* Since they too (those horribly acting people) function in this world, their life force comes from the sound of Torah (coming from the voice of Hashem), which then (through their own free-choice) becomes the sounds of evil words." [See *Aish Kodesh*, Parshas Mishpatim, p. 163. See also, Alter Rebbe, *Likkutei Torah*, Re'eh, 21b, regarding King David being 'cursed']

Even when he was walking in the shadow of death, this holy teacher was able to hear the sounds of Torah speaking to him.

TEN UTTERANCES,
TEN COMMANDMENTS, TEN PLAGUES

Our mission is to connect the Ten Utterances of Creation with the Ten Dibros or 'Commandments' of Revelation, the Ten with the Ten. This is subtly alluded to in that the full spelling of the letter Yud (10) equals 20: Yud (10) + Vav (6) + Dalet (4) = 20. Then we are to connect these words back to One. In other words, we must transform the Beis of *Bereishis* back into the Aleph of *Anochi*. When we do not connect all the myriad sounds of the world back into oneness, what we get instead are the Ten *Makos* / Plagues of Egypt.

When we do not hear the word of Hashem, the *Ko Amar Hashem* / Thus said Hashem within every experience, we then experience *Makah* / plague or hardship. [The word and idea of *Makah* originates in a distorted version of the word *m'Ko* / 'from Ko': *Zohar* 3, 145b]. Instead of sensing the Ten Utterances and Dibros within Creation, Hashem's words of creativity and revelation, we experience the Ten Makos, Hashem's destruction and concealment, so-to-speak. Instead of sensing that everything comes *m'Ko* / from Thus (i.e. from Hashem's voice), we sense hardships.

Perhaps this is a tall order, aspired to by many but only achieved by a few, and yet there will come a time as the prophet says, "...when all flesh will see that the 'mouth' of Hashem is speaking"[*Yeshayahu*, 40:5]. This means that our understanding and spiritual sensitivity will be so refined that we will be able to comprehend and 'see' the vibration of the Divine Word within every single thing/word. This is the experience, as explained, which we glimpsed at Sinai [*Nefesh haChayim*, Sha'ar 3:31].

The profound Chasidic Rebbe, the Sefas Emes explains [*Yisro*, Tav/Reish/Lamed/Dalet], that what actually occurred at Sinai, was that we were given the spiritual ability to tune into and hear the inner sound of the universe, the voice of Revelation, expressing the *Devar Hashem* / the word (sound/vibration) of the Creator's Unity. This inner sound of Creation was openly revealed to us following our refinement in Egyptian slavery, our subsequent redemption from that physical/emotional/mental/spiritual constriction, and our gradual process of refinement while wandering in the Desert.

Today as well, we are able to tune into this Divine frequency when our thoughts, words and deeds are attuned in sincerity and purity to the precepts of the Torah. Perhaps we may not experience a revelation like at Sinai, but a tangible sense of the Devar Hashem is something we can all access and open to in our day-to-day lives.

THE ART OF RE-HEARING
AND INWARDLY MANIPULATING SOUNDS

A simple practice traditionally suggested to help us learn to hear the 'sound of Hashem' within everything we experience is the art of *Tziruf* / letter combinations and manipulations. Let's say, for example, you are walking down the street and you overhear someone cursing another person (G-d forbid), saying, "May your life be filled with *Tzarah* / hardship!" Immediately as these words are being vocalized, you could use your *Chochmah* / wisdom and instead of hearing the word *Tzarah* you could internally rearrange its letters and hear the word *Ratzah* / desire. You can choose to hear or 're-hear' another person's originally negative sounds as saying something positive — in this case, "Your life should be filled with what you truly desire".

The person who cursed was actually the one to 'manipulate' the Kol of the Compassionate One. Using the 'potential' of his mouth he arranged the three Divine letters Tzadik, Reish, Hei, to say something destructive. When you chose to rearrange these letters to create a positive effect, you brought them back to their original creative source and thus original purpose.

In this way, your hearing becomes proactive and not merely passive reception. By performing a Tziruf you neutralize and transform negative speech into positive vibrations. You thereby become a participant in curating your own state of consciousness and decide what registers in your ears. We always have the choice to creatively select what and how we hear.

THE NAME OF HASHEM
WITHIN EVERYTHING

In addition to the type of redemptive listening described above, we can train ourselves to hear Hashem's name being spoken within every single sound and silence that we perceive. In the words of the Chasidic Rebbe, R. Tzvi Hirsh of Zidochov (1763-1831), "If a person is refined and experienced in the path of...seeing the Name of Hashem in front of him at all times, then he can speak to his friends in matters of business and within these words he can find the letters of one of Hashem's many names through the use of acronyms, Gematriyos, or Tzirufim [*Sur meiRa veAsei Tov*, Kesav Yosher Divrei Emes, p. 35].

In other words, a person can be speaking with someone about regular day-to-day events and detect hints and allusions to the sacred patterns of Hashem's Divine Names. In fact, even within the sounds of overtly negative speech, as in the case of a curse as explored above, you are able to hear the *Kol Hashem* / the voice of Hashem and the *Kol haTorah* / the sound of spiritual instruction and guidance.

It is important to keep in mind when discussing such practices that when someone is talking to you, you should be fully present and listening attentively, without using mental space to try to decode or reconstruct their words to form hidden patterns of the Divine Names. A solution is to listen deeply in the moment and then afterwards try to re-hear the conversation with a more creative sense of interpretation.

If you are on a higher level of practice, these two dimensions of hearing can occur simultaneously, without one canceling out the other. Then you could be fully present and focused on the person's words in the moment and yet also hearing the coded, unspoken letter patterns being formed. For most people, however, this is not yet an option. So it is best just to listen deeply and then later ask yourself, 'What did I really hear? What was the deeper message in that conversation? What was the reason I needed to hear those words at that moment?'

Both hearing and speaking occur on multiple levels. Firstly, we need to be fully present with whomever we are speaking with or listening to. Secondly, we need to make sure that whatever we hear is 'heard' as a blessing. Through the practice of Tzirufim we have the power to re-arrange sounds to transform their energy and impact. We may even find intuitive positive interpretations using double meanings, similar-sounding words and free associations even in our own vernacular. We can also find sacred names of Hashem hidden within what we hear through associated acronyms, Gematriyos, and Tzirufim. For example, you might hear the name *Moshe* being called and right away hear it the way it could be pronounced backwards: *Hashem*. Finally, and equally as important, we can hear the Kol Hashem and the Kol haTorah within the sounds of nature.

In short, we must always ask ourselves questions such as: 'What is Hashem telling me this very moment? Why am I hearing the sound of a siren? What is it waking me up to? Why did I hear someone speaking negatively? What is the lesson I can learn from what I heard?' Through the art of proactive hearing we may be surprised at how many blessings there are in our lives that we have never even noticed. Now let us turn to the more technical details of various practices related to letters, words and sounds.

PART TWO

PRACTICES

CHAPTER 1

···

PUTTING IDEAS TO MUSIC AND REPETITIVE SOUND:

AFFIRMATIONS, THE PATH OF MUSSAR & RABBI YISRAEL SALANTER

THIS CHAPTER WILL MOVE FROM ETHICAL PRACTICES BASED ON SOUND TO MINDFULNESS PRACTICES OF GAINING CONTROL OVER THOUGHTS, TO MYSTICAL PRACTICES INVOLVING CHANTING AND CONSCIOUS UNITY WITH HASHEM. Let's begin with a series of repetitive sound practices that were utilized by Rabbi Yisrael Salanter as part of his Mussar movement, a movement focused on the ethical development of individuals. But first, a bit of context.

RABBI YISRAEL SALANTER

Rabbi Yisrael Salanter was born in 1810 and as a boy he showed remarkable qualities, both as an intellectual genius and as a man with an open heart and refined sensitivity. At a young age he was already a towering Talmudic scholar and considered worthy to be named Rosh Yeshivah at a Yeshivah in Vilna, Lithuania. His genius extended beyond the sacred texts to include a deep understanding of the inner workings of the human heart and psyche.

It was during his younger years that he encountered the saintly and humble Rabbi Yoseph Zundal (1788-1868), who became his primary teacher. Reb Zundal impressed upon the young Yisrael the idea that intellectual erudition is important, yet the main objective of our intellectual learning is to live our truth and transform our *Midos* / character traits. This transformation, Reb Zundal taught him, occurs through the classic teachings of Mussar, teachings based on selections of ethics literature. To engage with their transformative power, one must study these teachings with an intent to implement them in one's conduct.

In the year 1842, Reb Yisrael established the first Mussar society dedicated to studying and implementing this material. Later on, when he moved to Kovno he opened a Mussar *Shtiebel* / house where ethical texts were pondered, discussed and practiced.

Without going into a full biography, Reb Yisrael felt strongly that rabbis and other Torah personalities should be fully engaged in community life and care for the welfare of all Jews, both spiritually and materially. Towards the end of his life he spent a lot of time on the road, far away from his birth place in Eastern Europe and away from its large centers of Torah learning, either raising funds or helping the various local Jewish communities that he encountered. In the year 1883, during one of his many travels, he fell ill in a small town and passed away with no one there knowing who he was. Years later, when some of his students asked the owner of the home in which Reb Yisrael passed away if he knew who this great man was, he answered, "No." "Was there anything special about his dying?" asked the students, "What were his last words?" The man contemplated for a moment and said, "As he was about to depart from this world, he saw that I was petrified of a man dying in my home. So, even as he was dying, he kept on reassuring me that everything would be fine, and there was no reason to be afraid."

During Rabbi Salanter's last moments on this earth he was more concerned with the psychological state of his fellow man than he was about his own spiritual well-being. This is the way he lived and this is the way he died.

One Yom Kippur Eve many years earlier, R. Salanter was quite late for the Kol Nidrei service. After patiently waiting for a while, his community realized that something must be wrong, so they set out to look for the Rabbi. They finally found him in a neighbor's house cradling their poor child who had been left home alone so his parents could go to Shul.

Another time, the Rabbi was walking with a young man during the month of Elul, the days of heightened Teshuvah prior to Rosh Hashanah. The young man was so intensely preoccupied with analyzing his own life and spiritual state that he failed to respond to a passing person's morning greeting. R. Salanter rebuked him, saying: "Must your own Teshuvah be at the expense of his *Good Morning?*"

MUSSAR

Mussar, in general, is a set of teachings that are specifically focused on ethical and interpersonal behavior, character refinement and self-transformation. This all begins with self-knowledge. One of the earliest, post-Talmudic writers of Mussar, Rabbi Bachya Ibn Pakudah (1050-1120), writes in his classic work, *Chovos haLevavos* / Duties of the Heart, that the purpose of all Torah-based philosophy is to achieve self-knowledge [*Chovos haLevavos*, Sha'ar haBechinah 5].

Over the years many important works of Mussar have been published, including *Sha'arei Teshuvah* by Rabbeinu Yona of Gerona (Spain, 1194-1263), *Orchos Chayim* by Rabbeinu Asher ('the Rosh' of Ashkenaz / Spain, 1250-1327), the anonymous *Orchos Tzadikim*, and the *Mesilas Yesharim* by the great Italian rabbi, mystic and poet, Rabbi Moshe Chaim Luzzatto (1707-1747), known as the Ramchal. Yet, an actual Mussar movement, with dedicated houses and programs to study and teach this form of ethical refinement, only began with Rabbi Yisrael Salanter.

Bettering and perfecting ourselves by working on our inherent character traits and ennobling them is the foundation of the entire Torah. [See *Rabbeinu Yonah* on Avos, 3:17. *Meiri* on Kidushin, 41a. *Sha'arei Kedushah*, 1:2]. "The purpose of the giving of the Torah is the refinement of man." [See *Tanchumah*, Shemini 7. *Medrash Rabbah*, Bereishis, 44:1]. The Baal Shem Tov would quote the great 10th Century sage, Rabbi Saadia Gaon (882-942), as teaching that the main purpose of Hashem creating human beings is that they will overcome their negative tendencies [*Ben Peros Yoseph*, 27b].

The objective in self-transformation is not to 'break your nature'. That would be a form of misplaced existential aggression. As the wise Rebbe of Kotzk once quipped: "If you try to break yourself, all you get is two *Yitzrei haRa* / evil inclinations." Rather, it is to learn to channel your natural tendencies for positivity.

Up until the time of R. Salanter, this kind of focus on individual development was not the pedagogic norm. Yeshivos, Shuls, other Torah institutions and the home itself, were more focused on learning the text than learning the self. The

Mussar movement placed a special emphasis on attending to each individual personality. This engendered a heightened awareness to personal and interpersonal patterns and processes. The study of Mussar became a primary focus for many, and not just an added dimension to one's regimen of learning. Once someone asked R. Salanter, "I have only a half hour a day to study. What should I study — Gemara (Talmud), Halacha (Jewish law), or Mussar?" "Certainly Mussar," R. Salanter answered, "for when you study Mussar for a half hour you will realize that you actually have more than a half hour to study." In other words, the clarifying power of Mussar study allows us to realize that we have much more time on our hands than we think. It also teaches us how to manage our time better.

In general, the method of the Mussar movement is the 'head on' approach. Each negative trait of the human psyche is to be directly confronted and combatted. The basic practice involves studying a work of Mussar or ethics, coupled with rigorously finding, acknowledging and contemplating each negative trait brought up in the text. One is to meditate on numerous aspects of each trait with the intention of refining its root and reconnecting it to holiness. For this process to be effective, according to some Mussar teachers, we need to concentrate on each character trait individually. [See Rabbi Yoseph Yuzal Horowitz (1848-1920), *Madreigas haAdam*, 1, p. 107-110].

R. Salanter used to say, "Man is a drop of intellect drowning in a sea of instincts." What this means is that, for the most part, our objective intellect that has the capacity to make conscious, free-will decisions is merely a drop of water in our oceanic constitution. We are primarily driven by our instincts. Most of our actions are reactive, not proactive; we go through life reacting to circumstances and not choosing our actions consciously. Our responses to life are already predetermined by our instincts.

What creates our instincts? Partly our genetics, but also patterns of learned behavior that are repeated over time. When we do something over and over again it becomes deeply ingrained: "Repetitious behavior becomes our *Teva Sheini* / second nature." [See *Shevilei Emunah*, Nasiv 4:2. *Teshuvas Maharam MiPanu*, 36] When we do something over and over again it becomes our mode of operation, and when a certain sensation triggers us we automatically react based on this inner template of behavior.

Let's say, for example, a person has a tendency to get angry. Basically, this means that when someone or something bothers him, his learned instinct is to flare up in anger. Now let's imagine that this person desires to overcome his behavior pattern. Perhaps he will delve into the Torah teachings regarding the harmfulness, both for others and for oneself, of anger, and will intellectually understand every nuance of these teachings. Will this effect change? The answer is most probably not. All too often we know intellectually how to act, but we do not actually do it. We know we are not supposed to become angry or judgmental, and yet, when we are faced with a predicament that normally triggers these behaviors, they tend to arise despite everything we 'know'. This is because the conscious or rational level of the mind is just one level among many. There are deeper regions of self. When something triggers us, our deeper unconscious instinctual self can override our conscious moral compass. No matter how clear we are intellectually, we may return involuntarily to our unconscious instincts and reflexes.

There appears to be a real disconnect between our rational and non-rational minds, between our logical conscious self and our deeper unconscious self. So how do we bridge this gap? How can we transform our subconscious mind, if not through intellectual or conscious effort? How do we work on ourselves to the point where even our instincts are positive? How do we transform our inner template?

R. Salanter calls our conscious self the "light side" of self, and the deeper conscious self the "dark side". This is not to be confused with anything negative; nor with the 'shadow side', which refers to parts of self one has swept under the rug. The reason he calls the deeper aspects of our consciousness 'dark' is because we are most often simply 'in the dark' regarding what and how we actually feel and think on a deeper level. It is like our blind-spot. On the other hand, with even the slightest awakening and illumination, these hidden impulses and behavior patterns are revealed.

Writing many years before the terms *conscious*, *subconscious*, *unconscious*, *Id*, *Ego* and so forth, were used, he spoke of the two layers of self. The lighter side is our outer self, whereas the darker side is our inner, deeper self.* The root and cause of most of our thoughts, feelings, words and actions, certainly those which spring forth unintentionally, can be traced to the caverns of our psyche, the parts of self that are beyond the reach of the 'light' part of our consciousness. To quote him:

> "All learning begins with more clear (or simple) issues, and yet these are more difficult to truly understand. Take a child who is beginning to learn Hebrew. How hard it is for the teacher to help the young student understand the shapes of each letter and their sounds, and then to understand how to connect letters to create words. (So, although he is teaching just the basics) it is very difficult for the child (at first) to read the letters and words. Yet,

* An even deeper, 'darker', or paradoxically 'lighter' side of self is 'beyond' our emotions and identity narratives altogether. This is the realm of the 'feeler' as opposed to the feeling, the 'experiencer' not the experience. This is the part of self that is empty of all form, and in constant union with the Creator, and is thus innately in 'love' and connection with Hashem. See, Alter Rebbe, *Likkutei Torah*, Shir Hashirim, "Shechura Ani". The "lighter" side is our conscious self, the "darker" side is our subconscious self, and the even "deeper/darker" self is our "soul". R. Yisrael in interested in transforming ourselves via penetrating our "darker" self. The Chasidic teachers speak about the revealing of the deepest parts of self, our soul.

once the child is accustomed to these letters, he will be able to read the words with little effort and not even require conscious thought. This is what the philosophers of the soul call 'clear verses; dark (or faint) powers'. The 'dark' powers are stronger (more deeply ingrained), and with little arousal they are awakened. A parent's love for his or her children is rooted in these 'dark' powers, as it is completely instinctual and unconsciously learned. Often, once the child is older, this raw love is not openly revealed or tangibly felt by the parents as when the child was young and completely dependent. And yet, with very little arousal, these powerful feeling can be awakened with great and overwhelming passion. The same is true with deep-set desires (such as lust, gluttony, honor, etc.); although not always felt, (they are deeply ingrained) and are thus able to control the human being." [Ohr Yisrael, 6]

How do we transform our 'dark side' as he calls it? How do we get ourselves to the point where our instincts are aligned with the way we intellectually understand how we need to act? How do we penetrate the dark side of our consciousness so that we can truly change? How do we release the light of our soul that is even more real and deep than our learned, unconscious, or darker side? How do we uncover the light of holiness and true greatness that we all possess? These are the burning existential questions that Mussar asks of each of us. Throughout the years, there have been numerous explanations and exercises offered to assist the person who authentically desires to transform their inner nature. For the sake of our focus in this text on sound-based meditation practices, we will focus primarily on the suggestions of R. Salanter himself, as he prescribes specific novel techniques that overtly utilize sound. To render the underlying concepts behind such practices in a more comprehensible manner, we will explore five progressive stages of R. Salanter's teachings.

THE FIVE STEPS
OF THE ACTUAL PRACTICE

Let's focus on judgmentalism as a trait that one wishes to overcome. Say a person finds himself constantly judging other people negatively. Now, the person knows that the reason he always judges others unfavorably is because his 'darker' consciousness has an existing pre-programed pattern created by many previous cumulative reactions. And yet, he also knows that he wants to reset and reprogram his instinctual reactions to not judge others negatively. So, how does he go about effecting such a seismic shift of consciousness?

1. Self-knowledge, getting to know himself and his issues, are is his first requisite step. Without this step, advancement on his path is all but impossible.
2. The second step is for him to choose a teaching in the Torah or by the Sages that explicitly addresses his identified

issue. For example, the teaching, "You shall judge each person (or, the "entirety" of each person) favorably" [*Avos*, 1:6], could be a perfect antidote.

3. Step three is for him to believe in the absolute truth of this teaching.

4. Step four is for him to learn the ins and outs of this teaching with excitement, passion and a harnessing of his entire imagination.

5. The fifth and final step is to repeat this teaching over and over again with a *Nigun* / melody, in a chant-like form.

THE FIVE STEPS IN GREATER DETAIL

STEP ONE:

The first and most crucial step is to figure out what aspect of your character really needs to be worked on. To initiate this process of self-discovery and honest self-evaluation, ideally you should sit down once a day, or at least once a week, and conduct a rigorous examination of your life. Who are you? What are your strengths? What are your shortcomings? What about you is worth developing? What about you needs work? What is your purpose in life? Are you moving towards that purpose, or are you off-track? If you are off-track, what is holding you back from becoming who you truly are? This is called a *Cheshbon haNefesh* / an accounting of the soul. The practice of Cheshbon haNefesh is absolutely crucial for any real, sustainable, spiritual development and growth.

There is a common custom to perform a Cheshbon haNefesh each night before going to sleep. [See *Zohar* 1, p 191a. *Sheivet haMussar* 20:17.] If one is not able to do this each night, then it is recommended at least once a week [*Ma'amarei Admur haZaken* haKetzarim, p. 359. *Sefer haBris*, 2:12:1], and preferably on Thursday nights [*Likkutei Sichos* 5. p 362]. When performing a Cheshbon haNefesh in the evening, one reviews the preceding day or week and thinks deeply about what they have accomplished during that time. What were the high points, and also what were their lows? Where did I excel and where did I lack? What good behaviors or responses were noteworthy, and which ones still need assistance? It goes without saying that absolute honesty with oneself is essential for the effectiveness of this practice.

Normally, one performs a Cheshbon haNefesh during the nightly recitation of the Shema before retiring to bed. The Shema is a declaration of Hashem's ultimate unity. This regularly repeated verse is intended to instill one with the unshakeable awareness that everything is always Hashem's doing. The prayer that introduces the Shema is an affirmation of forgiveness. Within this prayer one whole-heartedly forgives anyone who has wronged him in this incarnation or in any previous incarnation. One is asked to forgive both those who have wronged him intentionally or unintentionally, by coercion or by will. And one concludes the prayer by asking that no one should ever be punished on account of him.

In the context of Cheshbon haNefesh one reviews the previous day and takes a short reckoning of all their actions, words and thoughts throughout the day. If, when reviewing the day, one feels that there were thoughts, words or actions that could be improved upon, one resolves that tomorrow will be completely different and one will do better. Every night before retiring to bed, the legendary Chabad Chasid, Reb Gershon Ber Paharer [others report the same narrative with Rabbi Levi Yitzchak of Barditchev] would declare: "Tomorrow is going to be completely different!" And then, as he was not naïve, he would continue: "Even though I said this yesterday evening, tonight I really mean it" [Rebbe Rayatz, *Sefer HaSichos 5706*, p. 5].

Writing a daily journal can help with doing an honest and accurate Cheshbon haNefesh. It is a simple way for one to observe patterns of behavior without the ego clouding one's memory and obscuring what really happened. When you do this daily, you can review your journal, say on Thursday evenings, and acknowledge the trajectory and pattern of the week as a whole. You can also look back to remind yourself what your state was one week ago, one month ago, or even a year ago. This can help you determine if there are any repetitive, habitual behaviors, whether positive or negative. We can only correct things that we know about.

This is an important note: do not only look for the negative when performing a Cheshbon haNefesh. Do not beat yourself up. Acknowledge your small victories.

Of course we need to go deeper into our psyche than a retrospective review can take us. We need to take specific notice of our instinctive, reactive behaviors in the moment as well. The way to really know what is going on in your subconscious self is to observe your first responses and immediate impulses, even when you do not follow them. Your unpremeditated first reactions are indicative of your deeper or 'darker' self.

To illustrate these points, R. Salanter offers a parable of a father and son who are estranged. The father, a wise teacher, has a gifted student who he loves very dearly. He also has a rebellious child who is estranged from him and continually disappoints him. Both of these boys live in the father's home. If the father were to awake from sleep while a fire had broken out in his home, he would instinctively rush to wake up his own child before he would run to the room of his student. Deep down, parents' instinctual love for their children runs deeper than any other love.

It is an interesting parable, especially taking into consideration the biography of R. Salanter, as he himself had a child named Yom Tov, who was estranged from his father and became a well-known mathematician. R. Salanter once wrote publicly in the periodical "HaMagid" about how troubled he was by his son's choices, and he openly expressed his displeasure. We can surmise that R. Salanter's parable comes from a deep place of personal experience, possibly the result of his own Cheshbon haNefesh process.

The point is that our unconscious reactive behavior is indicative of our deeper inner state. Because of this, R. Salanter had a custom to write down his unintentional thought-streams. Or when an idea appeared out of the blue, he would immediately write it down in order to observe what was going on within himself on a subconscious level.

STEP TWO:

This step consists of choosing a teaching from the written or oral Torah that explicitly addresses the issue you are dealing with. Years ago, one would need to leaf through an old tome of Mussar and try to spot a specific teaching that addressed one's particular issue. Today, with various kinds of search engines, this process can be much simpler. It can also be highly effective to ask your rabbi, teacher or any other friend that you trust for their suggestions. Ultimately, you are looking for a phrase or teaching that speaks literally or figuratively about the issue you are confronting. It is important that you resonate deeply with the phrase as you will be working with it intensely over a period of time.

STEP THREE:

This step introduces an interesting concept, which is that one needs to absolutely believe in the fundamental truth of the selected teaching or saying. In other words, it is not enough to simply choose a beautiful or inspiring teaching. You must believe in your mind and heart — and even in your body — that this teaching or saying is absolutely true and binding. Without this requisite absoluteness it would be all too easy for the 'dark' mind to distract you, to undermine your commitment to the practice, or conceal the inner light of the teaching.

Quite frankly, the reason many people do not actually change their patterns of behavior, even though they know all the 'information' and 'understand' all the reasons that they should change, is that they do not believe in the absoluteness of their target. As a result, they slip up and let themselves off the hook by fashioning excuses: 'Well, I said I would not get angry, but this situation is different,' or, 'I resolved to stop eating fatty foods, but this time won't count, and then I'll commit afterwards.' These types of resolutions never work because we aren't relating to them as absolutely and unequivocally binding.

Much of the difficulty in keeping resolutions comes from our ego. The ego is only interested in the preservation and perpetuation of itself to the exclusion of all others, making it inherently self-centered and self-serving. Secondly, our ego is accustomed to certain pre-programmed patterns of behavior. These are in fact what define the ego's boundaries and provide it with a stable sense of self. When asked to change any of its ways the ego will always be resistant, as change is an affront to the ego itself.

R. Salanter would say, "The human being is equipped with such far-reaching vision, yet the smallest coin can obstruct his view." This visionary capacity is from the soul; the coin is of the ego. Seemingly, our ego often gets the upper hand. Over and over again we are inspired to change, we take on new resolutions, and when we do so — we do so whole-heartedly. Almost inevitably, a few days later we revert back to our old patterns.

One way to circumvent this predicament is to accept the selected teaching upon yourself in the form of a *Chok* / a supra-rational Torah commandment. This transforms the teaching into an objective truth instead of a subjective one that you can reason yourself into or out of. This way, no matter how you feel about your resolution the next day, you are bound to persevere, as a Chok is non-negotiable.

In the words of R. Salanter: "Indeed, from where does the awareness and understanding come from, and what actually awakens and arouses the person to sublimate his free-flow-ing (i.e., untrained and unharnessed) desires and emotions?

The primary foundation (to ensure that we take control over and mindfully direct our desires and energies) is that we accept our resolution as a *Chok* of the Torah from Hashem" [*Ohr Yisrael*, 31].

STEP FOUR:

Now that you have chosen a resonant teaching or saying from the great canon of the written or oral Torah, and accepted it upon yourself as a kind of 'commandment', step four is to learn that teaching inside and out with excitement, passion, and your entire spectrum of imagination. To study and ponder this teaching with vigor, it is helpful to conjure up all types of images of how this teaching can manifest.

In the paradigm of Mussar, it is also suggested that one imagine all the potential ills and harsh consequences that may arise from not following the dictates of this teaching as a method of self-coercion to do the right thing. Indeed, the ego can be like a thief, attempting to rob us of beneficial change. Just as we would go to great lengths to protect our most valuable possessions from theft, we need to protect our commitment to our chosen teaching. A Mussar teacher once chanced upon his student calmly engaged in Mussar study and rebuked his complacency, thundering, "Is this the way to handle a thief? Where is the passion and intensity in your studies?" [*Sefer Ohr haMussar* 2, p. 166].

In general, there are two ways to ponder a text or an idea. There is an abstract, detached, purely intellectual or left-brain form of learning, and there is a more personal, emotional and experiential type of learning. When our motivation in learning is only to gain information, we can calmly read and retain it, but when our purpose in learning is transformation, then we ought to learn with excitement and passion. We need to engage our imagination, our body and our entire self, in the process of living our truth. This is where sound comes in.

Chanting our chosen teaching with a melody or rhythm is a way to stimulate excitement in our learning [*Megilah*, 32a]. It also ensures that we remember and recall the teaching. It is powerful to repeat the teaching with an evocative melody, or one that can bring us to the point of tears. This way, the teaching will impact you not only mentally and emotionally, but on the deepest level of your psyche.

In the words of R. Salanter:

> "It is thus very important that the manner in which one learns these moral and ethical texts of Mussar should be with great arousal of the soul and a correct heart. (You shall recite these teachings) with bitter voice, and with your lips aflame. One shall also broaden the concepts with visualized imagery. The power of *Tziyur* / imagery and positive imagination helps tremendously with the work of Mus-

sar, to arouse the soul and to sense that arousal in the body.... As we have seen, the power of song and music can arouse a person and awaken his spirit to joy or to sadness. And so, when a person reads the teachings of the Sages and the texts of Mussar...he should do so with a bitter tune to arouse his heart. Then, his heart will warm up inside and his soul will be moved and all his senses will be aroused...even if this brings him to tears...(this eventually) will bring about a renewed spirit...."

[*Ohr Yisrael, Sha'arei Ohr* 9:2].

STEP FIVE:

The fifth and final step is to passionately repeat the selected teaching over and over again in a chant-like form with great concentration. Repeat it over and over again with a tune until these words ring in your head and become embedded into the depths of your bones.

The notion of repetition was taught by many of the great classical masters of Musar. For example, Rabbeinu Yonah of Gerona, teaches that one should "continue to repeat to himself words of *Yiras Shamayim* / awe of the Transcendent such as [the words of the Mishnah, *Avos*, 4:4]: "Be very, very humble" [*Sefer haYirah*]. This is perhaps rooted in a teaching by our sages: "Rav said, 'The ox call (the sound you make to chase away or urge an ox) is *Hen Hen*; for a lion, it is *Zeh-Zeh*;

for a camel, *Da-Da*'"[*Pesachim*, 112b]. In effect, Rav is saying that animals are aroused by repetitive sounds. Inwardly this could mean that to arouse our own inner animal, to 'chase it away' or urge a transformation of our inner negative, animalistic, reactive instincts, we need to use repetition [*Meshech Chochmah*, Bo]. The repetition of the exact same sound or teaching over and over again has the power to 'chase away', harness or transform the inner animal.

R. Yisrael Salanter adds another layer to this idea; to inject emotions, passion and imagination into the practice. When we are learning on an intellectual level, we are, for the most part, harnessing and tapping into the peripheral parts of the brain. This is effective for theoretical or abstract thought. When, however, we are learning with our body, breath, aroused emotions and engaged imagination, the wisdom lodges itself into deeper and deeper parts of our psyche. In the words of R. Salanter:

> "Therefore, it is good (for a person) to repeat a teaching of...Mussar many times. Especially when he is reading a teaching that he knows will inspire him and penetrate his heart. He should repeat the teaching over and over with excitement and arousal until the teaching becomes ingrained upon his heart. And then, even when he walks in the street or lays on his bed, the teaching will ring in his ears and will not fade from his memory."
>
> [*Ohr Yisrael, Sha'arei Ohr* 9:10]

Rhythmic repetition coupled with emotional arousal allows for the idea represented in the teaching to pierce the realms of the inner subconscious and thus transform the 'darker' levels of self. The more you learn, practice and repeat the teaching, the deeper the teaching settles into your soul. Our Sages teach that we should learn Torah with a melody [*Megilah*, 32a] so that we better remember what we learned [*Tosefos*, ad loc]. Yet, the method of R. Salanter is aimed at more than simply remembering teachings. Rather, it is to ensure that these teaching become encoded into our subconscious mind and transform the inner wiring of our brain for the better. This practice can help us transform our behavior on the deeper instinctual levels of our consciousness so that our highest intentions become second nature.

AFFIRMATIONS:

This practice of repetitive verbal self-influence is similar to the popular contemporary concept of 'affirmation' — short, positive statements that you repeat to yourself out loud or quietly, over and over again. Reb Aharon / Arele Roth (1894-1947), known as 'the *Shomer Emunim*', was another advocate of using mostly positive affirmations to assist oneself in stimulating spiritual development.

An affirmation takes a concept and concretizes it, as the verse says "I believe(d), because (or 'as') I have spoken" [*Tehilim*, 116:10]. Spiritually speaking, a verbal affirmation brings an ethereal thought-form from the world of *Beriah*

/ mental reality further down into the world of *Yetzirah* / verbal reality. This is the goal of transformative learning: not just understanding a truth intellectually, but to live it on all levels of being. Doing so takes an alignment of thought, speech and action. Speech is the bridge between the world of thought and the world of Asiyah / action and physical manifestation. By repeating a verbal affirmation over and over again, you strengthen the connection between your intellect and your actions, making it much more likely that you will be able to act in alignment with your ideals.

Again, Hashem created the world through speech. Speech is therefore the primary metaphor and instrument for manifesting new realities in this world. Because humans are created *b'Tzelem Elokim* / in the image of the Creator, we too have the creative power of speech, albeit on a microcosmic level. By speaking something over and over again, we are thus making it more real. Neurologically, because the act of repetition rewires the brain, the more you repeat it the more real it becomes.

A positive affirmation, such as, "I am a good person," or better yet, "I am really a Tzadik," is a declaration that what we desire is already true. It is a way of strengthening our desire and potential to be that which we hope to become, and helping our 'dark mind' rewire itself and think of itself in a positive and empowering light. Over time, the continuous affirmation that "I am a good person," or "I am a Tzadik," will inevitably lead you to acting from and manifesting those very qualities.

This form of affirmation is more consistent with the path of the Baal Shem Tov, where the focus is always on the positive and employing a positive wording. Yet to be more aligned with the teachings of Mussar in which negative traits are battled head on, here is an affirmation suggested by Reb Arele to eliminate the negative:

"I hereby nullify all negative, despicable and damaging thoughts that enter into my heart and mind, at all times when I pray or study Torah. They are as nothing to me and I have no desire for them at all."

[*Shomer Emunim*, Ma'amar Hashgacha Peratis, 3]

THE POWER OF A VERSE:

When a person is choosing an ethical teaching to use as their audible affirmation, it is important to note that there is an additional spiritual power to the practice when they select an actual verse from the Torah.

For instance, there is a practice mentioned for a person who finds himself lusting after or desiring something that is not rightfully his, in which he should visualize the words of the Torah commandment "Do not covet," and repeat these words to himself over and over again. [See *Ohr Haganuz leT-zadikim*, Parshas Yisro. *Darchei Tzedek*, 1:11. See also; *Tzetel Katan*, 7]. The visual and audible aspects of this repetition combine to give a person the extra strength and support to not slip deeper into the emotion of coveting, or G-d forbid acting on it.

"Hashem looked into the Torah and created the world" [*Medrash Rabbah*, Bereishis, 1:1]. The Torah is therefore understood as the blueprint of Creation. All reality existed first within the Torah and only then manifested in actuality. In the words of the Gaon of Vilna (1720-1797): "All that was, is and will be, until the end of time, is included within the Torah. Not only the general ideas, but even the details of every type of creation, and specifically every individual person, from the day of his birth to the moment of death, including all incarnations, and all details of details...."[See *Gra, Sifra deTzniusa*, Chap. 5. See *Ramban*, Devarim, 32:40].

As such, every issue that we find in the world is metaphysically rooted in the Torah — specifically where that issue is mentioned in the Torah. For example, the source of all relationships is rooted in the story of Adam and Chavah / Eve. Similarly, the source of all sustenance is rooted in the Torah portion that introduces the *Mon* / Manna. When a person repeats to himself the phrase "Do not covet," he is tapping into the root of this idea, and also connecting to the Torah's infinite wellspring of empowerment. Thus he has an additional infusion of empowering energy which helps him not to covet.

In summary, the five steps for these verbal repetition practices based on the Mussar teachings of R. Salanter are: 1) knowing yourself and your particular issue, 2) selecting the appropriate teaching that matches that issue, 3) believing in the absoluteness of the teaching, 4) learning the ins and outs of the teaching with excitement, with a Nigun, with passion and imagination, and 5) repeating the teaching with rhythm and melody over and over again.

CHANGE DOES NOT HAPPEN OVERNIGHT

It is important to note that while the aim may be a total transformation of self, the steps taken need to be incremental. [See *Sefer HaYashar*, Sha'ar 6. *Sichos HaRan*, 27]. We need to take one step at a time, without attempting to remodel, re-wire and transform overnight. Whatever method we use, all dramatic changes which come about too suddenly rarely endure. The moment the high or the inspiration fades, so does the desire to change. It is better to make small changes successfully, than fail in making drastic ones.

A classic book of Mussar, *Orchos Chayim* by the Rosh (Rabbeinu Asher, 1250-1327), is divided into seven parts corresponding to the days of the week. Each day, one is to study a part of the text and attempt to rectify the specific character trait that is described on that day. Every single day we should aspire to become a better person than we were yesterday. Indeed, "tomorrow is going to be completely different," and today we "really mean it."

It is never too late to work on yourself. Once, R. Salanter noticed an older tailor toiling at a very late hour in his home, so he gently knocked on the window and asked, "Why are you still working?" The tailor responded, "As long as the candle is still burning there is still time to accomplish and mend." R. Salanter was struck by this and later taught: "So long as one is alive there is still time to mend!"

PRACTICE

INTRODUCTION

Every practice must begin with the commitment to show up fully in this present moment.

We are not present when our mind is reminiscing about the past or worried about the future.

We need to clear the clutter from our mind, reduce potentially distracting forces and open ourselves up to presence.

It is preferable to carve out a specific time that can be fully dedicated to your practice, free from other commitments and distractions.

Before going to sleep is a most opportune time for this practice, although it can be done during any time of the day.

It is important to familiarize yourself with the space you are in and establish it as a safe and comfortable place to settle in for the duration of your practice.

Put aside any expectations of how this experience should be.

Turn off your ringer.

Begin.

PRACTICE

....

PUTTING IDEAS
TO A REPETITIVE MELODY

Select a phrase or teaching that stirs
and strengthens your soul.

For example:

VeTaher Libeinu leAvdecha beEmes
Purify our heart — render it transparent — so that
we can serve You in truth.

First, think about what the words mean.

Open yourself up to listen and be receptive to their
deeper meanings.
Allow the words to speak to you.
Make them personal.

Think about how your heart is so often
closed off or blocked.
Think about how your heart is so frequently
Tamei / impure, stuck, lifeless.

Feel how you truly desire a *Lev Tahor* / pure heart. *Tahor* comes from the word *Tzohar* / illuminated or transparent.

Think about what it really means to live your life transparent to truth and in service of truth.

Use your full range of thought and imagination.

Think about times in your life where you were not authentic or truthful to your deeper self.

Now, slowly begin to chant these words over and over in the rhythm and melody of your choosing.

Chant them with fervor and excitement, feeling deeply what each word means.

What does it mean to live from a place of truth? What does it mean to be pure?

Feel the words in your body, the visceral sensations they arouse.

Repeat the phrase over and over again with passion, allowing any tears of sadness or joy.

After one to four weeks of repeating these words with rhythm and melody, you will find yourself

almost constantly repeating them verbally
or mentally, often without them consciously
registering in the surface mind.

Slowly, these words will fill the mind, leaving little
space for other thoughts to intrude.

Eventually, the words and the sounds will begin to
overflow the mind.

Allow the words to trickle down from the
conscious mind into the deeper strata of mind,
heart, body and soul.

Feel the words in your very bones.

To conclude the practice, slow down your
repetition until you come to a place of
silence and stillness.

Allow the silence to speak to you and the
stillness to move you.

When you are ready to return, engage
and greet the world.

CHAPTER 2

....

EXPLORING
THE USE OF
REPETITIVE SOUND

QUIETING THE MIND & SELF
THROUGH REPETITIVE SOUND

THE SOUND REPETITION TECHNIQUE EXPLORED IN THE LAST CHAPTER IS A FOCUSED AND STRUCTURED PRACTICE, allowing you to ingrain a selected teaching into the deeper layers of your consciousness. This is one function of repetitive sound. You can also employ a repetitive sound to simply clear your mind from all distracting thoughts on the spot.

In the following series of practices, the objective and purpose does not reside in the meanings of the actual words
chanted or recited. It is even possible that the words you
choose for this practice are rationally meaningless. Here,
the words or sounds are used simply as a means to clear the
mind.

This method is much like the path of *Hashkata* / quieting
the mind through detached observation, which we explore
in great depth in the text *Breathing and Quieting the Mind*.
The objective of both methods is to slowly ease the onrush of distracting thoughts. Instead of acknowledging the
many thoughts that rise and fall, as in Hashkata, repetitive
chanting allows the mind to become absorbed in a specific
activity. The immediate experience of repetition both awakens and focuses the mind. The sound itself marginalizes and
silences all other sounds and stimuli until the mind is quiet
and still.

In Hashkata one empties the mind of chatter and thoughts
to achieve inner quietude.

In sound repetition practice one is filling the mind and
body with sound and vibration to achieve a similar state. It
is a beautiful poetic paradox to find silence through sound.
The great quieting power of repetitive and harmonious
sound is exhibited when we use it as an induction into a
transcendent experience. Repetition can create a hypnotic

and trancelike state. It is only via the sense of hearing, not sight, taste or smell, that a person can be catapulted into any form of *K'los haNefesh* / expiration of the soul, as it were. Through sound, rhythm, melody or music we can reach the highest levels of *Deveikus* / unification with the One, as well as achieving a total silencing of 'separate' consciousness and ego.

Through the sense of sight, for instance, we can be inspired to awe and we can lose ourselves for a moment. However, only through sound can a person experience an emptying of all sensations and impressions and arrive at total stillness.

Let's say, for example, you go to a museum and see a beautiful painting. The painting you are viewing is so exquisite that you become completely mesmerized and enchanted by its beauty and form. You feel like you are 'losing' yourself and becoming enveloped within the field of color and texture. This is certainly a powerful experience, but it can only go so far. Through sound, on the other hand, the Sages teach you can lose yourself completely. You can hear an enchanting melody and be so overwhelmed by its beauty that you experience a literal "K'los haNefesh". [Rebbe Rayatz, *Sefer haMa'amarim* 5699 (1939) Ma'amar "Ivdu Es Hashem"].

K'los haNefesh / expiration of self means a ceasing of all of one's egoic will, desire and self-definition. [*Nefesh* is our desires, wants and wills: *Rashi, Ramban, Sforno,* on *Bereishis,* 23:8]. One forgets about himself, letting go of any attachments or identities, and slips away into the melody, the rhythm, the music. Harmonies and melodies enter into your consciousness, resonate throughout your entire body, and without one noticing, initiate a *Kelayon* / expiration of one's Nefesh.

This is a form of *Hashkata* / quieting as well, although not just of the mind, but of one's entire being. In this practice, as well as the previous ones, we find that the repetitive use of sound and vibration allows Hashkata to pierce beyond the mind and impact the whole system.

REPETITIVE SOUNDS
TO QUIET & OPEN THE MIND

Our voices are primary tools for these practices, but sounds other than the voice are also capable of clearing the mind of all intruding and involuntary thoughts, allowing us to fill our mind with thoughts that are consciously chosen. In any case, the first step to clear your thinking is to shut out all clutter and static.

Our Sages mention that the sound of a continuous flow of water is a good *Siman* / symbol to help us with our studies. "...A Siman has value.... When you study, do so by water, for just as the water is drawn out, so will your learning be prolonged" [*Kerisus* 6a. *Horius,* 12a]. What does it mean that "your learning will be prolonged"? According to Rashi, the great 11th century French commentator, it means you will not forget your learning; it will never leave your lips [*Horius*, ad loc]. To prolong your learning means to 'remember' it, to prolong its presence and impact.

This example speaks of more than mere 'symbolism'. A deeper relationship between yourself and the material you are learning is established through the presence of a gurgling stream. It is obvious that if you learn with a quiet, still and focused mind, the information will penetrate deeper into your consciousness. There are few sounds more soothing and quieting than a stream of water. The sound of dripping or running water can help a person relax and also be therapeutic [*Eiruvim*, 104a]. In fact, there is a discussion in the *Shulchan Aruch* / Code of Jewish Law of whether one is allowed to put a utensil under a dripping vessel to help one relax and fall asleep on Shabbos. [See *Shulchan Aruch*, Orach Chayim 338, *Magen Avraham* 1].

Therefore, pondering an intellectual idea with the background 'music' of water calms the mind, and it also connects the idea itself to the influential flow of sound, allowing the concepts to lodge deeper into the psyche.

WATER, SOUND & CALMING

A lack of peace and calm contributes to an inability to fall asleep. You need to let go and trust your environment and the Creator of life in order to sleep well: "If you will rest you will not worry, you will lay down and your sleep will be pleasant...for in Hashem you will trust" [Mishlei, 2:24-26]. 'Surrender' is thus a central element in achieving peaceful sleep: "Sleep is one sixtieth of death" [Berachos, 57b]. Here, "death" means releasing your conscious control over your body and life. You need ease and relaxation to allow yourself to 'die' in this way. For some people this surrender is frightening, and they have anxiety around trying to fall asleep. The Rebbe Rashab said that a person who is able to fall asleep easily is likely a person who has an easier time dropping into a calm and relaxed state in prayer. The sound of dripping water, and other soothing repetitive sounds, can stimulate such a calmer state.

'Entrainment' is the synchronization of our internal organs and systems with an external rhythm or sound-pattern. In entrainment, our bodily pulses, including our heartbeat, automatically synchronize and align with any beat, rhythm or music that we hear. This is how listening to the gentle sound of continuously tumbling water calms your mind, body, heartbeat and general consciousness. Sitting near a seashore with the sound of waves also has a universal appeal for its calming effect.

On average, a healthy mature adult, when not exercising, takes 12 to 20 breaths per minute. We can round this out to about 18 breaths per minute. The number 18 is represented by the letters Yud (10) and Ches (8), which spell the word

Chai / 'alive'. [In a 60 minute hour the total breaths would be 1080: *Reishis Chochmah*, Sha'ar HaYirah, 10. R. Abulafia rounds this number down to 1000 breaths per hour: *Ohr HaSechel*, Chap. 6.] This is three to five seconds per inhale-exhale cycle. When a person is relaxed or sleeping, the breath cycle can last from six to eight seconds, as we breathe slower when we are asleep. The rhythm of breaking waves often occurs in a cycle of eight seconds. With the effect of entrainment, our body and mind absorb this rhythm and synchronize with it. As a result, we can begin to enter the eight second cycle with our breathing. This slower breathing creates deep calm and relaxation.

In contrast to the regular sound of running water or the crashing of waves, sounds that occur at irregular intervals, like sirens or traffic, will often keep people awake at night. These sounds rattle our nervous system rather than calm it. In addition to the suddenness of these sounds, there is another element which keeps us awake. Our brain constantly tries to categorize stimuli, to place all sounds in a neatly organized pattern. Since these sounds are irregular the brain tries in vain to create some kind of predictable order out of them. The mind therefore becomes disturbed and keeps itself awake searching for calming, regular patterns.

Whenever there is a constant, gentle rhythmic sound, our mind and body — and our soul, as we will explain later on — tune in and synchronize with that rhythm. This allows us to let go, lay back and relax into the rhythmic pulse all around and within us.

VOICE TO CALM TO SLEEP

Besides allowing dripping water to make sounds in a vessel, our Sages also mention using one's own voice to rhythmically induce oneself into a more meditative and calm state and fall asleep.

We are told of a certain sage of the Talmud that would fall asleep by repeating the Shema over and over again [Yerushalmi, *Berachos*, 1:1]. Accordingly, if a person is anxiously lying in bed trying to fall asleep, he should repeat the Shema to himself as a method of holy relaxation.* In this practice, you are using your own self-generated rhythm and continuous sound as a means to calm your nerves and fall asleep.

REPETITION OF A VERSE
TO ERADICATE INTRUDING THOUGHTS

During the 1500's, many great mystics, teachers, poets and

* *Shulchan Aruch,* Orach Chayim, 239, Ramah ad loc. See also Orach Chayim 61:10. To avoid suggesting any dualism in Hashem, it is forbidden to repeat the word *Shema* consecutively. Rather one is to recite the entire Shema all the way through, over and over again: *Biur haGra, ibid,* 61:10. *Mishnah Berurah,* ibid, 25. Or, wait after every time you recite the Shema and see if you fall asleep. See Shaloh, *Maseches Chulin,* Derech Chayim 18.

philosophers gathered from Spain, Portugal and Turkey in the holy city of Tzefas, Israel. Among them were great luminaries such as Rabbi Yoseph Caro, Rabbi Moshe Cordovero ('the Ramak') and Rabbi Yitzchok Luria ('the Arizal'). At that time, it appears there arose a methodology that was used to rid oneself of intruding thoughts by using a sound repetition technique.

A *Magid* / a channeled prophetic voice [the "Voice of the Mishnah"] revealed to R. Yoseph Caro (1488-1575) that to calm his mind and purify his consciousness of unwanted thoughts he should repeat a specific verse to himself seven times, followed by a specific exclamation. The verse was, "How fair and how pleasant you are, a love with delights" [*Shir Hashririm*, 7:7]. The exclamation was, *Kera Satan* / rip open Satan. [See also The Chida, *Devash L'phi*, Erech, Mem].

The Ramak (1522-1570) writes that he heard an instruction from the "old man", *Eliyahu haNavi* / Elijah the Prophet: If you are in the middle of your prayers and a negative thought comes to mind, such as one of jealousy or hate, and it is a place in the prayers that you are halachically permitted to interrupt, repeat the verse, *Aish Tamid Tukad al haMizbe'ach, Lo Sichbeh* / An eternal flame shall be kept burning on the altar, it must not be extinguished [*Vayikra*, 6:13]. Repeat this verse over and over again and then gently wipe your forehead with your hand while having the intention to wipe away the extraneous thoughts from your mind.

[See Shaloh, *Sha'ar haOysyos*, Lev Tov. *Chemdas HaYamim*, Shabbos Kodesh, 1. *Kaf HaChayim*, Orach Chayim 98. The Arizal also teaches a practice of wiping the forehead three times: *Sidur haAri*, R. Shabsi Rashkaver, p. 16].

In the following generation, a teacher and mystic named Rabbi Yeshayah Halevi Horowitz (1570-1630), speaks of a technique to clear the mind involving pronouncing a specific phrase from the Torah three times. He writes that if a person is distracted by extraneous thoughts before praying and he desires to rid himself of these, he should gently move his right hand across his forehead three times while saying each time the verse in *Tehilim* / Psalms: *Lev Tahor Bara Li, Elokim, veRu'ach Nachon Chadesh beKirbi* / Create in me a pure heart, O G-d, and renew within me an upright spirit [*Tehilim*, 51:12]. During the prayers, if you are in a place within the service that you are not permitted to interrupt, you may repeat this passage within your mind, without actually 'interrupting' your prayers through speech. [See also *Machtzis Hashekel*, Shulchan Aruch 98:1. *Mishnah Berurah* 98:2].

Rabbi Avraham, the son of the Rambam (1186-1237), writes that the above verse is a prayer and invocation of prophetic insight. The verse is referring to a state of internal isolation, which is a requisite for attaining prophecy. [See *HaMaspik LeOvdei Hashem*, Hisbodedus. This cultivated state is also connected to becoming a 'new person'. Arizal, *Sha'ar Halikutim*, Tehilim, 51]. It could therefore be said that the repetition of this verse not only helps to clear the mind of all distracting thoughts, but also to induce a more 'prophetic' or transparent (prayerful) mood/mode of consciousness.

WIPING THE FOREHEAD

As we mentioned, the Arizal, the Ramak, and the Shaloh all mention a practice of passing the hand over the forehead while reciting specific verses. How does wiping the forehead erase distracting thoughts?

Bodily movement shifts consciousness. The Chasidic Rebbe, Reb Pinchas of Koritz, a student of the Baal Shem Tov, teaches that physical movement disperses negative, habitual, self-centered thoughts. A physical shift and movement triggers a mental shift and movement [R. Pinchas of Kortiz, *Imrei Pinchas*, p. 136].

A similar idea is found in the teachings of the Baal Shem Tov, which implies that even slight movements of the eyes can shift focus and release the 'density' (distractions) of the body. This is perhaps related to the contemporary therapy E.M.D.R., in which eye movement is used to help release trauma from the body. In the words of a student of the Baal Shem: "There are times when a person has to look this way and that way to keep his mind/heart cleaving to Hashem. This is because the density of the body conceals the soul" [*Tzavaas haRiVaSh*, 80]. The movement of the head back and forth re-engages a person's ability to focus. It is like a shaking out of negativity, especially if done in rapid movement. When a person is anchored in negative or in-truding thoughts, the mere act of refocusing your attention on something else forces your attention away from where you were previously fixated.

Reb Pinchas of Koritz teaches that a person should con-tinuously recite the verses *Shema Yisrael...* / Hear Israel, Hashem is our G-d, Hashem is One, and *Baruch Sheim...* / Blessed be the Name of His glorious kingdom forever and ever, to himself [*Medrash Pinchas*, Os 8]. This, says R. Aaron Roth, helps with the quieting of intruding thoughts.*

Besides these meaningful verses, there is also a more 'magi-cal' or non-rational phrase used by certain *Poskim* / codifiers of law to calm the mind and clear it of distracting thoughts. They suggest saying *Pi-Pi-Pi* while passing a hand across the forehead, symbolically erasing the thoughts. This pro-cedure is concluded by softly spitting to the side, symboli-

---

* Rabbi Nachman of Breslov teaches that if a person wants to openly speak with the Creator (i.e.; *Hisbodedus*), but finds himself stuck and un-able to express himself or even say anything at all, he should repeat one word or saying over and over again until finally a breakthrough will occur and he will be able to express himself [*Likutei Moharan* 2, 96]. In other places he specifically suggests the repetition of the phrase *Ribono Shel Olam* / Master of the Universe. [See *Chayei Moharan*, 44. *Likutei Eitzos*, Hisbodedus, 16.] It is, however, clear in this case that the repetition of the phrase is not to eradicate unwanted thoughts or induce a deeper meditative state. Rather, it is a technique to help a person express himself. It is meant to jump-start the process of speech. This is precisely the rea-son why R. Nachman chooses the phrase *Ribono Shel Olam*, as it is (was) a familiar expression of many people of his time, certainly his followers. Much like today's English expression "O my G-d".

cally ejecting the thoughts. [See *Shulchan Aruch*, Orach Chayim, *Mishnah Berurah* 98:2. *Beir Heitiv* ad loc. The *Magen Avraham* (ad loc) writes that this is not a proven technique].

The repeated sound *Pi-Pi-Pi* seems 'meaningless'. While the syllables are in themselves nonsensical and they are meant to clarify the mind by their mere percussive sound, they also possess a deeply encoded semantic meaning. *Pi* (Pei-Yud) is an acronym for *Palti* and *Yoseph* / Joseph [*Sanhedrin*, 19b]. These two Biblical figures overcame their desire in the face of temptation. *Pi* literally means 'mouth' — *Pi* repeated three times refers to the three 'mouths' that 'opened' miraculously in the Desert: the "mouth of the earth", the "mouth of the donkey", and the "mouth of the well" [R. Tzvi Elimelech of Dinov, *Devarim Nechmadim*, Avos]. Numerically, *Pi* equals 90. Three times 90 is 270, which is equivalent to the word *Ra'* / evil or negativity. In this way, saying *Pi* three times is meant to eradicate any harmful distractions from one's thoughts.

INDUCING PROPHETIC CONSCIOUSNESS

The Medieval Kabbalists used repetitive chanting toward deeply mystical ends. The illustrious sage R. Yoseph Caro practiced a form of repetitive recitation of passages from the Mishnah, the essential text of the oral aspect of Torah. [See *Magid Meisharim*, Hakdamah, by R. Shlomo Alkabetz. *Shaloh*, Meseches Shavuos, p. 4]. During this same time period, Rabbi

Chayim Vital records the same or a similar practice involving the Mishnah. In his documented practice, one recites a Mishnah over and over again, evoking heightened states of 'prophetic' consciousness.

Repetitive chant can create a hypnotic or trance-like state in which the chanter or listener is induced into a receptive state, allowing them to experiencing something beyond normative consciousness. We must keep in mind that for any type of transcendental consciousness or 'out of body' experience to transpire, a person needs to be properly prepared. They need to enter the experience with an 'open mind', meaning with no distraction. Thus, we need to know how to clear the mind of the deluge of everyday thoughts.

The objective of this advanced practice is to reach the inner spiritual quality and *Magid*/angel or Guiding Spirit of the Mishnah. A full treatment and understanding of this technique and the revelation of the Magid requires more than a few passing paragraphs and is beyond the scope of the current exploration. G-d willing, in a future text we will expand upon it. For now, we are looking at how high spiritual elevation is available through verbal repetition. This is what Rabbi Chayim Vital writes:

> ...To attain any type of higher awareness and spiritual intuition you need to be alone in your home, so that you will not be distracted.... To isolate yourself further, wrap yourself in a Talis. Sit and close your

eyes, and divest yourself (in your mind) from your corporeal self, as if your spirit had left your body and is rising above the atmosphere.

After you feel that you have divested your consciousness from your body begin to read a Mishnah, whichever one you choose. Read it aloud many times over and over again. Do so with great speed, as long as you are able to pronounce each word clearly and not skip even one word.

Have in mind to attach your spirit to the spirit of the teacher that is mentioned in the Mishnah. This is accomplished by imagining that your mouth is the vessel through which the words of the Mishnah are externalized and animated. The words, once spoken, are not just 'dead' letters on the page. Your voice, which emanates from the *K'li* / vessel of your mouth, is comprised of internal sparks from your own deepest soul that are now reading the Mishnah. When we speak and externalize sound, we are using breath, the inner energy of the body, and our soul. And now, your soul (expressed through your mouth) is and can be a *Merkavah* / chariot for the soul of the *Tana* / teacher of the particular Mishnah (that you are chanting). And his soul (the soul of the author) will thereby become vested within your soul.

And when you are overcome with exhaustion from chanting the Mishnah, if you are worthy (refined and inwardly cleansed) it is possible that the spirit of the teacher (of the Mishnah you are chanting) will rest upon your lips while you are reading the Mishnah.

And the spirit of the teacher will offer you peace (through your own lips but with the energy and spirit of the teacher's soul, i.e., the teacher will speak through you. The phrase "offer you peace" suggests a greeting such as "Shalom Aleichem.")

Everything that you will think in your mind to ask, he (the spirit, teacher) will answer you by speaking through your own K'li or mouth, so that your ears will be able to hear. You are not, at this point, doing the talking. Rather, he (the spirit of the Magid, the teacher) is talking through you. This is the secret of the verse, "The Spirit of Hashem spoke through me, and His word was on my tongue" [*Shemuel 2, 23:2*]; (i.e, the Spirit of Hashem speaks through the prophet's own mouth).

If you are not worthy of this high level (of revelation), it is also possible to achieve another state through this practice. As a result of the rapid movements of the mouth during the repetitions of the Mishnah, your mouth will eventually stop moving on its own, and you will begin to fall into a kind of waking-sleep (a hypnagogic state), and then in this liminal state you will 'see' how you are receiving an answer to your question, whether obscurely or clearly. This all (what level of 'revelation' you experience) is dependent on your level of preparation.

If you do not experience either one, know that you are either not yet worthy (refined enough), or you do not yet know how to divest yourself from your corporeal self.

[*Sha'arei Kedusha*, Chapter 4,
Sha'ar 2, Hakdamah 1]

//

PRACTICE

....

REPETITION OF A PHRASE, WORD OR SOUND TO QUIET THE MIND

Every practice must begin with the commitment to show up fully in this present moment.

We are not present when our mind is reminiscing about the past or worried about the future.

We need to clear the clutter from our mind, reduce potentially distracting forces and open ourselves up to presence.

It is preferable to carve out a specific time that can be fully dedicated to your practice, free from other commitments and distractions.

Before going to sleep is a most opportune time for this practice, although it can be done during any time of the day.

It is important to familiarize yourself with the space you are in and establish it as a safe and comfortable place to settle for the duration of your practice.

Put aside any expectations of how this experience should be.

Turn off your ringer.
Begin.

Select a short phrase or Torah teaching,
for instance the one we mentioned above:
Lev Tahor Bara Li, Elokim, veRu'ach Nachon Chadesh beKirbi /
Create in me a pure heart, O G-d, and renew within me an upright spirit [*Tehilim,* 51:12].

Repeat your phrase or sentence slowly and quietly three times.

Remain still, in silence.

Notice if the mind is settled and clear.
If not, repeat the verse again three times.

Feel the visceral sensations that the words and
vibrations arouse in your body.

When you are chanting these sounds, do not think
about the semantic meaning of the words.
Rather, try to *experience* them with all your senses.

Slowly, these words will fill the mind, leaving little
space for other thoughts to intrude.

When this occurs, the mind will become full and
empty at the same time.

Once your mind has become clear and settled, sit
quietly within this speaking silence.

Allow the silence to speak to you and the stillness
to move you.

When you are ready, return and greet the world.

CHAPTER 3

....

MOVEMENTS OF SOUND CREATING INTERNAL MOVEMENTS WITHIN

MOVING SONOROUS & HARMONIOUS SOUNDS

MUSIC HAS THE POWER TO SHIFT OUR MOOD AND CONSCIOUSNESS. Music can make us happier when we are feeling melancholy, help us to be more introspective when we feel scattered, make us feel at ease when we are anxious, and open our mind when we feel intellectually stifled or stuck.

Yet, the real question is, what is music? What differentiates music from noise? On the simplest level, music is nothing more than the meaningful movement of sound and vibration. But where does the meaning come from, and is that what qualifies a series of sounds as meaningful?

There is a world of silence and stillness beyond our normative consciousness and beyond the created world. Our world is a realm of sound, movement and vibration; whatever is manifest and observable here is manifest through sound and movement. It is a world filled with *Osyos* / letters, words and sounds. Music is the fullness of this world. We can reach beyond and transcend this world through silence, and we can become more present, embodied and immanent through sound, speech and music. We 'divest' in silence and 'invest' through sound.

As music is, at its root, movement, it also moves us. When the movement of sounds and vibrations enter into our consciousness, they arouse a corresponding inner movement within us. When we are internally moved we can awaken to a deeper understanding of ourselves and of life. Music is thus sound with a purpose, and its meaningfulness is the purposeful movement which transmits to us a certain non-verbal understanding.

PHYSICAL MOVEMENTS SHIFT FOCUS

External movement stimulates inner movement. When a person moves his physical body, he can cause a movement within consciousness. A shift in the body's position can affect a shift in mind-set. For this reason, if you are in the middle of praying and you find that your intention is not focused on the prayers, it may help to "lift your eyes upwards, towards Heaven to awaken intention" [*Shulchan Aruch haRav*, Orach Chayim, 95:3]. A simple shifting of the head and eyes to a higher angle can refocus and shift your intention. This movement can facilitate a mental, internal movement. The Baal Shem Tov teaches: "Sometimes you need to gaze this way and that in order to attach your thoughts to the Creator, blessed be He. This is needed because of the materiality of the body which is an obstructing barrier to the soul" [*Tzavaas haRiVaSh*, 80]. A simple rapid back-and-forth movement of your eyes can break the monotony of your thoughts, and shift their overall pattern.

A more subtle form of movement is that of a melody, when it generates internal warmth and stimulates emotional, intellectual and spiritual movement [Rebbe Rayatz, *Likutei Dibburim* 3, p.445]. The *Chidush* / novelty of music is that these sonorous movements of air, sound and vibration compel inner movements within us. There are physiological, emotional and intellectual reasons why we 'move' along with these subtle movements. Let's attempt to understand how this works.

OUR 'LOWER' SOUL IS DYNAMIC
AND REQUIRES MOVEMENT

There is a world of stillness and silence, lacking any movement and sound. This higher or deeper, inner world is referred to as Atzilus; it is a perspective of oneness with the Creator. This is the world of the Divine 'thought' beyond the Divine 'word'. In the consciousness of Atzilus there is no *Tenuah* / movement, as there is no here or there, inside or outside, before or after.

Our world, by contrast, is created and defined by movement and sound. It is thus a world of *Pirud* / separation, as movement suggests a separate here and there, a separate inside and outside. This world, as we know it, begins with words and letters. It is literally and metaphorically filled with sounds and vibrations, both subtle and not so subtle movements. This world manifests by means of Divine vibration: "And G-d said, 'Let there be light', and there was light.... and G-d said...and so it was." Correspondingly, our normative consciousness, which is part of this realm of movement, needs stimulation, sound and *Tenuah* / movement.

Our most embodied level of soul is called *Nefesh*. This level of soul animates the body and enables it to persevere, organizing the cells and transforming them into a coherent whole that can sustain itself. It is the Nefesh that gives the body motion [*Avodas HaKodesh*, 2:28]. Beyond this level of soul is our *Ruach*, literally 'wind'. Cravings for self-expression are a manifestation of Ruach. Love, passion, being moved by a work of art, a symphony of music, a beautiful person or object, are all associated with this soul dimension of Ruach. *Neshamah* is the cognitive and intellectual dimension of the soul, the part of us that seeks knowledge and wisdom.

These three levels of self that comprise our normative consciousness operate within the world of *Tenuah* / movement as physical, emotional and intellectual movement. Because we exist within this world of movement, we must be in constant movement, and we need to be stimulated by movement.

Meaningful movement of sound can move us on the level of Nefesh. It can move us to dance, or motivate us to get up and act. On the level of Ruach, music can open us up emotionally to love and pain, joy and sadness, connection and yearning, excitement and anxiety. Each type of music arouses emotion in a different way. On the level of Neshamah, music can move us to focus our mind, settle our thoughts, or even achieve deeper insight, depending on the type of melody.

A phenomenon called 'acoustical resonance' occurs when two fine-tuned violins are placed in a room. When a string on one is plucked or bowed, the other violin, even if it is at the other side of the room, will respond and vibrate in a similar fashion. Our bodies also vibrate and pulsate to rhythms and tones in our environment. We, too, are fine-tuned instruments. This is why, for example, we become calm at a seashore. Our heartbeat and pulse begin to synchronize with the calming, slower paced rhythm of the breaking waves.

Repetitive sound-movements — from the natural music of waves crashing on the seashore, to man-made music — have the power to stimulate us or calm us down, to focus or quiet the mind, to open or break the heart, to motivate us to act or to rest.

This is all within the realm of Tenuah and separation. Yet, music can also catapult us beyond Tenuah and separation. Music can even take us on a journey 'beyond' the world of sound into a world of transcendence, silence, stillness, unity and oneness with The Transcendent One. Melody can bring us to a place of *Kalos haNefesh*, an expiring of the normative consciousness, in which we are no longer operating from the level of movement and sound (i.e., the Nefesh, Ruach or Neshamah). Through sound, rhythm, melody or music we can be catapulted into the highest, deepest, most unified levels of *Deveikus* / unification with the Only One and experience a total silencing of the conscious ego.

The holy Zohar teaches us that the Torah, which is the secret of *ZA* (*Zeir Anpin* / the emotive Sefiros or Divine attributes), is elevated through *Nigun* / song, and so is the Shechinah (the divine presence within this world). The people of Israel as well are elevated from their exile through Nigun [*Tikkunei Zohar*, Tikkun 21]. In other words, song, melody and music inspire elevation. Music is movement of the highest order and thus it ignites and arouses movement throughout the entire world. Everything moves with music, and it is through music that we move out of exile and into Redemption.

In the world of Pirud and movement, the world of sound, we are presently in exile. Music helps us move out of exile and into Redemption because it can catapult us to a 'space' beyond Tenuah, a 'space' where Redemption is always already present. Music moves us out of our state of exile into the ever-present 'future', our essential state of Redemption. This is the 'movement' of Kalos haNefesh in which you 'experience', even if indirectly, a glimmer of the *Olam haBa* / the World to Come in the present moment.

MOVEMENT CAN BE UPWARDS INWARDS OR OUTWARDS

Now let us delve into the world of Tenuah and explore the movement of inspiration or motivation that music can stimulate in our Nefesh, Ruach and Neshamah. Let us observe how music inspires us on the level of Nefesh to use the body, as in to clap or dance. Let us observe how music inspires our Ruach and opens our heart to deeper feeling, and how music can move us to open our minds on the level of Neshamah. Melody helps us act, feel and think, or to even quiet the mind.

On the level of Nefesh, music 'entrains' living organisms and synchronizes them with its external rhythm. The simplest example is when we respond by tapping our feet, clapping our hands or moving our body to the rhythm. This is our innate ability to infer beat from sound — a virtually automatic response. An almost involuntary motor response to hearing and absorbing external rhythm that makes us move in some way. The next time you hear an upbeat rhythm, try to keep your feet grounded or head and body still and notice that it is almost impossible. Your body seems to want to move in rhythm with the music. When the music moves your soul your physiological rhythms of breath and heartbeat will alter accordingly as well. The beat and movement enters us fully and moves us on all levels.

The deeper reason for this automatic movement is that the external movement becomes linked with our inner movement of the bio-energy of Nefesh.

MUSIC TO ROUSE THE MOVEMENT
OF OUR EMOTIONS

The physical and emotional movements of music move us 'outward', sparking a desire to dance or to act. They can also entrain us to decrease in activity and go 'inward', enabling us to be more introspective and aware of subtler emotions. Inward movement can lift us 'upwards' into greater spiritual sensitivity and also send us 'downwards' to the depths of an emotional abyss. Music, melody and song in the realm of Ru'ach have the power to shift our emotional states and arouse positive or negative responses.

Music can lead one to rebellion or bring him to the remorse of Teshuvah; it can elicit tears of joy or tears of abject sorrow. [See *Divrei Yisrael*, Mikketz, Ma'amar Echad meRemazei Rosh Hashanah]. A single song or sound has the capacity to wake one up from emotional slumber [Rambam, *Hilchos Teshuvah* 3:4. Avudraham, *Ta'amei haTekiyos*, in the name of the Rasag, 7], while another may soothe him to sleep [*Eiruvin*, 104a. *Magen Avraham*, Orach Chayim 338]. Songs can arouse love as well as hate. Certain music can induce a form of prophetic consciousness [Rambam, *Yesodei haTorah* 7:4], or shift our focus from the mundane to the sublime [R. Shem Tov Falaquera (1225-1290), *Sefer haMevakesh* (1970) p. 86]. And other types of music can pull us down to the level of idol worship [Rambam, *Hilchos Akum*, 11:6].

Music is played at both momentous moments [*Bereishis*, 31:27] and mundane moments [*Yirmiyahu*, 48:33. *Sotah*, 48a]. Music is played at weddings [*Radak*, Tehilim, 78:63], and music is played at funerals[*Kesuvos*, 46b]. Music is played in war [*Bamidbar*, 10:9. *Devarim*, 20:30, *Rashi ad loc. Sotah*, 42a], and music is played in victory [*Shmuel* 1, 18:6. *Melachim* 1, 5. *Tehilim*, 18]. Music is played at every occasion throughout the cycle of life. Every human emotion can be stimulated and amplified by music and thus every human emotion has its unique song.

The psychological and neurological power of sound, rhythm and music can evoke deep sentiments when the music is associated with a childhood memory. For example, a certain lullaby may soothe you to sleep, while another tune may bring you to tears. This is not because of a physiological reason, but rather because the tune reminds you of being put to sleep as a child, or it reminds you of a sad experience from your past.

JOYOUS AND EXPANSIVE MOVEMENTS

"The Holy Spirit does not rest upon a person except in the midst of joy" [*Shabbos*, 30b]. For this reason the prophets of Israel had music played for them to lift their spirits and bring them to the joyous state necessary to receive prophecy. [See Rambam, *Yesodei haTorah* 7:4. R. Avraham ben haRambam, *HaMaspik leOvedei Hashem*, haPerishus. R. Chayim Vital (1543-1620) *Sha'arei*

Kedusha, 2:4]. When the prophet Elisha, for instance, desired to enter a prophetic trance-state he would say, "Now, bring me a harpist," (and) while the harpist was playing, the hand of Hashem came upon Elisha"[*Melachim* 2, 3:15].

One of the easiest methods to bring joy into your life is singing or playing joyful melodies. The Alter Rebbe wrote that for a person suffering from existential (as opposed to physical) depression, the simplest way to extricate himself from this condition is through singing happy tunes. [See *Ma'amarei Admur Hazoken*, Inyonim, p. 403]. For this reason, many Chasidic Rebbes would not allow themselves or others to sing melancholy or more somber tunes. [See: e.g; *Igros Kodesh Admur haZaken, haEmtza'i, Tzemach Tzedek*, p.324, and p. 326]. Singing joyful songs arouses inner joy as we begin to move in a positive and elevated direction along with the uplifting music.

Rabbi Yehudah haChasid (1150-1217), the legendary Tzadik from Germany, writes that if someone wants to pray with the right intentions they should sing melodies that correspond to their desired intentions. For instance, one should sing a happy tune to arouse joy [*Sefer Chasidim*, 158].
We move in sync with the movement of the melody. If our inner movements are upbeat, coherent or suggestive of positive emotions, we are uplifted or opened up. If our inner movements are chaotic or suggestive of emotional upset, we can be be pulled down into a state of despondency, craving, frustration or rage.

On one level, a love-song is a simple expression of love. As Rabbi Elazar Azikri (1533-1600), the great Kabbalist and poet, writes, "The finest way for a lover to express his love is through a love song" [*Sefer Chareidim*, 10:6]. The various tones within an octave represent the various levels of a person's feeling of love. For instance, the higher the note, the higher and deeper is the emotional expression of love. [See R. Levi Yitzchak of Berdichev (1740-1809), *Kedushas Levi*, Likutim, p. 206. *Divrei Yisrael*, Mikketz, Ma'amar Echad meRemazei Chanukah]. Yet, a song is not only an expression of the particular feeling that one is already experiencing. Rather, the song itself awakens and inspires the listener, and even the singer, to shift and move their consciousness along with the movement of the music.

In general, people function either from *Mochin d'Katnus* / immature or constricted consciousness, a state of disempowerment, incapability and lack of insight — or from *Mochin d'Gadlus* / mature or expansive consciousness, a state of empowerment, capability, and clarity of insight. There are multiple levels in between these two, and most people vacillate between them constantly. In order to pinpoint our state of consciousness and know why we are feeling Katnus or Gadlus at any given moment demands subtle self-awareness. Still, a simple truth is that sometimes a good song, melody, or piece of music can propel us out of a state of Katnus and into a more expanded and empowered state. [And even bring on a state of Deveikus. *Likkutei Halachos*, Hilchos

Nesias Kapayim, 5:6. See also *Reishis Chochmah*, Sha'ar haAhavah, 10]. The movement of the expansive music expands the listener as well.

MUSIC TO OPEN THE LEFT
AND RIGHT SIDES OF THE BRAIN

Beyond enlivening and inspiring our emotions on the level of Ruach, meditative music can also open the mind and awaken the power of the intellect [Rabbi David Kimchi (1160-1235), known as the Radak, *Tehilim*, 33:2]. Faster rhythms can encourage beta brain wave patterns and thus induce the state of a person who is alert, attentive, focused and engaged in problem solving or decision making. This positively charges the nervous system and stimulates mental capacity.

Recent studies have shown that music with a defined structure and pattern can make a significant impact in helping people articulate their intellectual capacities. This is especially true of Western classical music, which is defined as 'goal oriented', and has a definitive beginning, middle and crescendo. Students who listened to pieces of classical music before taking college tests performed better than those who did not.

Even at a very young, pre-linguistic age, such structured music has been proven to help a child's intellectual development. One study took 30 three-year-olds and divided the group in half. One half received weekly piano lessons and daily group singing sessions, and the other half did not. Eight months later these two groups were tested. Those who were musically active showed greater proficiency in working with puzzles, a standard way to test children for their mathematical reasoning. And in fact, over a longer period of time, the children who received musical training showed increased spatial-temporal awareness, which again is another form of mathematical and dimensional thinking. The mind learns to sequentially assimilate data and to process information in a coherent manner via the deeply learned patterns of 'rational' and 'goal-oriented' movements that exist within music. Math, spatial perception and music all seem to be deeply linked and intertwined in the structure of the brain itself.

In fact, on one level, music *is* mathematics. Music is the sound of numbers in sequence, where one sound relates to and builds upon the next. When the brain becomes accustomed to process these subtle relationships and movements of sounds, it also learns how to process data in more logical and elegant ways.

This type of goal-oriented and structured music seems to help us develop our rational thought process. It helps us to mentally move within and through the logical structures we are trying to grasp. We learn to move forward with the music. The 'left-side' of the brain becomes more alert and refined by listening or playing these types of melodies and compositions. The study and grasp of logic, including Gemara and Talmudic dialectics, arguments and counter-arguments, is greatly enhanced when such forms of music are engaged during study. This is precisely why you will hear people singing the text aloud in a Yeshivah study hall as they learn. The melodies help the intellect move from question to answer, and answer to question, and so forth, in ever-deepening understanding.

In addition to the above, there appear to be many other parts of the brain that are activated through music. Neuroscientists studying the brain as it listens to music have determined that the cerebellum tracks rhythm, while melody is perceived by the temporal lobes. Additionally, it has been shown that the right side of the brain interprets the music holistically.

Certainly, not every person is a neuroscientist, but most everyone knows that a powerful song moves us in ways that are much deeper than could a mere orderly or logical sequence of sounds. There is a mystery and magic in music that is unexplainable by quantification or science.

Despite the fact that different genres of music affect people differently according to their conditioning and preferences, still it seems that there is a magic in certain kinds of music that touches people more deeply than other kinds. It is safe to say that there is a palpable 'super-rational' element to many forms of music. Often, profound music touches something transcendent in us, beyond our normative, rational consciousness.

The venerable Chasid, Rabbi Hillel of Paritch (1795-1864), once said, "He who does not appreciate and understand song can never really understand *Chasidus* / the deeper, more mystical teachings of the Torah. [Quoted by the Rebbe Rayatz on the first night of Pesach 5697 / 1937].

A similar teaching is transmitted in the name of the Gaon of Vilna (1720-1797), who once stated that without a working understanding and appreciation for music one cannot truly know the inner secrets of the Torah or the secrets of the [Tikkunei] Zohar. [See *Pa'as haShulchan*, hakdamah, a tradition from R. Menachem Mendel of Shklov, who heard this from the Gaon]. Parenthetically, the *Tikkunei Zohar* explains the inner meaning of the Hebrew vowels, which is part of the 'music' of the Torah.

The 'left side' of the brain is a very useful apparatus for understanding and deciphering law and logic, yet a different type of awareness is required to access something of the ungraspable, the Transcendent, the mystical, and the musical. Mystical teachings, by definition, tether around the sublime and the ungraspable. To connect to and 'understand' the mystical depths of the Torah, the rational 'left side' of the brain needs to be stretched to its limit, while at the same time the 'right side' of the brain — the more imaginative and poetic dimension — needs to be awakened.

Music speaks to that part of the brain and reaches those deeper recesses and creative dimensions of self. It is thus not by coincidence that every time there was a renaissance and explosion of deeper mystical teachings and practices, there was simultaneously an explosion of musical creativity. For example, in 16th Century Tzefas / Safed Israel, the Alshich, Alkabatz, Elazar Azikri and the Arizal created a renaissance in Torah, and there was a simultaneous proliferation of *Piyutim* / hymns and sacred poetry. Later in the 18th Century Ukraine, the Baal Shem Tov, the Maggid of Mezritch, and the Toldos Yaakov started waves of powerful revelation in Torah, and there was a concurrent musical awakening in the form of Chasidic *Nigunim* / wordless melodies. These two forms of 'revelation', the mystical and the musical, are deeply connected. Heightened mystical consciousness manifests in partnership with heightened musical appreciation and sensitivity.

This is the power of music, especially trance-like, circular, repetitive, non-goal-oriented music. The mystics teach that the heavenly chamber of music is architecturally situated next to the heavenly chamber of prophecy [*Likutei Moharan*, 1:3]. This form of music opens up the more imaginative, creative dimensions of the mind and facilitates a more prophetic type of consciousness. For this reason, the ancient prophets would employ music to induce states of consciousness conducive to prophetic revelations.

A prophet would listen to music in order to stimulate a meditative state. The music would inspire a transformation of the prophet's normal, 'logical' state of consciousness into the intuitive and imaginary state of open awareness needed to prophesy. The repetition of the instrumental or vocal melody would become hypnotic and bring the prophet to a higher state of consciousness, ready to receive and open to express.

EMPTYING THE MIND THROUGH GENTLE SOUND / MOVEMENTS

As we explored earlier, our Sages teach that a good omen to succeed in one's studies is to learn in close proximity to a stream of water. The continuous soothing sound of flowing water serves multiple purposes: it relaxes the person, it fills the mind with white noise to empty the mind of all distracting thoughts, thus allowing the person to study with clarity and ease, and as a result it ensures that what is learned is deeply ingrained.

Flowing water is just one of many possible examples of a continuous, gentle, soothing sound. Any form of music or sound that contains these same characteristics could have a similar effect. Such music or sound relaxes the person and rids the mind of all intruding thoughts.

One of the words for song in the Torah is *Zimrah*. The word *Zimrah* is similar to the word *Zamir*, which means "to cut off". As in the verse, *Zamir Aritzim* / The branch of the terrible ones shall be brought low (i.e. cut off) [*Yeshayahu*, 25:5]. The art and power of a Zimrah is that it cuts off all distracting and unwanted thoughts. [see R. Yoseph Gikatalia (1248-1323) *Sha'arei Orah*, Sha'ar 1. Alter Rebbe, *Likkutei Torah*, Parshas Netzavim, 51d]. Such is the nature of all music and song. The tune fills the mind with its own movements and as a byproduct, empties the mind of all other 'movements' or thoughts.

This is one of the distinctive characteristics of music, this power to fill the mind with vibrations and patterns and clear the mind of all extraneous thoughts. The resulting clarity of mind opens the door for deeper and higher states of consciousness. Rabbi Avraham the son of the Rambam writes that the prophets would employ song and music to clear their minds and hearts from all thoughts other than Hashem, and that this would allow them to enter into a prophetic state.
To quote:

> "To achieve this inner form of isolation, a state where man is unified with his Creator, the proph-

ets and their students employed music and musical instruments. Music awakens, arouses…and purifies the internal from anything outside of Him…."

[*HaMaspik leOvedei Hashem,*
Hisbodedus, p. 177-185]

CALMING & RELEASING ANXIETY

Just as an upbeat musical movement can inspire and move you to joy, to wake up or think sharply, slow, repetitive sounds can quiet your brain and entire system. Faster tempos or higher frequencies enliven us, charge us, and force us to get up to ride the sound, as it were. Slower and calmer tones in lower frequencies tend to slow down the rush of mind and relax the body.

Sustained, slow, regular rhythms can help relax the body and, in turn, the mind, much like how the ebb and flow of the ocean or the pulse of the wind can soothe a splintered psyche to the point of putting the person in a state of total ease.

A repetitive melody or rhythm has a soothing nature. As explored earlier, our Sages speak of the sound of continuously dripping water upon a hard surface as a means to help a person relax and fall asleep. Certainly, this is even more true with intentionally produced rhythms and constructed music. Soothing music has the wonderful ability to calm a person's nerves and lessen their anxiety. [See R. Shem Tov Falaquera, *Sefer haMevakesh*, p. 12. See also; *Maharsha*, Berachos, 57b, Shelosha Moshivim]. A person suffering from nagging anxiety and shredded nerves would do well to listen to calming music. [See Rambam, *Shemoneh Perakim*, Chap. 5. *Sefer Shemiras haDa'as, Imrei Tal, Ma'amar Nigun*, pp. 5-7]

Calming sound to our nervous system is similar to healthy food for our bodies. Food nourishes the organism on a cellular level and sound nourishes our electrical impulses that charge our neocortex. Calming sounds therefore calm us down.

Anxiety is a form of erratic and brash internal movement. The mind jumps from one dramatic, devastating scenario to the next, relentlessly and unforgivingly. The mind, left to its own devices, will paint, in rapid succession, one horrific narrative after the next until the person feels utterly crippled and powerless. The paranoid thoughts begin to fill up the mind with every possible situation in the future going terribly wrong. As a result, the mind spins out of control as it confronts the unknown future, asking itself unanswerable questions such as: "Will I have enough money?" "Will I be healthy?" "Will I find love?"

Slower rhythms encourage alpha brain waves, the brain state of a person who is relaxed and mindful. Soothing, slow music can ground us in the present. The unhurried movements of sound take us on a journey, albeit a journey from distraction towards presence and being mindful in the now. This grounded presence inevitably lessens the allure of the unforeseen and apprehensive future. This form of music 'teaches' us and gently guides us to be more open, alert, and focused in the moment.

In addition to being an aid to help us relax in general, these forms of downtempo music and movements enable us to reach a state of *Hashkata* / quiet, meditative mind, eventually allowing us to enter into deeper, more spiritual states of stillness.

Sometimes we become so relaxed and free of anxiety that we are induced into a semi-sleep state. When we enter such a semi-sleep state while remaining awake and alert, similar to a lucid dream, we gain access to the 'behind the-scenes' parts of our self that are usually off-limits during our normal waking state of self-conscious awareness. When we are fully conscious in an awake state, our default setting is generally defensive and does not allow us to venture deeper into our psyche. This meditative semi-sleep state relaxes our ego-defenses and subjective biases, enabling us to see ourselves more objectively and allowing us to get closer to our deepest selves.

INTERNALLY GENERATED SOUNDS
AND MOVEMENTS

Just as you can listen to external sounds that arouse you or calm you, you can also tune into and listen to your own internal vibrations and sounds. There is an unceasing inner sound pulsating through you and you can learn to be sensitive enough to hear it. When a person learns how to shut out all other externally stimulated sounds he will be able to discern these very faint vibrations occurring within.

Even apparently inert matter is emanating vibration; how much more so does a living system such as the human body produce a spectrum of sounds, some easily audible, some less so. The mouth is not the only orifice that emits sounds. The entire body vibrates and is pulsing with life, movement and sound. The holy Arizal, Rabbi Yitzchak / Isaac Luria (1534-1572), refers to the sounds released from a person's ear as the *Hevel* / breath of the ear. Today we know there are otoacoustic emissions which are very subtle, nearly inaudible sounds given off by the 'inner ear' when stimulated. Remain still for a few moments, close your eyes and mouth and let yourself become inwardly focused. Let all external sounds pass through you without holding onto them. You will begin to hear the inner sound of the body humming with aliveness.

Once you get used to this sound and allow it to fill your consciousness completely, you will become one with this sound and no longer hear it. Following this stage, another new sound will emerge.

We could understand the various internally generated sounds as related to the Ten Sefiros, the ten primordial frequencies, strings, or tonalities of this world. We could also relate them to the 22 letters of the Aleph Beis, the basic, vibratory building blocks of Creation and of the human being. Various Kabbalistic texts map the Ten Sefiros upon the human body, and many texts also map out the 22 letters upon the human form. In this way, each general part of the body and subtle body is connected with another one of the ten Sefiros and one of the letters of the Aleph-Beis. Perhaps what we are hearing when we tune into the body on a deep level is the 'sound' or frequency of these Sefiros and letters.

FOUR TYPES OF MELODY

Speaking generally, certain vibrations and melodies are more meditative and others are more upbeat and enlivening. There are movements that inspire love and those that stimulate awe, there are movements of joy and movements of melancholy. All these types of sound are simplistic in that they arouse or quiet just one emotion to the exclusion of others. There are also deeper or higher forms of movement and melody that can simultaneously spark contrasting emotions, for instance both arousing and quieting the mind, or inspiring both introspection and action. These types of melody have a more complex palette and function. Essentially, there are four kinds of song. These are: *Shir Stam* / a regular melody, *Shir Merubah* / a square (four-sided) melody, *Shir Kaful* / a double melody, and *Shir Pashut* / a simple melody. [See *Tikkunei Zohar*, Tikkun 21. Zohar 3, p. 227b. Rabbi Yehudah Muscato (1520-1590) *Nefutzhos Yehudah*, Derush 1, Higaon Bechinor. Alter Rebbe, *Ma'amarei Admur haZaken*, MaRazal, p. 25-28. *Torah Ohr*, Bereishis, 7c. Rabbi DovBer of Chabad, *Sha'arei Teshuvah* 1, p.35].

Shir Stam is an 'ordinary', uncomplex melody. It can express and evoke joy, such as in a more upbeat tune, or it can be a melody expressing and arousing bitterness, such as in a slower, more somber tune. However, each Shir Stam expresses just what the composer was feeling at the time the tune was composed, and in turn it stimulates that same feeling within the listener. The defining factor is that a single emotion is being expressed.

A more complex kind of melody is the *Shir Merubah*. As squares are formed with four sides, this musical formation is also a type of quadrangle: there are usually two or more stanzas, with each movement expressing a different emotion — for example, joy in one stanza and hope in another, longing in one movement and love in the next. Not every Shir Merubah expresses four emotions or sentiments, yet any melody that contains more than one trajectory is called *Merubah*, a four-dimensional tune. The reason is that the root of such tunes is in *Da'as* / knowledge, which is the fourth Sefirah counting from Keser. [See Rabbi DovBer of Chabad, *Shaarei Teshuvah* 1, p. 35]. *Da'as* is the ability to divide, separate, compartmentalize and contextualize, all of these being cognitive necessities for this type of composition.

An even more subtle and sophisticated form of melody is a *Shir Kaful*, a 'twofold melody'. This is a composition which expresses opposite feelings, sentiments or values, *simultaneously*. In a single stanza it can express feelings of both joy and longing, desperation and consummation, or hope and redemption. In this form of music one is able to embrace emotional paradoxes and seeming contradictions. A high level of sophistication is required from both the composer and the listener to articulate and assimilate such music.

The highest level of song is called a *Shir Pashut*, which literally translates as a 'simple melody', although the simplicity of a Shir Pashut is a bit deceiving. On one hand, the melody indeed seems unsophisticated and straightforward. There appears to be a simple rhythm and movement to it, and yet, despite (or because of) its simplicity there is something very profound occurring in the tune. Without all of the complications, complexities or sophistication of the Shir Kaful, a Shir Pashut seems to generate and maintain a myriad of diverse emotions and sentiments simultaneously and with ease [See Rabbi DovBer of Chabad, Ma'amarei Admur haEmtza'i, Kuntresim, *Kuntras Hispaalus*, p. 159]. The accessibility of such a composition is its power. Without being a master of music, every person who 'has ears to hear' can be moved by such an uncomplicated yet profound melody, feeling its multidirectional feelings and effects.

This Pashut form of music is reminiscent of the *Mon* / Manna that the Israelites ate in the Desert. The Mon was a very simple looking seed, and yet it contained all the flavors in the world in potential. Mon was a form of *Pashtus* / simplicity that was not empty of all forms or tastes, rather the opposite. Because Mon was on the level of *Ayin* / no-thing-ness, it had the potential to contain everything. The same dynamic is found within this form of music. Its simplicity is the empty canvas upon which many emotions are projected. This is a very high and deep form of melody, one that the greatest masters and the simplest novices can both appreciate. Its magic is that there are no extreme dramas, no deep valleys or high peaks, no thundering sounds or deafening silences, just a pure and simple tune — and yet it contains everything within it.

REACHING DEVEIKUS THROUGH MELODY

Some melodies, certainly if they are of the deeper forms that we have discussed such as Kaful or Pashut, can propel us to a state of *Deveikus* / cleaving in unity with the Divine in unconscious ecstasy. This is a type of music that can take a person out of the body, in contrast to the kinds of music that inspire one to become more fully embodied and present with their emotions. This type of music does just the opposite; it literally lifts a person out of his emotions and out of the drama of life, inspiring a movement towards an 'expiration' of ego, *Hispashtus haGashmiyus* / detachment and divestment from materiality, and Deveikus. This is one of the remarkable powers of trance-inducing and transcendental forms of music and song.

In the words of Rabbi Chayim Vital, the prime transmitter of the teachings of the Arizal: "Through the sweetness of the music, a transcendence (separation) settles upon the prophet and his soul divests (from his body), whereupon the music ceases and the prophet remains in a state of deep Deveikus." [See *Sha'arei Kedusha* Part 4. In addition, when one is in isolation, which is an important ingredient to attain prophesy, one usually sings. *Sefer Shemiras haDa'as, Imrei Tal,* Ma'amar Nigun, p 24]. This music is created and received with specific intentions.

It is interesting to note that all sound creates a sensation of separateness. How do we hear sounds? Sound waves enter our ears and travel into the ear canal. The vibrations create fluid in the inner ear, which causes electrical signals to move from the inner ear up the auditory nerve to the brain. When these electric signals hit the brain, the brain interprets them as sound. Perhaps because of this 'upward' movement of vibration and current, from the ear canal to the brain, sound has a separating illusion. It is as if the reception of sound causes the head, where the sound enters, to separate from the lower part of the body.

Try snapping your fingers around the circumference of your head at ear level. For many people, it will feel as if the top part of your head, from the ears upward, is detached from the rest of the body. This physiological sensation is perhaps connected to the spiritual sensation of Deveikus. If so, the physiological phenomenon is not the cause but rather the effect of the spiritual sensation. In any case, there is a similar 'detaching' movement in Deveikus music, a force of 'separation for the sake of unification' with the Divine.

As we explained earlier, it is only through the medium of sound that a person can truly experience a form of *Kalos haNefesh* / expiration of the ego. Through repetitive trance-inducing sounds, we can reach the highest levels of Deveikus, unification with the One and a total silencing of the conscious ego.

BEYOND SENSE OF SELF

Pain is one of our body's greatest defense mechanisms. It is the way our ego protects us and warns our mind that danger looms and that we should do something about it. Without an alert of pain, G-d forbid, a person would get injured and possibly die from his injuries, not knowing that he had to seek medical attention. Pain is a manifestation and agent of our self-preservation instinct. This instinct to survive is prevalent and dominant throughout all of nature. It is primal and essential. And yet, even more powerful than this primal impulse is music. Through music and song, a person can transcend and override the world of pain.

Chasidei Modzhitz is a group of Chasidim that originated in Modrzyc (pronounced *Modzhitz* in Yiddish), a village near the town of Demblin, Poland. The Rebbes of Modzhitz were known to be exceptionally musical and composed many melodies. The founder of this dynasty was Rabbi Yisrael Taub (1849-1920) R. Yisrael suffered greatly from diabetes and in 1913 he traveled to Berlin to seek a cure. He was informed that the only way to save his life was by amputating his gangrenous leg. At that time, although anesthesia was generally applied, there were still some risks involved and significant complications were the norm. The Rebbe requested that the doctors perform the amputation without anesthesia.

Certain that the Rebbe would beg for anesthesia once he began the painful surgery, the doctors reluctantly agreed. However, to their utter surprise, from the very moment he was laid upon the operating table, the Rebbe began to compose a melody bemoaning the desolation of the holy city of *Yerushalayim* / Jerusalem. The Rebbe was elevated through his extemporaneous melody to another world, a world with no pain, and he was able to survive his surgery successfully without recourse to anaesthesia.

It is true that pleasant music activates the brain's limbic system, which causes a release of pain-killing endorphins. Yet, a person needs tremendous levels of concentration to be fully present in the melody in order to not be pulled down into physical discomfort or pain, to say nothing of an amputation or surgery. The Rebbe was able to use the power of his mind to focus on the melody he was composing, and in turn, he was elevated through the melody to a higher state of consciousness in which he was oblivious to what was occurring to his physical body.

The above narrative illustrates the extreme power of music to transport a person to an alternate reality. Instead of being inevitably wedded to a world of physical pain, the Rebbe was transported via his heavenly melody to a world of unity and bliss. He was able to induce an out-of-body experience, as it were. Some people have used melody and music to help them transcend physical life all together. There are numerous stories of people who have on their deathbed sung themselves, or been sung, literally out of their body and out of this world. In this sense, music can be a bridge or a chariot that can carry us between worlds.

TRANSCENDING BODILY LIFE

"Exile is transcended through song "[*Tikkunei Zohar*, Tikkun 21]. All forms of limitation or constriction — whether physical, emotional, or mental — can be transcended through music and song. When the holy teacher Rabbi Yisrael Baal Shem Tov (1698-1760) was lying on his death-bed surrounded by his beloved disciples, he requested that they sing a song together. As they sang and his soul be-gan to gently drift from this world, he whispered a prayer: "Oh Hashem, please do not bring me to the foot of con-ceit" [*Tehilim*, 36:12]. At that point his soul departed from his body. Thus it was through a melody of deep yearning and longing, a tune with an inherent 'upward' movement, that his soul was elevated from this world. The process of his holy soul's ascension was initiated through song.

The Baal Shem entered eternity in exactly the way he lived in the moment. He lived a musical life, he died a musical death, and ultimately he *became* music — a *Pashut* / simple yet powerful vibration that continues to be felt today.

TRANSITIONS THROUGH MUSIC

Not only dramatic transitions such as death, but every tran-sition, every kind of movement, can be aided by music. Our Sages declare, "All bearers of collars go out with a collar and are drawn by a collar" [*Shabbos*, 51b]. The literal meaning of this statement is that although it is forbidden on Shabbos to allow your animal to carry anything out from a private domain to a public domain, it is permitted to allow an animal to go out with its collar around its neck. The word used for 'collar' in this passage is *Shir*, which also means 'song'. As such, the statement can mean: "All masters of song go out (transcend) with song and are drawn in (return to immanence) through song."

All upward movement occurs through song [*Emek haMelech, Seder Tikkunei Shabbos*], as song is essentially movement. We come and go, move inward and outward, upward and down, all through song. Every transition and movement warrants its own tune. In fact, there were Rebbes that sang different tunes throughout the day, each tune specific for the particular activity and time of day. There were also songs sung only on Shabbos, as well as songs uniquely suited for the weekday. There were special songs sung when putting on Shabbos garments, and songs sung when they were taken off. [As recorded by the Rebbe Rayatz, *Sefer haSichos* 5704, p. 95. *Likkutei Dibburim* 1, p. 103]. Every mundane or lofty transition demands its own song and is greatly assisted by the movement of its suitable melody. Every form of transition vibrates on a unique frequency and those who are attuned to life and attuned to their own inner frequency know how to identify the particular tune for whatever transition they are experiencing.

The truth is that everything in reality is in the process of transition. Nothing is static, fixed or stationary. Time moves forward and our subjective present is different from our past. As we and everything around us are changing, our relationship with everything in our life is also always changing. All things are in constant movement, and thus everything in the world has its own tune, rhythm, vibration.

Every person, as well, has their own vibrational resonance. Everyone is living and singing the song that belongs to him and to no one else. Additionally, every person has his own type of music he is connected to and resonates with. While certain people are inclined towards a particular genre of music, others are repelled by it. There are certain gustatory tastes and flavors that some people relish and others despise depending on their soul type and soul-connection. The same is true with different types of music and song [*Sha'arei Teshuvah*, 2, p, 15]. Certain people resonate with slower, meditative tunes, whereas others are inspired by more upbeat rhythms. Each person is connected to the music, rhythm, and movement of their own inner *Ruach* / 'spirit'.

EXPERIENCE NOT OBSERVATION

As insightful as all of these theories about music may be, it is self-evident that to get the most out of any form of practice, it must be experienced. It is simply not enough to study the ideas intellectually. We must experience music first-hand to truly grasp its power. This includes, but also goes far beyond, casual listening to background music. To tap into the transformative potentials of music, we must enter into it and allow it to enter deeply into us.

As a practice, we ought to learn to cultivate an appreciation for song, melody and music and even build a personal repertoire of tunes — wordless or with words — that we can recall at will. Any time or any place that we feel small, constricted, sad, down, clouded or discombobulated, we can pull up a certain composition or Nigun and hum gently to ourselves. A single tune sung with openness and intention will help us re-focus or perk up, depending on what we need in the moment. If we gather a big enough repertoire we will have a song for every occasion and for any circumstance. Singing or humming to yourself does not need a special time or place. On the contrary, you can do it in any place, at any time. All you need to do is sing a song and allow yourself to be transported by it.

CHAPTER 4

··

THE LETTERS, VOWELS & THE NAME OF HASHEM

THERE ARE 22 LETTERS IN THE HEBREW ALEPH-BEIS. AN ANCIENT AND MYSTERIOUS TEXT, SEFER YETZIRAH/THE BOOK OF FORMATION, DIVIDES THESE 22 LETTERS INTO THREE DIFFERENT CATEGORIES:

1) The three Mother Letters,

2) The seven Double Letters, and

3) The twelve Simple Letters (which we have explored, earlier).

What are these categories and what can they teach us?

Over the centuries, the mysterious text of Sefer Yetzirah has been contemplated and probed by the greatest rabbis and Sages. Many of them from the 10th through the 15th Centuries tended to interpret it as a book of philosophical cosmology. In other words, they read it as a text that explains the nature and make-up of the universe. For them it was a cryptic and symbolic explanation of how the world began from a state of ultimate oneness, the Oneness of Hashem, and gradually revealed and manifested itself as a world of seemingly infinite multiplicity. Read in this way, the text becomes an ancient book of physics, just on a deeper, more metaphysical, level.

Sefer Yetzirah has also been explained as a mystical and meditative text. From this perspective, it is not just an abstract treatise on lofty metaphysical ideas, but also a condensed and coded manual for actual mystical practice. For the most part, certainly from the 16th Century forward, with the Arizal and his school of thought, the book has been expanded upon in what can be called a 'left-brain' methodology, which privileges the more analytic and rational cognitive capacities as opposed to the more imaginative and intuitive faculties.

THE PATH OF SIGHT & MEANING

One of the main topics of Sefer Yetzirah, if not its primary focus, is the Aleph-Beis. The interpretive path laid out by the holy Arizal makes meaning out of the text by focusing on the shape, form, and numerical value* of each letter of the Aleph-Beis. Take the 'Mother Letter' Aleph for example. To decipher the inner meaning of this foundational letter according to the path of the Arizal, it would behoove us to take stock of each of these specific categories of shape, form, and numerical value, as well as the semantic meaning of the word Aleph itself.

One reason that Aleph is considered a primary Mother Letter is that its shape alludes to all the other letters via a deeper numerical value. In addition to the primary 22 letters of the Aleph-Beis, there are five 'final-letters', bringing the overall total to 27 letters. The letter Aleph is shaped as two Yuds with a slanted Vav in between them (א). Numerically, Yud equals 10 and Vav is 6, so the two Yuds and Vav

---

* The letter Aleph is 1, Beis is 2, Gimel is 3, and so forth. The first 9 letters are the single digits, 1-9. The next 9 letters are the double digits, 10-90. And the final 4 letters are the triple digits, 100-400. The final letter of the 22 letters is Tav, which is 400. Parenthetically, if Aleph is considered the highest letter and Tav is the lowest, shouldn't the numbers go from 400-1? The Ramak explains [*Shiur Komah*, 7] that the root of the letters is the *Ohr Ein Sof* / the Infinite Light beyond all numbers and manifestations. And so, as the letters are moving away from the Source of Unity and Oneness they become more revealed and multiplied. In this respect, the 'lowest' number is actually the highest, as it is closest to its Source, which is beyond all number and form. The Baal Shem Tov teaches that Aleph is an expression of the One beyond all form and letters. Beis is therefore considered to be two Alephs, Gimel three Alephs, and so on...until Tav, which is 400 Alephs. [See *Toldas Yaakov Yoseph*, Bereishis. *Toldas Aaron*, Likutim, p. 493.] In essence, there is only one Light. This One Light is first reflected in a single, unified vessel, the Aleph, and then into the vessel of two, the Beis, and then three, the Gimel, and so forth.

add up to 26. Adding 1 for the Aleph itself, the number 27 corresponds the total number of letters in the Aleph-Beis [*Likutei HaGra*, 29]. Twenty-six is also the numerical value of the name of Hashem, the Ultimate Source of Creation (Yud/10, Hei/5, Vav/6, Hei/5 = 26). [See Radbaz, R. David Ben Zimra (1470-1572) *Magen David*, Oys Aleph. See also: R. Yaakov ben Yehudah Landau.[?-1493) *HaAgur*, Hilchos Tefilin. *Levush* on Orach Chayim, 36:1]. Aleph is the source of the 26 letters of the Aleph-Beis, the building blocks of Creation, and Aleph symbolizes the Four-Letter unpronounceable Name of Hashem.

We can also zoom in on the Aleph and see two Vavs as well as two Yuds; separating the upper half of the slanted Vav from the lower half yields two separate Vavs [symbolizing the upper and lower waters of Creation]. This brings the inner numerical value of Aleph to 32 (Vav/6 + Vav/6 + Yud/10 + Yud/10 = 32), representing the 22 primary letters together with the 10 vowels.

Another interpretive strategy within this same path is to look at a letter's placement within the overall sequence of the Aleph-Beis in order to more fully understand its inner significance. The letter Aleph is the first letter, is numerically 1, and thus it represents 'the One'. Additionally, the full numerical value of the letter Aleph is 111: Aleph is spelled Aleph-Lamed-Pei. Aleph/1 + Lamed/30 + Pei/80 = 111. This sum represents the Oneness of Hashem that permeates the oneness of Creation (space/time) and the oneness of consciousness.

In addition to the Aleph's ordinal position, numerical value and actual structure, we need to also unveil the meaning of the word itself. The word *Aleph* is related to the word *Aalefchah* / learn or train in the verse *veAalefchah Chochmah* / and I will teach you wisdom [*Iyov*, 33:33]. The letter Aleph is thus connected to learning, highlighting the fact that the first step in growth is learning about the possibility to grow. Aleph is also related to the word *Aluf* / chief, and thus the first letter of the Aleph Beis refers to the *Alufo Shel Olam* / the Chief of the Universe, the Creator. Aleph also contains the same letters as the word *Peleh* / a wonder or miracle. All of this taken together suggest that learning and growth are connected to wonder, to the miraculous and relationship to the Divine. All of this touches on why Aleph is the first, most fundamental letter and building block of Creation.

THE PATH OF SOUND

The above analyses of graphic design, numerical value and etymology are based on the methods of the path of 'sight' and the path of the 'intellect'. There is, however, an alternative path to arrive at the secrets of the Aleph-Beis: the path of 'sound'. How does each letter sound when uttered? How does it resonate in its own unique way, and what does this communicate to us? In this path, the mystical and spiritual meanings of the letters are discovered through sounds and vibrations. The actual chanting of the letters reveals their essence. This is a non-intellectual, left-brain activity, different than our more analytic, intellectual methods. The path of sound is a more visceral, vibrational approach to deeper understanding.

In the path of sound, Aleph is the first letter because it is literally and tangibly the beginning of all sound. It is the opening of the mouth and voice, like the sound *Ah*. This 'musical' sound is the beginning of all voice and eventually speech; it is the almost imperceptible sound of the mouth or throat opening to vocalize. Aleph therefore opens up the potential for language, communication, and ultimately prayer. Every word, every vocal tone, begins with the *Ah* of Aleph. Aleph is the sound produced by the very desire to communicate.

As a sound or word, *Ah!* expresses the beginning of an understanding, the opening of a process of 'learning'. It also communicates wonderment as in, *Peleh*. Thus, the resonance communicates the same meanings discovered through visual and intellectual analyses — only through a more visceral, tangible, non-intellectual medium.

The same is true regarding all of the letters. The depth of each letter is revealed through its auditory resonance — how it sounds, how it is physically produced, and how the sound reverberates within us, triggering subtle understandings. When you say *Ahhh-leph* slowly, for example, how does your mouth and breath move? How does the vibration of this letter register in your body, and how does it shift your consciousness?

The 'path of sound' is much less abstract than the intellectual path of sight. It also seems to have been the dominant path of many of the early Kabbalists. For example, it is the mystical path delineated by the Spanish Kabbalist, R. Avraham Abulafia (1240-1291). His primary source of mystical insight and inspiration was his intense immersion in *Sefer Yetzirah*, and specifically the commentary of R. Eliezer of Worms (1176-1238), who was one of the luminaries of the *Chasidei Ashkenaz* / German Pietists.

The Chasidei Ashkenaz were a mystical, ascetic movement in the German Rhineland during the 12th and 13th Centuries. It appears that their mystical path, in addition to their asceticism, was based on an understanding of the Hebrew letters and their corresponding sounds and vibrational qualities. This letter-based auditory foundation is clearly displayed in the writings of R. Eliezer of Worms. Yet, it was not until the emergence of R. Avraham Abulafia that the path of sound was expressed as a fully articulated and structured system of mystical transcendence. R. Abulafia's teachings exerted an enormous influence upon the Ramak in the 16th Century, who quotes lengthy teachings by Abulafia, although not by name. But before going any deeper into the particular theories and practices of R. Abulafia, who was this enigmatic figure?

A SHORT BIOGRAPHY OF
R. AVRAHAM ABULAFIA

R. Abulafia was born in Saragosa Spain in 1240, an auspicious year, since in the Hebrew calendar it marks the beginning of the Sixth Millennium, the beginning of the era of world redemption and Moshiach. In his younger years, he studied Torah, Talmud and the commentaries with his father R. Shmuel. During this time, he involved himself in Jewish philosophy and was especially interested in the Rambam's *Guide to the Perplexed*. In fact, he wrote a Kabbalistic interpretation to this classic of Medieval Jewish philosophy.

At the age of 18 he lost his father, his primary teacher. Two years later he decided to travel to Israel to find the legendary River Sambatyon and the Ten Lost Tribes of Israel. Finding the Land of Israel in a state of desolation and lawlessness, a result of the last Crusade and the war between the Mongol Empire and the Mamluk Sultanate, he turned around and returned to Europe. There he married.

While in Italy, he began to learn under the tutelage of a certain Rabbi, philosopher and physician named Hillel — perhaps R. Hillel ben Shemuel of Verona, the author of *Tagmulei haNefesh*.

It was also in Italy that R. Abulafia began to teach and gather students. A prime disciple of his was R. Yoseph Gikatalia (1248-c.1305), who would become the renowned author of such Kabbalistic works as *Sha'arei Orah* and *Ginas Egoz*. Like his teacher R. Abulafia, R. Gikatalia occupied himself with mystical combinations and transpositions of letters and numbers. His great knowledge and piety earned him a reputation as a miracle worker. He was in fact referred to as R. Yoseph *Ba'al haNisim* / the Miracle Worker. Interestingly enough, there was never any controversy surrounding this holy mystic; he was always widely accepted. The same cannot be said of R. Abulafia.

At age 31, R. Abulafia returned to Spain. He reports that when he was in Barcelona and was deeply meditating on the Sefer Yetzirah with the commentary of R. Eliezer of Worms, the Divine spirit rested upon him and he saw fantastic visions. As a result, he wrote numerous books of wisdom and prophecy. He also writes that jealous spirits — however we understand that — attached themselves to him and he struggled mightily against them. In his book, *Otzar Eden haGanuz*, he writes, "I saw imaginary false visions and my mind was greatly confused, as I did not find a person to show me the way I should travel. The Satan was on my right side, causing me to deviate for 15 years. [Parenthetically, he also writes that the word Satan equals 359, the same value as the words *Zera Lavan* / 'white seed', i.e., wasted seed]. But in the year *El'yah* / 46 (meaning when 46 years old), Hashem desired me and brought me into the holy chamber."

In the year 1280, when he was 40 years old, he went to Rome to speak with Pope Nicholas III about the condition of world Jewry, and ultimately to persuade him to change his ways. At that point, the Pope was in Suriano, and he ordered the Vatican to detain 'Raziel' and publicly burn him as soon as he would reach Suriano. (Raziel was R. Abulafia's own code name for himself, as the name is numerically the same as his first name, *Avraham*: 248.) In close proximity to the inner gate of the city, a stake was erected. R. Abulafia knew of this edict but traveled nonetheless to encounter the Pope. He predicted the fall of the Pope if he refused to meet with him. When he was passing through the outer gate, news arrived that the Pope died the night before from an apoplectic stroke. The guards of the city of Suriano took this as a sign not to harm or even touch R. Abulafia, and so he went free and returned to Rome.

When he got back to Rome he was thrown into prison, but was liberated after a few weeks, perhaps also because of that prophetic prediction. From Rome he went to Sicily and gathered many disciples. It was there that he began to attract a lot of attention. Many people turned to the great Spanish scholar R. Shlomo ben Aderes of Barcelona, the Rashba, and asked him how to handle this mystical, messianic rabbi. The Rashba sent a sharply worded letter against R. Abulafia. Today, we have a letter from the early 1290's within the *Teshuvos* / responsa of the Rashba: in Teshuva 548, the Rashba denounces R. Abulafia in very harsh terms.

This ruling of the Rashba, and the surrounding controversy, was one of the principal reasons for the exclusion of R. Abulafia's teachings from the various schools of Kabbalah during his lifetime, and for some time later.

The Rashba's edict had a devastating effect on R. Abulafia and he once again picked himself up and left the Sicily area. He went into an 'exile', settling on a small island near Malta, today called Comino. It was there, in the year 1291, at the age of 51, that he wrote his last known work called *Imrei Shefer* / Words of Beauty, a meditational manual of sorts. After this, all details of R. Abulafia's life are lost. Perhaps he passed away on the island shortly after writing this work, or perhaps he just removed himself even further from public view.

Although a tragic figure, spending most of his lifetime in exile and condemnation, history has been a bit more kind to him, so to speak. A few centuries later, in 16th Century Tzefas / Safed Israel, R. Abulafia's teachings and texts became accepted and integrated into the wider mystical tradition by the great luminaries of Kabbalah such as the Ramak and R. Chayim Vital. However, perhaps out of reverence for the Rashba, they do not quote him by name.

Again, although he was born in Spain, R. Abulafia was greatly influenced by the Sefer Yetzirah, and specifically by the commentaries of the Chasidei Ashkenaz. In fact, his mystical, sound-based practices can be traced to his en-chantment with the teachings and practices of the Chasidei Ashkenaz. The Chasidei Ashkenaz were the first group of mystics and teachers who focused their attention on the Aleph Beis in general, and specifically focusing on the 'let-ters of the prayers'. The Chasidei Ashkenaz were the initi-ators of the then popular practice to count the letters and words of the prayers to uncover hidden meanings and sig-nificances based on their structural compositions.

These early Chasidim of Ashkenaz, such as the Rokeach, R. Eliezer of Worms [*Siddur Chachmei Ashkenaz*, p. 121], were the ones who fine-tuned the *Nusach* / version of the prayers as we have them today. They counted and measured every letter in the *Amidah* / the essential standing prayer.*

---

* Regarding the 'counting' of the letters of the prayers: The Spanish Rab-bi, R. David Avudaraham (14th century), who some believe was a student of R. Yaakov ben Asher, the Tur, was one of the foremost authorities on the ritual and meaning of the prayers. He writes that he too original-ly counted the words and letters of the Amidah but then realized that there is no good foundation for this practice, as there are various (slight) variations of the Amidah. [See *Beis Yoseph* on Tur end of Siman 113.] Nonetheless, the opinion of the German Kabbalists and the Arizal [*Pri Eitz Chayim*, Sha'ar Ha'Amidah] is that the amount of words are meant to be counted and that they are exact, no matter what the Nusach. The renowned scholar Rabbi Yaakov Yehoshua Falk (1680-1756) writes in his work the *Pnei Yehoshua* (*Berachos*, 28b): "The very nature of the num-ber of letters and words can have an effect on High to draw down the intention of the blessings." So much so that when we pray the words of the Amidah we should say them slowly, as if counting jewels [Semak, quoted in the *Siddur Shaloh*, "Kavanas veHanhagas haTefilah"]. It seems that the Alter Rebbe's opinion is that there is no exact amount of words and letters in the blessings of the Amidah. [See *Sha'ar haKolel* 8:5.] Yet,

The Tur, R. Yaakov ben Asher (c.1269- c.1343), who was born and raised in Cologne Germany, and thus influenced by the Chasidei Ashkenaz, passed down the custom of counting the words of the prayers and relating the numerical totals to particular verses in the Torah. [See *Orach Chayim*, Siman 113. See also, the Tur's father, the Rosh, *Teshuvas haRosh*, Kelal 4:20]. Alternatively, he passed down the practice of counting the numerical value of the first letter of each word of the prayers in order to tease out their spiritual and symbolic significance. [See Tur, *Orach Chayim*, Siman 118, see *Perisha*, ad loc, Yud].

Not only were words and letters noted, which suggests a basic sensitivity to the letters themselves, but even 'missing letters' were noted. For example, *Kol Bo*, a text by an anonymous author, notices that in the entire Amidah, the final letter Pei never appears [*Kol Bo*, Siman 11]. In any case, R. Abulafia's heightened sensitivity to the letters and sounds of the Aleph Beis can be traced back to his fascination with the Sefer Yetzirah and the Chasidim of Ashkenaz.

---

the Alter Rebbe does explain why, for example, in his Nusach one does not say *Tzur Yisrael* right before the Amidah, and bases his reasoning on the idea that there should be exactly 41 words from the words *Mi Kamochah* / who is like You until *Go'al Yisrael* / who Redeemed Israel. If *Tzur Yisrael* is added, there would be more words, making the total more than 41 [*Ma'amarei Admur haZaken* — HaKetzarim, p. 581-582]. The Alter Rebbe also writes about the number of words in the ending passages of the Amidah [*Shulchan Aruch haRav*, Orach Chayim, Siman 101:1].

The 'Mother Letter' Aleph is very prominent in the prophetic, meditative practices of R. Abulafia. He even adds
an Aleph to the Name *Yud-Hei-Vav-Hei* in his chanting
(breathing) system based on the Four Letter Name [*Ohr Ha-
Seichel*, p. 104]. Yet, as we explained previously according to R.
Abulafia, the majesty and importance of the letter Aleph, as
with all the letters, lies in and is revealed through the *sound*
of the Aleph.

This understanding and revelation of meaning through
sound can also be found in the writings of Rabbi Eliezer of
Worms. In his mystical text called *Sod Raziya* [*Sefer Alpha Bei-
sa*, *Os* Aleph], he writes that the letter Aleph has three letters
when pronounced — Aleph, Lamed and Final Pei, which
represent the 'beginning, middle and end', transforming
the Aleph into a kind of cosmic storyboard containing the
meta-narrative of Creation, Revelation, and Redemption
within its very pronunciation.

We pronounce the *Ah* of the letter Aleph using our throat,
the innermost part of the mouth; this is the 'beginning'. The
Lamed sound is created using our tongue, the middle of our
mouth; this is the 'middle'. The *Ph* sound of Pei is fashioned
using our lips, the outermost part of the mouth; this is the
'end' [*Sefer Razie-l haMalach*, (Bnei Brak, Ayin Hei), p. 36].
These physical locations of the mouth are part of the secret
of the letter Aleph's inclusion of 'beginning', 'middle', and
'end'. The macrocosmic dynamic is reflected in the human
physiology of pronunciation. This is why Aleph is an el-

emental 'Mother Letter'. It is connected to the basic elements of sound — the beginning, middle and end of the
mouth. Thus, according to R. Eliezer of Worms, the meaning and attributes of a letter are discovered through its vocalization. This idea is a clear link between the prophetic
path of R. Abulafia founded on the sounds of the letters
and the Chasidei Ashkenaz.

It is beyond this present text to go much more deeply into
the actual path and practices of R. Abulafia; such a topic
would demand its own book. Let it suffice to say that the
method he advanced involved the sounding and chanting of
the letters accompanied by simultaneous head movements.
The purpose of these practices was first of all to clear the
mind of all unwanted and distracting thoughts. Following
that stage, which is no easy task, the ultimate purpose of
this practice was to induce transcendental, prophetic-like
state of consciousness. Practical details and instructions will
follow, G-d willing, in a future text.

THE WORLD OF *MALBUSH* / GARMENTS OF LETTERS

The primordial sounds of the Aleph-Beis are the vibrational building blocks of the universe. Everything in the world
is created by a combination of Divine sounds and continues
to vibrate with a Divine pulse. The micro- and macro move-

ments of everything in the world are a manifestation of corresponding spiritual movements and vibrations emanating from the 'stillness' and Oneness of the *Ohr Ein Sof* / Infinite Light, which are then immediately reflected back Above.

Letters/sounds are the very 'first' expressions or movements from the inside-out of the *Ohr Ein Sof* / Infinite Light.

"Then I was by Him, as a nursling, and I was daily *Sha'ashu'im* / delighting or playing, always before Him" [*Mishlei*, 8:30]. The word *Sha'ashu'im* comes from the *Shah* / to turn. A double *Shah*, as in *Sha'a-Shu*, means 'turning for the sake of turning', which is an act of pleasure or play, as opposed to an act of necessity. The Sha'ashu'im referred to in the verse, is the Torah. The 'source' of the letters of the Torah as they exist in the highest realms ("always before Him"), is known as the world of the *Malbush* / garments. [See *Emek HaMelech*, Sha'ar 1:4. See: *Nefesh haChayim*, Sha'ar 4:10].

There is a mysterious, hidden teaching by the Arizal about the world of Malbush that is not brought down in the canonical transcriptions of Rabbi Chayim Vital, but rather in the teaching of R. Yisrael Sarug. Between the years 1594 and 1600, the Egyptian Kabbalist Rabbi Yisrael Sarug disseminated his version of the Arizal's teachings in Europe, and especially in Italy. Although R. Sarug was not one of the Arizal's official pupils in Tzefas, and he is not listed among the students who sat with the Arizal and learned Torah, he claimed to have been one of his main disciples. Perhaps he studied with the Arizal when he lived in Egypt, before he immigrated to Israel. This scenario does indeed make some sense, considering that R. Sarug was himself Egyptian. It is entirely possible that immediately after the passing of the Arizal, or even before the Arizal went to Israel, R. Sarug went, or was sent, to Italy in order to spread the teachings of the Arizal. At that time Italy was considered a vital center of Jewish philosophy and mysticism, making it an attractive and receptive location for a budding Jewish mystic to spread the seeds of a new Kabbalistic dispensation.

What follows are highlights from R. Sarug's exposition of the world of Malbush and the innermost world of Divine delight. Initially (and forever), before the concept of 'time' was created there was (and always is) One, a total Unified Stillness and Silence, as it were, of the Infinite Light. Then, as the concept of time was created, there arose a 'ripple of joy' an indent, a movement within the One, at the thought of the pleasure it would receive from the spiritual work and good deeds of all the righteous people that would be born into the world. This rippling is similar to the wave-like movement that occurs in one's belly when one begins to laugh. In other words, the body generally has a uniform position, upright and straight. When the person starts laughing, the body collapses slightly and bends in and out and the belly ripples. The Divine inner ripple is a kind of *Tzimtzum* / a contraction, so-to-speak, of the Essence of the Infinite Creator. As a result of this ripple of joyful laughter within the One, a finite space manifested within It. In this space it was possible to reveal an infinite light; light could begin to move and emerge within the 'innards' of the Creator, as it were. This is referred to as a "Tzimtzum from Himself into Himself" [*Leshem, Hakdamos veShe'arim*, Sha'ar haPone Kadim, 1].

Think of the Essence of Hashem as a black hole where no light can escape due to its dimension-warping gravitational pull. It is only when the intensity of this gravity is lessened that light can 'escape' and emerge. In this sense, Hashem's laughter allows for Creation to occur in two ways: 1) it creates the necessary space within the One by contracting G-d's Essence, and 2) it introduces a degree of levity or lightness sufficient to lessen the deadening 'gravitational pull' of Absolute Oneness. These quantitative and qualitative movements within the One, initiated by a holy chuckle at the thought of Creation, are what allows the world to come into existence. Before this, there was no room within the One even for the Infinite light; there was only Ein Sof, which includes and transcends infinity and finitude, light and darkness. Only after the 'ripple' of Hashem's laughter can the Infinite Light begin to emerge and fill the finite space created within the One. This is precisely where the Creation of the world takes place.

This divine laughter is an expression of the Sha'ashu'im, the immeasurable delight of the King within His Essence. This 'belly laugh' is the first arousal of movement of Creativity, revealing Infinity within the Essence of the Creator, and as a consequence, the potential for finitude. The desire to reveal and to be revealed is the essential characteristic of the world of *Malbush* / garments.

The 'garment' referred to is composed from the 231 possible Hebrew letter combinations. Since there are 22 basic letters in the Aleph-Beis, combining each letter with the next creates 462 combinations [22 letters x 21 letters = 462]. There are 231 possible 'forward combinations' of letters, also called *Panim* / face-combinations, such as Aleph-Beis, Aleph-Gimel, Aleph-Dalet, etc. There are also 231 backward combinations, also called *Achor* / backward combinations, such as Beis-Aleph, Gimel-Aleph, Dalet-Aleph, and so forth. Adding all possible forward and backward combinations brings the total potential letter combinations to 462.

These primary letter-compounds are the supernal 'sound-bank' from which all sound, vibration, frequency, energy and matter emerge. This sound-bank houses the vital potential to reveal the Infinite Light and then the finite vessel of Creation. But still we are only speaking of the potential to create finite reality. There still needs to be another process which allows this to actually happen. We need to move beyond pure potential.

Following the first movement from desire to potential, there was a second Tzimtzum that created the possibility to evolve the creative process from potential to actual. This is called the "Folding of the Garment". Folding creates edges, representing the potential of finitude. This Tzimtzum is also called the "Tzimtzum of the Square". Within this 'square' there is the revealing of *Avir Kadmon* / the Primordial Vapor. This Avir is also the *Ohr* / Light of the *Yud*. The letter Yud is the prima materia of all the other letters, as every letter in the Aleph-Beis, when written out, begins with a small letter Yud, a single point [*Chesed l'Avraham* (Kalisk), Va'eschanan]. This is demonstrable by the fact that you must first touch the pen to paper in order to form a letter. The very moment that the point of the pen makes contact with the writing surface, you have created a Yud.

Yud is the Nekudah /point of every letter, the point from which every letter arises. The letters that spell the word Yud (Yud-Vav-Dalet) spell the word *D'yo* / ink. Yud is the drop of ink that starts every letter. In other words, the Yud is the point that expands into manifestation, the small dot of ink, the pure potential that is expressed and articulated in each letter of Creation.

DOTS, LINES & DIMENSIONS IN METAPHYSICAL REALITY

Malbush is the inner dimension and highest/deepest reality of the Letters of Creation, but 'before' the Malbush (i.e., before the emergence of 'Letters') came the *Sha'ashu'im* /

Divine delight and desire to create. When the inner movement of the Sha'ashu'im was stimulated, sparks of light and energy were released, much like when we bend a straight metal rod. These sparks were first revealed as small *Nekudos* / points or dots.

When two or more sparks or dots were connected, they created a line. These conceptual lines became the (root of the) letters [*Leshem, haKedamos veShearim*, ibid], as each letter is essentially comprised of many small dots that make up lines of various lengths. Every straight or curved line, and even circles, are fundamentally comprised of tiny dots that come together to create something beyond themselves.

In other words, the Sha'ashu'im, which generated 'dots' and then 'lines', is what brought about the possibility of Malbush, the world of Letters, as the Letters are comprised of various combinations of dots and lines. The inner world of Malbush is thus the root of all the letters of the Torah, and the Torah is the root of all created matter in the universe. The Ten Utterances of Creation (Bereishis) are in fact sourced within the Ten Commandments of Revelation (Matan Torah). In this way, we can understand that the world is an impression of the Torah, and the Torah is an impression of Divinity, as explored earlier in greater length. Ultimately, the root of all expression, duality and dialogue is the 'dot', the first 'point' that was released/expressed from within the Unified Oneness of Hashem.

This complex structure seeks to explain how the apparent multiplicity of Creation emerged from within the infinite Oneness of Hashem. First there manifested a primordial dot or point. This singular point then became a 'line', which ultimately led to the formation of the individual letters of the Aleph-Beis. These letters, as we have explored, then proceeded to give birth to all further formations and vibrations of created reality. This basic description of the cosmic creative process is also found within the writings of the early Rishonim (11th until the 15th Century), albeit in more philosophical terms. R. Shlomo Ibn Gabriel (11th Century), the Ramban (13th Century), and even the Zohar, all explain the unfolding process of Creation as a development from *Nekudah* / point to *Kav* / line to *Shetach* / volume. [See: R. Shlomo Ibn Gabriel, *Mekor Chayim*, Sha'ar 2, Chap. 22].

Thus, a single Nekudah is the narrow bridge between the Absolute Unified Oneness of the Creator and the multiplicity of Creation. It is important to note that we are not referring to a point in the sense of spatial reality, but rather to a point in a conceptual, mathematical sense. When a second point joins together with the first point, or when a point extends beyond itself, it creates a Kav. The appearance of this linear reality creates a conceptual 'first dimension'. If the Kav is then joined by a third point outside the trajectory of the line, this forms an abstract triangular plane or *Shetach* / surface area — giving birth to a conceptual 'second-dimension'. If then joined by a fourth point, a conceptual third-dimension emerges. The continuing evolution of this *Nekudah* / single point leads to formations of increasing complexity and represents the iterative creative process that perpetually manifests exponential levels of multi-dimensionality and multiplicity.

All the above is reflected in the letter Yud itself. Yud is written as a dot, but spelled out as Yud-Vav-Dalet. This spelling is a graphical display of expansion from a point to a line to an area. First there is a Yud a *Nekudah* / point (ʾ), then this point extends down into a *Kav* / line (ı). Then finally the Dalet adds a horizontal vector and becomes a *Shetach* / area (ᴛ). [Rebbe Rashab, *Sefer haMa'amarim* 5666 ["Samach Vav"], B'Yom haShemini, p. 490. The Rebbe, *Basi I'Gani*, Lamed/Vav] The Yud is the Nekudah that evolves into the Kav, that evolves into the Shetach.

DOTS, LINES & DIMENSIONS IN THE DEVELOPMENT OF LANGUAGE

Again, for the most part, the process above is understood as a purely abstract, philosophical, and even metaphysical description of how the world of duality came into being. Yet, this construct can also perhaps be understood in terms of 'letters' and even actual 'sounds'. In this way, we can move beyond the purely conceptual realm and enter into the experiential dimension of the creative process. The first 'sound' is the 'dot', the Yud. Then, through various connections and combinations of individual dots, multiple 'sounds' are created, giving birth to our multi-dimensional, sound-based reality.

The first cooing sound a child produces is much like a Nekudah or Yud. Conceptually, this rudimentary sound can be conceived of as a primal point from which all further communication commences.

From another perspective, primitive forms of speech and communication, such as when a person points to a chair because he wants to sit down, or grunts or says *Nu*, are also a kind of Nekudah. Young children often communicate in this Nekudah-like manner of speech, such as wanting something, pointing at it and whining, or seeing a toy and gurgling with happiness.

A more sophisticated form of speech is expressed when there is more than one syllable being vocalized. Or, for example, when someone points to a chair and utters two words or referential sounds; one 'ah' while pointing to the chair, and another 'ah' while moving his hand towards himself, indicating that he wants to sit down in the chair. This more deliberate level of speech is in the form of a Kav, which is comprised of two points, dots or sounds.

Real, evolved, developed language emerges when there is

actual *Shetach* / area, greater meaning and dimensionality to the sounds. This is when Nekudos and Kavin, dot and lines, begin to be structured into full letters, sewn together into words and words into sentences.

'HIGHER' LETTERS

This development and evolution of sound (and light) — metaphorically from a dot to dots, from a line to lines, area and volume — is rooted in the evolution of the actual *Osyos* / letters themselves, moving an abstract state of potential into a manifest material form. The letters themselves have undergone a process from a state of abstraction to sonic and graphic manifestation, and from Nekudos (Yuds) to Kavin (Vavs) to fully filled out letters.

The deeper teachings of the Torah speak about the various forms of the letters and the processes by which they arrived at those forms, including the letters we have today. For the most part, we are only familiar with the shapes of the letters as we know and use them today. Yet, there were other forms of the letters prior to these.*

* The various spiritual grades of the Aleph-Beis helps to explain the different shapes of the Aleph Beis throughout different periods of time, in the times of Moshe or in the times of Ezra [*Sanhedrin*, 21b]. The Aleph-Beis represents Divine energy that is being transmitted into the world, and at various revelational states of history, different letters were revealed. The shapes of the letters we have today embody the quality of what they represent. For example, Vav, shaped as a line, represents a movement of connection and drawing down. These letters were only 're-

There are the letters, as they exist in the upper/inner world of Malbush, and there are letters that are called the *Osyos* / letters of *Razie-l* the angel, also called the "seals of the angels". They, too, are a form of Aleph-Beis, just not in the shape and form that we are generally familiar with. They are the letters, as they existed 'prior' to the creation of physicality. There are 'spiritual letters' that are way beyond the manifest letters of the Aleph Beis [*Meah She'arim* (Chabad), Imrei Kodesh, 24]. The Maggid of Mezritch reported that the Baal Shem Tov taught him the mystical understanding of the Aleph-Beis of Razie-l the angel [*Magid Devarav leYaakov*].

The forms of the letters as we have them today, in the shape and Shetach as we see them, begin in the inner/upper world of Atzilus, the world of Unity. Yet, in the world of Atzilus they are formed solely out of Nekudos. For example, the letter Vav, a single line, would be written out in the shape of three vertical dots. Likewise, the letter Ches, which is made of three lines, is constructed of nine dots, three for each line. Metaphysically speaking, there are large, medium and small letters [*Zohar* 1, p. 3b].

---

vealed' to us after the Purim story, once the physical world was utterly refined. [See *Kedushas Levi*, Kedushah Sheniyah. Perhaps a manifestation of this refinement was that other nations (Ashur) began using the sacred Aleph-Beis as their own letters. See, *Ritvah*, Megilah, 2b.] It may be that the Torah was revealed to Moshe in one form of letters, and revealed to Ezra in another form. And there is depth and reason to both forms, as the Maharam Alshakar explains. [See, R. Moshe Alshakar (1466-1542) *Teshuvos Maharam Alshakar*, Siman 74.]

The large form is considered 'higher', and the smaller letters 'lower' [*Meorei Ohr* 1, 52]. 'Large' does not refer to area, nor even to being more pronounced or revealed. To the contrary, the larger letters are less separated from their Source and less detailed, and thus contain a larger amount of conceptual space. [See Rebbe Rashab, *Sefer HaMa'amorim 5659*, p. 56 (p.42) *Likutei Torah*, Tzav, 17b]. They are more like points, before they become lines, and with Shetach. Perhaps we could think of the higher letters as packets of atoms. Even though the size of a cluster of atoms is 'smaller' in size, it includes more energy than even an enormous mountain. The higher or larger letters, are clusters of energy-packed Nekudos.

The Aleph Beis of *Pirur* / individual Nekudos, are letters as they exist in the realm of Atzilus. The complete formation as we have them today, formed out of full lines, semi-lines, circles or squares, begins in the world of *Beriah* / creation. The Torah begins, "In (or with) the beginning, *Hashem Bara* / created (as in the *Beriah*) *Es* the Heavens and *Es* the earth." *Es*, a grammatical modifier, is understood as an acronym for Aleph-Tav, the first and last letters in the Aleph Beis, implying the entire Aleph-Beis. Thus, the verse can mean, 'In the beginning, Hashem created the Hebrew letters, through which came the Heavens and the Earth.'

TAKING THE LETTERS BACK INTO
THEIR SOURCE, TO THE POINTS

The profound and prolific Italian Kabbalist known as the *Ramdu*, Rabbi Moshe David Valle (1697-1777), writes about a metaphysical technique called *Nituach* / the art of surgery that involves breaking down the letters into their foundational constituent elements of *Kavin* / lines (like the letter Vav) and *Pirur* / dots, crumbs (such as the letter Yud) [*Sefer haLikutim*, p. 184]. Since everything in this world is a manifestation of a particular formation of the Divine energy transmitters of letters/sounds, and since each letter is made up of dots and lines, we are able to 'perform surgery' on reality itself, so to speak, by writing certain words or verses in their more primordial forms.

For example, if a person by the name of Moshe is *Choleh* / sick, his current reality of disease is being sustained through the metaphysical conduits of the letters that make up the words *Moshe* and *Choleh*. The art of Nituach involves 'breaking apart' these letters, and deconstructing them into the raw material of 'points', in order to then reconstruct them with the intention of drawing down a new reality of healing. After the letters that spell *Moshe Choleh* have been deconstructed into dots, one then begins to put them back together, first in lines and then in their final forms, in such a way that now Moshe is healthy. This practice, accompanied by prayer and *Teshuvah* / spiritual realignment, has the power to re-state reality, transforming sickness into health.

As above, every letter is made up of Yuds and Vavs, points and lines.* Additionally, every line is made up of three Nekudos that are similar to the shape of 'eyes'. [See Arizal, *Sha'ar Heichal Nekudah*, Nikudim. Parenthetically, there are 24, or according to some, 70, 'eyes' in the name of Hashem. *Regel Yesharah* (Dinov) Maareches Oys Yud. See also *Tikkunei Zohar*, Tikkun 70, p. 128a]. The art of deconstructing the letters to their original points (as they exist in the world of Atzilus) returns the letters to their primal source of energy and expression. One is then able, through prayer and intention, to reconstruct the letters in order to express or project an alternative expression that will manifest a new reality. This act can be accomplished through writing. Practically speaking, one would first write out the letters in dots/points, then in lines, and finally in their fully reconstituted forms, while praying and having *Kavanah* / intention on their desired outcome. Alternatively, this technique can also be practiced conceptually in the mind as a visual exercise, or vibrationally, as a spoken

---

* Each letter is made up of points and lines. See for example, how the letter Shin contains the letters Vav, which is a line, and Yud, which is a point. [*Eitz Chayim*, Sha'ar 39, (Sha'ar Ma'n uMa'd) Derush 5. *Mishnas Chassidim*, Meseches Shemos Z'a, 3:6-7] All letters, besides the seven letters that comprise the words Zocher Din [Sefer haTemunah, see, *Megaleh Amukos*, Beha'alosechah, Derush 1], are formed out of other letters, when broken apart. For instance, an Aleph is comprised of two points (Yuds) and a slanted line (Vav) in between. At the very least, every letter contains a Yud in it as part of its form.

exercise. To do this, one would sound out the words in a developing series of sounds starting with primal cooing or grunting, followed by longer multiple seed-sounds strung together, and then finally with the fully articulated letters and words.

COMBINATIONS OF SOUNDS

Another way to undo the sound/letter 'patterns' of *Dinim* / judgments, to deconstruct sound/letters patterns which give rise to your reality, is through the art of *Tziruf* / letter combinations and permutations.

The *Chochmah* / wisdom of *Tziruf* / combination is mentioned by *Chazal* / the Sages of the Talmud [*Berachos*, 55a], and apparently, this was a wisdom that they themselves were familiar with and proficient in [*Sefer haPeliah*, 1. p 17a.]. Throughout the ages, leading Kabbalists were also involved in the art of Tziruf. One older Kabbalistic text, called *Sha'arei Tzedek*, describes Tziruf as a method of transcending the body in order to see oneself from the outside the body, while one speaks and reveals future events. [See *Shushan Sodos* (Koretz: 1784) p. 69b. See also: *Dover Tzedek* (R. Tzadok of Lublin) p. 96a]. It is said that the 13th-14th Century Kabbalist, Rabbi Yitzchak of Aco (Acre), would communicate with angels through the manipulation of the letters. R. Yoseph Gikatalia writes that through Tziruf the depth of wisdom will be clarified and the wonders of Creation will be revealed [*Sha'arei Orah*, Sha'ar 5]. Regardless of the time period or source text, all agree that the practice of Tziruf is a very potent, very advanced and potentially dangerous practice [Rabbi Avraham Azulai, *Chesed leAvraham*, 2:11] which we will only deal with in a cursory fashion in the present text, but which will be explored in greater length in a future text, G-d willing.

The concept behind the practice of Tziruf is that all words that share the same letters are interrelated and connected at their root. Therefore, one may redistribute the resident energies within a particular word or phrase by literally rearranging its letters to spell something different. Letters are the transmitters of energy and Divine life force. A word with two letters contains two 'Divine lights', which refract their particular energies according to their presented sequence. When these two letters are arranged one way, their energies combine to revealed a particular 'hue', as it were, and when arranged in the reverse order, they reveal a difference hue. That is, both sequences would reflect the same general 'color', but different shades or hues of that color. A word with three letters creates six possible Tzirufim. Each of these six Tzirufim expresses another tint of this same light. Each added letter multiplies the variety of outcomes. Here is a simple method of Tziruf taken from the teachings of the Baal Shem Tov. We will explore it further in the next chapter. Every experience of life and any Heavenly decree, whether positive or the perceived opposite, is revealed through the medium of letters — images, sounds and vibrational frequencies. Say, for example, someone is experiencing a form of *Tzarah* / hardship and they want to eliminate it from their life. One way to achieve this through Tziruf would be to take the three letters that make up the word *Tzarah* (Tzadi, Reish, Hei), and rearrange them in their mind's eye to spell *Ratzah* / desire, thereby transform- ing the 'hardship' into a experience that they 'desire'. [See *Kesones Pasim*, p. 47b. *Baal Shem Tov al haTorah*, Amud haTefilah, 159. *Toldos Yaakov Yoseph*, Noach, 15d]. In essence, one should rear- range the letters of a particular word to read or visualize an opposite meaning. In our above case, moving from hardship to desire; or, as another example, transforming *Mes* / death (Mem-Tes) into *Tam* / complete or wholesome (Tes-Mem).

In addition to this simplified approach, there are other ways to perform Tzirufim: through acronyms (Nutrikun), letter exchanges (Temurah), or shared numerical values (Gimatriya).

The Zohar [*Tikkunei Zohar*, p. 71b] comments on the verse, "I went down to the *Ginas* / grove of nut trees." [See *Shir Hashirim*, 6:11, see also the *Yalkut*, ad loc]. It says the single word *Ginas* actually stands for *Gimatriyah, Nutrikun, Temurah*. These hermeneutic methods are not only utilized by the later Kabbalists.

The Sages of the Gemara also make use of these three methods of interpretation.* [See *Nazir,* 5a. *Shabbos,* 104a. Chasam Sofer, *Toras Moshe,* Vayigash].

Gimatriyah is the symbolic employment of letters as numerals, usually in comparison with other words, numbers or concepts. There are 22 regular letters and five final letters in the Aleph-Beis, totalling 27 letters. Aleph, the first letter in the Aleph-Beis, equals 1. Beis, the second letter, equals 2. Gimel, the third letter, equals 3, and so on until the 9th letter, Tes, which equals 9. The next nine letters represent the double digits. Yud is 10, Chaf is 20, Lamed is 30, and so on until Tzadik, which is 90. The next nine letters represent the triple digits, with Kuf equaling 100 and the final Tzadik equaling 900.

So, for example, if there is a word that has a numerical value of 26, we can deduce that this word is connected to the name of Hashem in some way, as the Four Letter Name of Hashem also equals 26. Gimatriyah is considered another form of Tziruf used to uncover and flesh out hidden or alternative meanings within a particular word or set of words.

─────────

* The *Geonim* / Sages who lived over 1,000 years ago speak about the five forms of acceptable letter manipulation, which are called: *Tikkun, Ma'amar, Tziruf, Michlal,* and *Cheshbon* [Rav Chamai Gaon, *Sha'ar ha-Shamayim* (a.k.a. Sefer haIyyun), at the beginning. See also: Rabbi Yoseph Tzayach, *Even ha'Shoham,* Chap. 8.]

Nutrikun is the art of creating or finding acronyms within a single word or set of words.

A word with four letters, for instance, can be interpreted as an acronym for a sentence comprised of four words. For example, *Anochi* / I, the first letter in the *Aseres haDibros* / Ten Commandments is comprised of four letters (Aleph, Nun, Chaf, Yud) and can be understood as an acronym for the phrase: *Ana Nafshi Kesavis Yehavis* / I have given Myself (to you) in Writing, i.e., in the Torah [*Shabbos*, 105a. *Zohar* 3, 73a]. This is yet another form of Tziruf, a way of expanding upon the overt meaning of a given word in order to reveal something apparently different or deeper.

Yet, it is also understood that the meaning or association revealed through the acronym was already latent within the word itself. The acronym merely unpacks what was always already present. This process can be reversed as well. Meaning that one can collapse multiple words in a statement to form a single word in order to arrive at a hidden subtext concealed within the statement itself.

Temurah is the method of substituting one letter for another related letter. There are many ways that this can be done. One way is according to the phonetic relationship between letters. If two letters sound the same or very similar, such as an Aleph and an Ayin, or a Samech and a Sin, these letters are considered interchangeable in Temurah. There are five primary phonetic families of letters according to the place in the mouth that their sound is pronounced, they are: 1) *gutturals*, from the throat, 2) *palatals*, from the palate, 3) *linguals*, from the tongue, 4) *dentals*, from the teeth, and 5) *labials*, from the lips. Any letter from within a particular family can be exchanged with any other letter that comes from that same 'family'.

Another method of Temurah is to substitute letters based on their order within the sequence of the Aleph-Beis. For example, one may exchange the first letter of the Aleph-Beis (Aleph) with the last letter (Tav), and the second letter (Beis) with the second to last letter (Shin). This particular form of Temurah is called *A-T Ba-Sh*. Additionally, one may exchange the first letter of the single digits (Aleph) with the last letter of the single digits (Tes), and the second letter of the single digits (Beis) with the second to last letter of the single digits (Ches); one may exchange the first letter of the double digits (Yud) with the last letter of the double digits (Tzadik), and so forth. There are many other ways to substitute letters that we will not go into here.

In our context, the purpose of these methods of letter/sound/energy exchange are intended to create new vessels to receive and circulate positively-charged divine energy. In place of any perceived sense of *Din* / judgment or conceal-ment, through the practice of Temurah, there is now a re-ceptacle for divine compassion and revealed goodness.

VOWELS ARE THE LIFE & MOVEMENT
OF THE LETTERS

In addition to the 22 (or 27) letters, there is also the world of *Nekudos* / vowel points'that are placed above or below the letters. The letters of the Aleph Beis have no 'sound' without vowels. For example, in English, the letter 'A' on its own can sound like *ei, ah,* or *aa* (as in 'apple'), however the letter Aleph on its own, without any vowel, attached to it is inaudible. This is because, in Hebrew, the alphabet is comprised solely of consonants. A vowel is what moves a consonant into a particular sound [*Pardes Rimonim,* Sha'ar 19, and Sha'ar 28].

As an example, take the word *Aleph,* spelled Aleph, Lamed, Peh. On their own, none of these letters have a vowelization, and they can therefore be pronounced in numerous ways. When pronouncing the word *Aleph,* we vocalize the first letter with an *ah* vowel (Patach), and the second letter with an *eh* vowel (Segol). But, as mentioned, this is only one way to pronounce these three letters. If you place an *ee* vowel (Chirik) under the first letter, and an *oh* (Cholam) under the second letter, 'Aleph, Lamed, Peh' would be pronounced *EeLoF.*

The vowels are what give particular sound and thus 'life' to the letters. The letters are considered the body or vessel, and the vowels are the life-force or lights that energize the letters. Without the light, the body is lifeless. Without the vowels, we have no way of knowing how the letters are meant to be read and so they are, for all intents and purposes, inert and illegible. A letter without a vowel is lifeless, so to speak. The vowels are "like the soul that lives in the body" of the letters. [See *Sefer HaBahir*, 115 and 116. *Maareches Elokus*, 3, *Minchas Yehudah*, ad loc. *Amud haAvodah*, "Kuntreisim leChochmas Emes"].

Another way to understand the relationship between the letters and vowels is that the letters themselves are the Nefesh, the basic life force, and the vowels are the *Ruach*, the wind, breath or spirit that moves the letters [*Tikkunei Zohar*, Hakdamah, 7b]. Without the vowels, there is no way of moving the letters into speech and meaning. In the words of the Nefesh haChayim: "Letters without vowels exist only in the world of *Asiyah* / action, such as letters written in a Torah scroll without vowels. One cannot articulate these letters without connecting them to vowels" [*Nefesh HaChayim*, Sha'ar 2:16].

Typographically, the structures of the letters are mostly comprised of lines, angles and squares, whereas the vowels are mostly rounded points [*Tikkunei Zohar*, Tikkun 18]. In the words of the *Sefer haBahir*, an ancient anonymous mystical text attributed to a First Century sage, Rabbi Nechunya ben Hakana, "Every vowel point is round and every letter is square. The vowel points are the life of the letters and through them the letters endure" [*Sefer HaBahir*, 116].

Roundness represents continuous movement, in the image and manner of a wheel. The vowels are the wheels of the letters — when we attach them, they make the letters into mobile vehicles. As we are enabled to read the letters as words, we can also move from one word to the next, revealing phrases and sentences. We ourselves can be transported by the meaning and communication that comes alive.

The vowels move the letters and give them definition. Letters themselves, without vowels, are open to multiple ways of sounding. They can be pronounced and read with any potential vowel, and as such, they are essentially illegible.
It is true that every letter has a 'natural vowel', for example *ah* for *Ah*leph and *ei* for B*ei*s and *ee* for G*ee*mel. Yet, clearly sometimes the Aleph, Beis or Gimel in a particular word is read with other vowels. So, without knowing the actual vowels for each word as it was intended we would not know how to articulate or understand the given set of letters.

THE 'KING' OR LARGE VOWELS
& THE 'SERVANT' OR SMALL VOWELS

There are a total of nine Hebrew vowel sounds, plus a the tenth 'vowel' which is silence.

The vowel symbols are as follows:

Kamatz is an *ah* or *aw* sound. The Kamatz appears beneath a letter as a dot topped by a short horizontal line: ㄒ

Patach is an *ah* sound. The Patach appears underneath a letter as a flat line: ━

Tzeirei is an *ei* sound. Tzeirei appears underneath a letter in the shape of two horizontal dots: ••

Segol is an *eh* sound. Segol appears underneath a letter in the shape of a downward pointing triangle comprised of three dots: •••

Sh'va is an *uh* sound. Sh'va appears underneath a letter as two vertically stacked dots: ⠆

Cholam is an *oh* sound. Cholam appears in the shape of a dot placed on top of a letter: ﬠ

Chirik is an *ee* sound. Chirik appears as a single dot placed beneath a letter: •

Kubutz is an *oo* sound. Kubutz appears in the shape of three dots, diagonally aligned and placed underneath a letter: ⠢

Shuruk is also an *oo* sound. Shuruk appears as a dot placed in front of a letter (most often a vav): ﬡ

The final 'vowel' is silence or 'no vowel'. This appears when a letter has no vowel attached to it. That letter becomes a silent letter or a consonantal stop in a word.

Among these vowels are the five primary, larger 'king' vowels, and the remaining secondary, smaller 'servant' vowels [HaK'damah, *Tikkunei Zohar*, 4b. Tikkun 70, p. 135b]. Rabbi Moshe Cordevero, the Ramak [*Pardes Rimonim*, 28, Sha'ar haNekudos 1], describes these categories in great detail. The primary vowels are Kamatz, Tzeirei, Chirik, Cholam, and Shuruk. The secondary vowels are Patach, Segol, Sh'vah and Kubutz. The 'vowel' of silence is beyond these categories.

Discussing the stones that were placed on the Ephod, the ritual garment of the *Kohen Gadol* / High Priest the Torah says: "With the work of an engraver in stone, like the engravings of a signet, shall you engrave the two stones with the names of the People of Israel "[*Shemos*, 28:11]. The words *Pituchei Chosam* / engraving of a signet, which appear in our verse, contain all five primary vowels: *Pi*- has a Chirik, -*Tu*- has a Shuruk and -*Chei* has a Tzeirei; *Cho*- has a Cholam, and -*Sam* has a Kamatz.

These five primary vowels are hermeneutically related to the five mentions of the word *Ohr* / light that appear at the beginning of the Torah in the account of the first day of Creation five times [Hakdamah, *Tikkunei Zohar*, 4b]. This correspondence points to the fact that vowels are the 'lights' of the letters, and the letters are the 'vessels' of Creation. In order for reality to manifest and be sustained by the Divine vibrations of Hashem's creative speech, the vowels must illuminate the inert letters, allowing them to shine as their own distinct identities, shapes, dimensions, sound vibrations and meanings.

Additionally, these five primary vowels are subtly connected to the five primary phonetic families of letters: 1) gutturals, letters that are articulated with the throat, 2) palatals, letters that are articulated with the palate, 3) linguals, letters that are articulated with the tongue, 4) dentals, letters that are articulated with the teeth, and 5) labials, letters that are articulated with the lips [*Tikkunei Zohar*, 14a].

THE VOWELS & THE SEFIROS

The ten vowels also correspond to the ten basic Sefiros. The ten Sefiros are likened to screens through which the Infinite Light of the Creator penetrates and permeates finite reality. The distinct form, shape and texture of each Sefirah serve as filters through which the Infinite, formless, unified Light is reflected and refracted into our world. Passing through the Sefiros causes the Light to appear differentiated and defined depending on which Sefirah it is passing or perceived through. Through these ten *Sefiros* / finite vessels, screens, circuits or prisms, the Infinite Undifferentiated Light of the Creator is revealed and manifest. The word *Sefirah* is related to *Sappir* / illuminated, like a sapphire [*Zohar Chadash*, Yisro, 41b]. The Sefiros are illuminated by the Divine Light as it passes through them on its way to finite manifestation.

The word *Sefirah* is from the grammatical root *Safar*, meaning counting [Ramak, *Pardes Rimonim*, 1:1. Gra, *Yahel Ohr*, 6d]. It is also related to the word meaning 'edge', as in the *Sefar /* edge of the city. The Sefiros are the finite 'edges' that allow the Infinite Light to be moderated, articulated, measured or 'counted', as it passes into the finite realm of Creation.

In the metaphor of sound and speech, each Sefirah could be understood as another part of the cosmic 'mouth', which allows the infinite, undifferentiated Divine sound to vibrate at a particular defined frequency. The word *Sefirah* is also related to the word *Sipur*, meaning 'story' — the Sefiros 'tell the story' of Creation, as it unfolds. They impart the cosmological history of the Infinite Unmanifest as it becomes manifest in finite form.

THE VOWELS AND THEIR THEIR CORRESPONDING SEFIROS

1) Kamatz **ָ** *Keser,* deep desire and primordial will

2) Patach **ַ** *Chochmah,* wisdom and intuition

3) Tzeirei **ֵ** *Binah,* reason and cognition

4) Segol **ֶ** *Chesed,* kindness and love

5) Sh'va **ְ** *Gevurah,* strength and restraint

6) Cholam **וֹ** *Tiferes,* beauty and compassion

7) Chirik **ִ** *Netzach,* victory and perseverance

8) Kubutz **ֻ** *Hod,* splendor and humility

9) Shuruk **וּ** *Yesod,* foundation and relationship

10) No Vowel (Silence) — *Malchus,* kingship and receptivity;

Malchus 'receives' from Above and has no 'light' of its own. So too, this vowel has no sound.

VOWELS: THE PATH OF SIGHT
VS. THE PATH OF SOUND

Just as there are two ways to decipher the meanings of the letters — the path of sight and the path of sound — so it is with the vowels. Take the vowel Kamatz, for example. The path of sight and intellect teases out its meaning by observing its shape. The shape of the Kamatz is a Yud (a point or dot) with a vertical line above it, in the shape of a Vav [Hakdamah, *Tikkunei Zohar*, 7b]. The numerical value of Yud is 10, and the numerical value of Vav is 6. Together these equal 16, which is the number of all the dots/points and lines that make up all of the other eight vowels. Patach, for example, is comprised of one line (–) and Tzeirei is comprised of two points (..). When you add all the dots and lines together from the other eight letters, the total comes to 16 lines and points. Since Kamatz is the highest vowel, the Sefirah of Keser, the crown, it contains all the other vowels within it.

In that path it would also be appropriate to analyze the word *Kamatz,* to get insight into its nature. The word *Kamatz* comes from a word meaning 'to close the hand' or 'a handful' [See *Vayikra*, 5:12]. Thus, *Kamatz* means 'to close' [Hakdamah, *Tikkunei Zohar*, 5a], or 'closed' [*Ibid*, 8a. Tikkun 5. Tikkun 70. *Ohr Torah*, 433]. Being the highest vowel, and embodying Keser, Kamatz is somewhat removed and closed off from full expression.

The numerical value of the word *Kamatz* would also be taken into consideration. In the system of *Mispar Katan* / reduced or small number, Kamatz equals 14. In Mispar Katan, every letter can only be a single digit, in contrast to the more commonly known system, *Mispar Gadol* / large number. For example, in Mispar Gadol Yud is 10, and Kuf is 100, whereas in Mispar Katan, both lose their zeros and equal 1. in Mispar Gadol, Chaf is 20, and Reish is 200. In Mispar Katan, both equal 2.

In Mispar Gadol, the word *Kamatz* (Kuf/100, Mem/40, Tzadik/90) is 230. In Mispar Katan, however, *Kamatz* is Kuf/1, Mem/4, Tzadik/9, equalling 14. The number 14 corresponds to the 14 parts of the hand: three parts in each of the four fingers, plus two parts in the thumb [Hakdamah, *Tikkunei Zohar*, 4b]. The word *Yad* / hand is 5 in Mispar Katan, alluding to the five fingers. But in Mispar Gadol, Yud/10 and Dalet/4 = 14. The vowel Kamatz therefore represents a 'closed hand'. It is like a fist, with all 14 bones flexed inward; this way the hand appears not as five revealed fingers, but as a singular, closed mass. Kamatz is by nature transcendent and unified — in some sense 'closed' to revelation, or 're-duced' in expression and manifestation.

Again, these have been examples of the interpretive strat-egies on the path of sight. They yield tremendous results, helping the earnest learner of Torah to develop and dimen-sionalize his understanding of Hashem's words. But there are other ways to enter into the words of Torah and truth, and notable among them is the path of sound.

On the path of sound we will need to delve deeper into the actual articulations and vibrations of the vowels in order to uncover experiential connections to their corresponding Sefiros.*

For this reason, there is no one-size-fits-all system of Sefirah/vowel/sound equivalence. There are, rather, different systems that are promulgated by various teachers throughout the ages. For example, Cholam is connected to the Sefirah of Tiferes according to the Arizal and the Kabbalists that come after him. Yet, in some older texts, such as Sefer Hakanah [Sod Hilchos Treifos, p. 273-4], Cholam is connected to the Sefirah of Keser. The path of sound is more subjective and diverse. This is an important point that has relevance beyond our immediate discussion of the Sefiros and their sounds.

---

* Before we venture off into the world of sound and start drawing fixed connections between vowels and Sefiros, it is important to note that sounds, like colors, mean different things to different people in different places at different times. As we explored in our text on visualization practices, there is almost no *inherent* meaning to any color. For example, pink can be seen as both a masculine and a feminine color depending on the culture and time period. Today, in the west, we think of pink as a feminine color, yet at one time little boys were dressed in pink, not girls. The same is true with sounds. Certain sounds can mean one thing to one people, during one era in history, and represent something quite different in another era to another people.

Nevertheless, in the spirit of the countless truth-seekers and humble Divine servants before us, let us select and focus on one specific paradigm for now. Let us explore the nature of the ten vowels and their corresponding Sefiros according to the way the later Kabbalists have correlated them.

Kamatz

Kamatz corresponds to Keser, the highest Sefirah, the innermost will and desire of a person or of the Divine. [Kamatz is "above and high", higher than Patach: R. *Bachya*, Vayeira, 18:3]. The word *Kamatz* is an acronym for *Kadmon Tzach Metzuchtzach* / Primordial One, Pure and Clear [*Me'Eiyn haChochmah* (by an early Mekubal), p. 5]. The *aw* of Kamatz is considered a 'closed sound', involving some retention and enclosure of the vibration. As we mentioned, the word Kamatz actually means 'closed'.

Why is Kamatz considered a 'closed hand'? Sound is a product of movement. Movement implies a separation or distancing from unity. The Ein Sof is One, a Unified Whole. From the perspective of Ein Sof, there is no interior and exterior, higher or lower. There is only Omnipresent Oneness. The Sefiros are the 'finite' screens through which the One is projected into and perceived from a perspective of 'the many'. This indicates a gradual process of perceptual separation. Keser is the bridge between the Ein Sof and all the lower Sefiros. Therefore, it exists at the dynamic intersection between Unity and multiplicity, stillness and movement, silence and sound. In this intermediary position, Keser contains both an initial stirring of sound as well as a 'reticence' to express sound. It is like a seed about to burst forth from its enclosed shell into blossoms and a process of individuation.

The Maggid of Mezritch teaches that the word *Kamatz* comes from the saying [*Rashi*, Devarim 32:50]: *K'motz Pichah* / Close your mouth (from speaking). There is a *Pih* / mouth in this verse, describing a capacity for speech and sound. And yet, the passage says to 'close' the *Pih*. The Kamatz is thus understood as the fulcrum between sound and silence, between opening and closing, between movement and stillness, separation and unity. Kamatz is on the cusp of the fullness of finitude and the emptiness of infinity.
Patach

The next vowel, Patach, corresponds to the aspect of *Chochmah* / wisdom and intuition. In Chochmah there is the beginning of a true opening. The word *Patach* actually means 'opening'. The *ah* of Patach is the sound of opening up: *ahhh…* This is the continuation and expansion of the opening that tentatively began with the Kamatz. It is called the "opening and revealing of the hidden thought". [See *Tikkunei Zohar*, Tikkun 70. According to certain sources there is a possibility that the Patach symbol actually indicates a Kamatz sound. "Haskamas R. Yehudah Leib meYanavitch", *Siddur Torah Ohr*. See also: *Rashi*, Berachos 47a. Hagahos Yaavatz]. Again, *ah* is the sound we make when an idea or concept becomes clear to us, as in, "Ah, now I am beginning to understand," or "This was an *aha* moment for me."

TZEIREI

Tzeirei is the attribute of Binah. Binah is full comprehension and understanding. The two dots of Tzeirei suggest a process of forming comprehension (as in *Tziyur* / 'forming'[*Tikkunei Zohar*, Tikkun 70]) through the drawing of parallels, analogy, association and analysis. Phonetically, the *ei* sound is associated with the point in the cognitive process when deeper understanding forms: after the initial *ah!* there is a corresponding *ei* sound (as in *hey!*) This shift in vibrational frequency represents the movement from an initial, intuitive grasp of an idea on a big picture level, to a more thorough understanding of its constituent parts. Birthing this level of comprehension can take patience and sometimes extended contemplation or 'incubation'.

SEGOL

Segol is associated with the attribute of Chesed, which is giving and loving-kindness. The *eh* sound of Segol is a generously expressive sound, with a large output of breath. In addition to its sound, the shape of the vowel is also significant. The triangle of three dots, with two on top and one on the bottom depicts a process of synthesis. It shows that something 'higher' wants to lower itself and contribute to an other.

SH'VA

Sh'va is connected to the Sefirah of *Gevurah* / strength and restraint. The root of the word *Sh'va* means 'to sit' or settle (i.e. pause) [*Bereishis*, 29:19. *Tikkunei Zohar*, Tikkun 70]. Sh'va is the sound *uh*, an inwardly-moving sound that indicates you are pausing in order to reflect. Sh'va functions as a small pause before a greater release of sound. It is a sound of withdrawal or restraint of energy, and a gathering of strength for the pronouncement of subsequent syllables.

CHOLAM

Cholam is associated with the attribute of Tiferes. Tiferes is beauty, harmony and compassion. The *oh* or *oy* sounds of Cholam are sounds of compassion, empathy and mercy. Many people make an *oy* sound when they feel pain, or witness the pain of others.

CHIRIK

Chirik is connected to Netzach, victory and perseverance. The *ee* sound of Chirik is a penetrating sound, a sound of persistence.

KUBUTZ

Kubutz is linked to the attribute of Hod, thankfulness and humility. The *oo* sound of Kubutz is a sound of wonderment, awe and splendor. This is the essence of Hod — the experience of being overawed, a *wow* moment. Being in awe is to be humbled by the majesty of both Creation and Creator.

SHURUK

Shuruk is associated with Yesod, which is 'foundation' and relationship. This too is an *oo* sound, but it is graphically placed in front of the letter, unlike the Kubutz, which is placed under the letter. 'Being in front' suggests an outward movement. This is the idea of Yesod, to connect and form relationships with others.

NO VOWEL

A letter without a vowel — or the absence of a vowel itself — represents Malchus, kingship and receptiveness. As Malchus simply 'receives' from Above and has no Light of its own, so too this vowel has no sound of its own. It only receives the resonances that are given to it from beyond it, or it may remain silent.

SHAPE OF THE VOWELS AND THE MOVEMENT OF THE MOUTH

Up until now we have been examining 'why' the *aw* sound of Kamatz, for example, is connected with the first Sefirah, and why the *oh* sound of Cholam is the sound of compassion. Now, let's go a little deeper and explore how the shape and configuration of each vowel corresponds to its sound. There is a relationship between the sound of each vowel and the movements the mouth and face make when vocalizing it. Our mouths move in particular directions as we annunciate each vowel. For example, when creating the *oy* sound, our lips move up, and when we make the *ee* sound, our lips move down. Furthermore, the form of each vowel — whether it is comprised of a dot, two dots, or a line — mirrors the movement of our mouths when we vocalize that vowel. In the paradigm of sound, the shape of a vowel, as well as its placement in relation to its host letter, is based on the shape, placement and movement of the mouth when it is pronounced.

Kamatz is a line with a dot under it. The reason why the Kamatz is shaped in this particular form is that our mouth assumes that shape when we pronounce it. That is, when our our lips part to vocalize the *aw* sound, the upper lip creates a 'line', while our lower lip drops downward like a 'dot'.

Tzeirei is shaped as two horizontal dots underneath the letter. When we begin to pronounce the *ei* of Tzeirei, our lips part very slightly and two small dimples appear on both sides of our mouth, like two dots.

Chirik is a single dot under the letter. When we begin to pronounce the *ee* of Chirik, our bottom lip drops down and creates a subtle dimple under it, on the chin.

Cholam is a single dot above the letter. When we begin to pronounce the *oh* or *oy* sound, our mouth parts slightly and our upper lip moves upward, creating a subtle 'dimple' above the mouth, in the philtrum.

Shuruk is a dot placed in front of a letter. When we pronounce the *u* sound of Shuruk, our mouth moves forward, lips puckered, thus creating a small, round space in front of the face.

Patach is shaped as a flat line underneath a letter. As the mouth makes the *ah* sound the lips become slightly ajar and create the shape of a thin flat line between them.

Segol is a downward facing triangle comprised of three dots placed beneath a letter. As we make the *eh* sound, the mouth opens up, the lower lip drops slightly, creating two dimples on both sides of the month, and a subtle dimple below the lower lip.

Sheva is formed by two vertical dots placed underneath a letter. When the mouth generates the *uh* sound, the lips are tightened and two subtle dimples are formed: one above the upper lip and one below the lower lip.

These are the experiential correspondences between the shapes and the sounds of the vowels. Beyond these specific shapes, there are also general graphic placements of the vowels. Some vowels are placed below the letters, while others are positioned above or in front of them. This too, as will be explained below, has an experiential counterpoint in meditative movement.

In the 13th Century, R. Avraham Abulafia developed an entire system of practices wherein one chants various letters of the Aleph-Beis with different vowels attached to them. As one does so he also moves his head in the direction of the vowel (front, back, up, or down).
To quote:

> "After you begin pronouncing the letter start to move your heart and head. Move your heart imaginatively as it is internal, whereas your head is external so you may move it literally. Move your head in the direction of the vowel that you are pronouncing." [*Chayei Olam Habah*, p. 150]

Each of the vowels are located in a specific location, either on top, on the side or below the letter. As we pronounce the letters in this practice, we move the head in the direction of the vowels. In this system (which will, G-d willing, be explored in greater detail in a future book), when we are chanting a letter with a Shuruk, for instance, we would move our head forward to indicate its position in front of the letter. If we were chanting a letter with a Cholam, we would tilt our head upward, and so forth.

The deeper experiential basis of R. Abulafia's practice can be understood as follows: The act of tilting our head upwards when sounding a Cholam, for example, is not merely to indicate a *symbolic* or *conceptual* relationship between physical movement and the placement of vowels. Rather, while the upward movement reflects the upper placement of the dot, that placement reflects the upward lift of the upper lip when producing the Cholam sound. In other words, the graphic vowel is not ambiguously chosen; it is based on a physical experience. The head movements of R. Abulafia in this practice are therefore magnifying the physical, experiential aspect of the vowels, within a meditative state of consciousness. The links between mind, body and spirit are thus revealed and emphasized.

Our bodily posture is directly linked with our consciousness. We have a bio-feedback loop in which our posture informs our state of consciousness and our consciousness, in turn, guides our bodily behavior. When we sit down, for example, we automatically become more settled mentally. And so too, when we lift our upper lip to produce the sound of Cholam, our 'head' (consciousness) and our heart can be elevated to focus on the One Above, and we can be uplifted by a recognition of the beauty and compassion of the Divine attribute of Tiferes. When our lower lip drops downwards to produce a vowel such as Segol (*eh*), our head and our heart can drop into a focus on the presence of Hashem in this world beneath the Heavens; we can become 'grounded' in the recognition of the Divine Chesed that descends to this world.

THE META-ROOT OF ALL SOUND: THE NAME OF HASHEM

As we explore the elemental sounds of the Aleph Beis and the vowels, it would behoove us to touch upon the most fundamental of all sounds, the essential Name of Hashem, the Yud-Hei-Vav-Hei. In general, when attempting to decipher the meaning of the Name Yud-Hei-Vav-Hei, one is guided to focus on analyzing the Name visually and teasing out its meaning based on how it can be read. Before we explore the sounds themselves, let us touch into these visual and intellectual ways of analysis.

One way to refer to this name is *HaVaYaH*, which is a permutation or rearrangement of the four letters. *HaVaYaH* literally means "the Exister who brings all into *Haviyah* / existence"; the Ultimate Being, which is the source and stuff of all beingness. The four letters, Yud-Hei-Vav-Hei, when rearranged, can spell out the words *Hayah* / it was (past), *Hoveh* / it is (present), and when you exchange the Vav for another Yud (the Vav is understood as an elongated Yud), it spells *Yehiyeh* / it will be (future).

Accordingly, the essential Four-Letter Name represents the simultaneous totality of all past, present and future. The

Primordial Being does not depend on anything else to exist. Rather, it is That which gives rise to all past, present and future manifestation, thereby bringing all things into existence *ex nihilo* / something from no-thing.

The last three letters of this Name, Hei-Vav-Hei, create the word *Hoveh* / being — the present tense verb. The first letter of the Name, Yud, serves as a prefix to the word *Hoveh*, modifying the verb to express perpetual action. Therefore, Yud-*Hoveh* means '(the Creator of) the ever unfolding present'. It implies a 'stateless' state of infinite transcendence, beyond any conception of time and space, expressing itself as the eternal present moment.

In addition to the thought on how the Name is read, there has also been much thought on the 'reasons', so-to-speak, that Hashem chose these particular letters to represent the essential Name, and why in this particular sequence. In this approach, the meaning of the Name is understood via the letters themselves, not merely by what the letters mean.

Every Hebrew letter has a numerical value, as explained earlier, and every letter is also a word. For instance, *Aleph* is spelled 'Aleph-Lamed-Pei', and *Beis* is spelled 'Beis-Yud-Tav'. So, we can see that each letter inherently gives birth to other letters [*Bnei Yissachar*, Kislev/Teves, Ma'amar 3:19]. The full numerical value of a letter is therefore arrived at by adding together all the letters that make up its name. For example, the letter Aleph numerically equals 1, but when spelled out, the numerical value is 111 (Aleph/1, Lamed/30, Pei/80). The letter Beis numerically equals two, but when spelled out, it comes to 412 (Beis/2, Yud/10, Tav/400).

The letters of the Divine Name, when spelled out, have the smallest numerical values of all the letters. Yud is 20 (Yud/10, Vav/6, and Dalet/4), Hei is 6 (Hei/5, Aleph/1) Vav is 12 (Vav/6 and Vav/6). This is one 'reason' that these specific letters were chosen to express the Infinite One. Infinity takes up the least possible space, as it were, since Infinity is beyond space and time.

Another reason, we could say, that these letters were chosen for the Name, is that between 1 and 10, only the digits 5 (Hei), 6 (Vav) and 10 (Yud), when multiplied by themselves, are still present in the total: 1x1= 2; 2x2=4; 3x3=9; 4x4=16; 5x5=**25**; 6x6=**36**; 7x7=49; 8x8=64; 9x9=81; 10x10=**100**. They thus represent the Eternal One, who is unchanging and ever-present.

THE PATH OF SOUND:

In the above methods, one is either seeking understanding by analyzing what the Name (Hashem) means, such as the above treatment of Yud-*HoVeH*, or by assessing what these letters represent in terms of their numerical value. To arrive at an even fuller understanding of what the Name Yud-Hei-Vav-Hei really expresses, we need to also explore its nature and power in the context of sound.

In addition to the letter-chanting of R. Avraham Abulafia and his disciples, many other spiritual practices dating back to the students of the Ramban involve verbally formulating the sacred name(s) of Hashem in one form or another.

As above, according to the Sefer Yetzirah, there are three 'Mother Letters': Aleph, Mem and Shin. These represent the beginning, end and balance of all sound. The letters of the Name, Yud, Hei and Vav, are not Mother Letters, however in a sense they are even 'higher' than the Mother Letters. Earlier we explained that on their own, without vowels, the Hebrew letters are inaudible, and that the vowels animate and give life to the 'dead' or inert letters. Vowels 'move' letters and create a way for one to pronounce them; vowels are to letters what the soul is to the body. A letter without a vowel is lifeless and inanimate, as a body is without a soul — they are "mere letters of the Aleph Beis" [*Baba Basra*, 168b], with no animation. The vowels are like the *Ohr* / light or *Ruach* / spirit or wind that moves and gives light to the letters. However, the three 'magical' letters in the Name of Hashem (Yud-Hei-Vav) serve both as letters *and as vowels*.

R. Yoseph Gikatalia writes in his book, *Sha'ar haNikud* (in the very beginning), that the letters of Hashem's name — the Yud, Hei and Vav can function as vowels that move letters.

To quote:

> "Just as the (intellectual) soul moves (animates) the body, but itself does not move (the soul is not susceptible to change or movement), the same is true of the Great Name (Hashem) that moves and animates all the world, as it is (seen in) the secret of the Name. This Name (of Hashem) moves everything, yet remains transcendent of what it moves... the letters Yud-Hei-Vav move the other letters yet remain transcendent of and hidden from them." (Perhaps this also means that although these three letters move the other letters and serve as vowels, when they are actual vowels they are hidden from the other letters by the fact that they are encrypted. A dot is a 'hidden' Yud, for example, as a line is a 'hidden' Vav.)

A little further on, R. Gikatalia goes on to explain how these letters (Yud, Hei and Vav) represent the signs of the vowels. The letter Yud, for example, is a dot, such as we find in the Chirik (*ee*), and the Tzeirei (*ei*). The Vav can be used in a word to create a Cholam (*oh* or *oy*). And the Hei can be used to create an extended Kamatz sound, as in *ahh*.

According to R. Avraham Abulafia, the teacher of R. Gikatalia, the Name of Hashem is sometimes written with an Aleph in the beginning, as in Aleph-Yud-Hei-Vav-Hei. The letter Aleph, too, can be used as both a letter and as a vowel: when a letter is followed by an Aleph it often indicates the articulation of the vowel Kamatz.

The form of a Yud looks similar to the dot of a Chirik, so it visually suggests an *ee* sound. However, it also suggests a vowel sound in its own right, apart from that similarity of appearance. This is the case with the other letters of the Name. Linguistically, Aleph, Yud, Hei and Vav are called 'consonantal vowels'. This means that when reading a text without actual vowel symbols, when you encounter one of these four letters, you immediately understand or 'hear' a vowel sound. For example, when a Beis is followed by an Aleph, you inwardly hear *ba*. When a Beis is followed by Yud, you hear *bee*. When a Beis is followed by Vav, you infer *bo*. When a Beis is followed by Hei, you infer *bah*.

Now that it is clear how these four letters are also vowels, we can understand something deeper about them. Vowels 'move' consonants, as a consonant cannot be pronounced without a vowel. Vowels transform a stream of letters into a readable and audible word. Vowels are also the *Koach* / power and energy that animates the Divine speech of the Torah, which is the blueprint for all Creation. Hashem created the world through speech, i.e., through the letters of the Torah — however it is the vowels of the Torah that move or 'sing' these letters into the manifestation of physical Creation. As these four letters function as both consonants and vowels, they represent both the letters and the 'space' beyond the letters, so to speak.

The Yud-Hei-Vav-Hei, Hashem is *HaVaYaH*, meaning, 'the Exister who brings being into *Haviyah* / being', the Ultimate Being, the Source of all beingness. It is the Four Letter Name — with the Aleph — that pronounces and moves all letters, the *Ruach haKodesh* / holy wind, that moves everything in life into existence, as all of life is rooted in Divine speech and letters.

This is a 'sound-based' reason that these particular letters are chosen to express the Name of Hashem. These letters are movers, flowing with dynamic, life-giving sound energy, like the Unmoved Mover, the Life of All Life, who enlivens all through the vibrations of Divine speech. The enlivening energy of these four letters is also completely integrated with the 'body' of the letters, showing the continuity between physical manifestation and the Divine sound that creates it. The vowel-nature of these letters and their consonant-nature are actually indivisible, in the image of the Indivisible Omnipresence.

THE NAME AS SUBTLE SOUND — BREATH

A more subtle sound than speech is the sound of breath. Originating in the lungs, breath gives rise to a 'wind' that circulates within the mouth. The wind in the mouth mingles with the potentials of the mouth such as the teeth, tongue and lips to create words. In this way, breath is the source of the voice.

Rabbi Yeshaya HaLevi Horowitz (c. 1565-1630), otherwise known as the Shaloh haKodesh, the illustrious Kabbalist and chief rabbi of Prague, writes [Shaloh, *Meseches Rosh Hashanah*, p.169] that the shape and sound of the Shofar, the ram's horn that is blown on Rosh Hashanah, mimics and embodies the Name of Hashem. The Shofar is in the shape of a logarithmic spiral helix with a small opening at the mouth and a wider opening at its end. Through the act of blowing the Shofar we become partners with Hashem, Who also 'blows' the breath of life into Creation to birth on the new year.

The small opening of the Shofar's mouthpiece, (or the small opening of the mouth that is placed on the mouthpiece), represents the letter Yud. The initial inhale of *Hevel* / breath that one takes before blowing the Shofar represents the first letter Hei, as Hei is the sound of breath itself. The final Hei is the exhale: *haaa*. And the actual *Kol* / voice or sound that comes through the Shofar is the letter Vav: *oo*.

The idea of encoding of the Name of Hashem in the Shofar is open to numerous other interpretations. Here is another way: Both Heis represent the sound of the exhale; the Yud and Vav represent the act of inhalation. From this perspective, the process might look something like this: Yud / Inhale, Hei / Exhale, Vav / Inhale, Hei / Exhale. Alternatively, if the Hei represents the breath in general, including both the inhale and the exhale, then the Yud and Vav would be the retentions or spaces in between the inhales and the exhales: Yud / Retention, Hei / Inhale, Vav / Retention, Hei / Exhale.

Thinking about the Four Letter Name in this way brings up the possibility that perhaps Hashem's Name was never actually vocalized as a linguistic pronunciation, but was rather sounded as 'breath', which is the dynamic template of the rhythm of life. Perhaps the Name thus represents the perpetual Cosmic Inhale and Exhale, the expansion and contraction, or running and returning, of all of Creation. In this sense, the Name can be understood as a micro-cosmic rendering of the very manner in which Creation is manifest and sustained. Essentially, this name can be understood as the constant motion and sound of the breath of life, the sound (*Keviyachol* / so-to-speak) of the Creator breathing Creation into being anew each and every moment.

Being that we are created in the 'image of the Creator', we represent the inverse of the Divine breath of life. We are the animated echo of Hashem's all-enlivening breath. Our inhale gathers in the Cosmic Exhale of renewed life and oxygen, and our exhale empties our lives into the Supernal Inhale. In this way, we are "saying" the name of Hashem with each and every breath we take. Indeed, everything is breathing in some way, taking in and letting go. All of life speaks the Name of Hashem as we — and all of life — are continuously 'being breathed', Divinely spoken and birthed into existence.

Every moment that we are alive and breathing, and certainly when we are speaking [*Sheivet Mussar*, Chap. 43], we are animating and channeling the Name of Hashem through our very bodies. When the verse says, "The Neshamah of every living being shall praise Hashem," [*Tehilim*, 150] our Sages reply: "With every *Neshimah veNeshimah* / every breath, a person shall praise Hashem." This can be understood quite literally, meaning not that we *should* praise Hashem with every breath, but that we are in fact doing so by virtue of our natural inhale and exhale. In this way, all of Creation cannot help but say the Divine Name of the Creator continuously. With every breath, we are giving 'voice' to and praising the Name of Hashem, HaVaYaH, That which is, was, and will be, That which is giving rise to all of life, every moment, anew.

CHAPTER 5

....

RIDING THE SOUNDS:

THE PATH OF THE
BAAL SHEM TOV ON PRAYER

IN ADDITION TO THE SOUND-BASED PRACTICES WE HAVE ALREADY EXPLORED, such as integrating a teaching through chant and repetition, or quieting the mind through music, there is also the idea of 'riding' the waves of sound during prayer to swim 'upwards' and 'inwards.' In this sense, one is first calmed by the sounds and vibrations, and then carried by them to a higher and deeper place. This is the path of the Baal Shem Tov in prayer.

THE BAAL SHEM TOV

Rabbi Yisrael ben Eliezer, also known as the Baal Shem Tov, was the most important and innovative spiritual master of his time, and in fact one of the great teachers of all times. Today, more than half of Torah-committed Jews count themselves among his followers.

Yisrael / Israel was born in 1698 in Okop, a small village in the Ukraine on the Polish-Russian border. He was still a very young boy when his parents passed away. Most of his early life is shrouded in mystery. We do know, however, that the young orphan was cared for by the community. During his youth, perhaps due to a lack of shelter and stability, he found solace wandering alone in the fields and forests. He would spend hours on end surrounded by nature, pouring out his heart to the Creator in great love and awe. In being alone, he came to realize that man is never alone, and that Hashem, the Creator, is always present in every place and in every moment.

As a teenager, he supported himself as a teacher's assistant. He eventually developed a fascination with the Hebrew Aleph-Beis and drew great mystical insight and spiritual inspiration from the simple sounds and shapes of the letters, as will be soon explored. This can also be traced to his many years spent with children, as they were learning the sacred letters of the Aleph-Beis for the first time in joy and excitement.

Throughout his younger years — as he was developing as a great mystic and healer of both body and soul — the Baal Shem Tov maintained an image of simplicity. He dressed, walked and talked like the average man of the village.

At the age of 36, he received a message from Heaven to reveal himself to the world. In a short period of time, his fame as a holy man grew exponentially and he became known as Yisrael Baal Shem Tov. The title *Baal Shem* / Master of the Name was a common name given to many holy men who were miracle workers in the region. In fact, his teacher was known as R. Adam Baal Shem. But only Reb Yisrael received the extra appellation of *Tov*, singling him out as the 'Master of the Name of Absolute Goodness'.

Once he was settled in the small town of Medzeboz (currently transliterated as *Medzhybizh*) in Western Ukraine, and began to be supported by the community as the local Kabbalist and healer, many noted scholars became the Baal Shem Tov's disciples. The foundation of the Chasidic movement was then established, and it would flourish after his passing in the spring of 1760.

The Baal Shem Tov himself did not write down his teachings. What he did leave us with are his disciples — 'living books': living, breathing embodiments and examples of his teachings, who naturally modeled the teachings to others. These disciples eventually wrote down some of the teachings of their master, and it is from them that we get a glimpse into this revolutionary, profound, yet 'simple' spiritual master. As the Baal Shem Tov spoke in Yiddish, and his books were written in Hebrew, one needs a finely tuned ear to discern when perhaps a nuance was lost in translation.

THE PATH OF THE BAAL SHEM TOV ON PRAYER, IN BRIEF

Since the whole world is filled with the 'letters', vowels and vibrations of the Torah (the 'blueprint of Creation'), everything in this world is merely another expression of Divine Speech, no matter how lofty or lowly. The redemptive path of the Baal Shem Tov is based on the understanding of the 'shattered vessels' and 'scattered sparks of Divinity' hidden within the world. This path is predicated on 'elevating' these sparks by gathering all the far-flung sounds of the universe into your *Tefillah* / prayer, thereby integrating them back into their source. This reveals the inherent wholeness and holiness of Creation.

Begin this process by orienting your life around the recognition that you are constantly in the presence of the Omnipresent. The most fundamental obstacle that stands in the way of a deep, fulfilling and transformative prayer experience is *presence*. It is essential that we recognize that we are standing, at all times, and especially during prayer, before the presence of the Omnipresent.

To arrive at this awareness and acknowledgement of Hashem's infinite greatness, it would be fruitful to ponder the sheer magnitude of Creation, from the highest of its levels to the lowest. When you consider the myriad ways that the macrocosm mirrors and is synced up with the microcosm of Creation, you cannot help but marvel at the limitless power and brilliance of its Creator. This contemplative instruction is designed to inspire a sense of *Yirah* / awe. The quality of Yirah is often translated as 'fear', but it should not be confused with being scared or panicked, which are both *Kelipos* / negative trait' rooted in the *Sitrah Acharah* / other side. Yirah, properly understood, is an experience of sensing the numinous mystery of being in the presence of the ineffable. It is being overwhelmed by the unfathomable immensity of and luminosity of the Creator. The awe and wonder that result from such an experience open us up to the possibility of *Ahavah* / love. The experience of Ahavah is a gift, not a state that we can achieve or occupy on our own. However, *Yirah* opens us to receive this gift.

Once the emotion of Yirah is awakened, you should contemplate and form a *Kavanah* / intention for your words of prayer. Then, when you begin to intone, speak or sing the words of prayer, you should have no further thought or heaviness attached to it. Rather, one enters fully into the letters and sounds of their prayers in order to actually ride the sound waves, as it were, ever upward and deeper inward. Ultimately, one simply surrenders themselves to the sheer sounds and vibrations of their prayer. This practice requires one to shift their focus from the semantic meaning of the words to the sonic quality of the sounds of the words. This serves to shift one's consciousness from the cognitive capacity of the intellect to the affective realm of feeling.

THE PATH OF THE BAAL SHEM TOV IN GREATER DETAIL

According to the path of the Arizal, the great master Rabbi Yitzchak / Isaac Luria (1534-1572), there are sparks and shards of holiness scattered throughout Creation, and the primary means to "elevate" these sparks is through intellectual / spiritual intention. For example, before one recites a blessing over a glass of water, in order to elevate the sparks of the Divine within the water, one should meditate on a specific *Yichud* / formula of unification while aspiring to draw down and connect the spiritual realm with the physical world. We could surmise, since this is for the most part an inner mental practice, that only the inner quality of Creation, the 'souls' and perhaps 'angels', can be elevated by it. This is in line with the Arizal's own thought that the elevation of the outer, physical world itself will only occur in the future, in the times of Moshiach [*Sha'ar HaKavanos* 2, Seder Shabbos]. The Baal Shem Tov's path of elevation, on the other hand, is very different in that a) it can elevate the entirety of the Creation; it is not merely sifting out the latent Divine, Infinite Sparks that exists *within* it, and b) the transformation and elevation occurs not merely intellectu-ally, but through the use of the actual physical world itself; in prayer this occurs through the vibrations of the words themselves.

According to the Baal Shem Tov, this deeply holistic prayer practice involves the six general stages: 1) Presence, 2) Awe, 3) Love, 4) Thought, 5) Speech, and 6) Surrender. We will now explore these stages one by one.

STAGE ONE

PRESENCE
BEING PRESENT

What does it mean to 'be present'? "*Shevisi* / I have placed Hashem before me at all times "[*Tehilim*, 16:8]. In response to this verse the Rama writes [*Shulchan Aruch*, 1:1. See Rambam, *Morah Nevuchim*, 3:51-52. *Rashi, Radak* ad loc. *Reishis Chochmah*, Sha'ar haYirah, 1]: "This is a great principle of the Torah and is a paramount attribute of the Tzadikim who walk in the ways of Hashem. For the manner in which a person sits, moves around, and carries out his daily activities while he is alone in his house is not the same way he would engage in these activities while standing before a great king (or a person he deeply respects). In addition, the way one speaks while among those in his home and the conversations he partakes of with his relatives is not in the same manner in which he would speak while in the presence of a mortal king. Surely when one considers in his mind that the mighty King — The Holy One, blessed be His Name…stands always before him and constantly sees his deeds…then everything he does will be with more caution."

In other words, by sensing that we are in the presence of the Omnipresent, our whole manner of being and doing, thinking and speaking will be transformed, refined and elevated. Our life becomes that much more infused with urgency, meaning, and ultimate purpose when we cultivate an awareness of living within the perpetual presence of the Creator.

In the path of the Baal Shem Tov, when you live your life in the presence of the King, the *Nochechus* / immediate presence of Hashem is observed experientially, not just conceptually. These teachings warmly invite each of us to sense Hashem's tangible presence surrounding us as we become aware of being within the presence of Hashem's light. To quote:

> "There is a great advantage when a person ponders and thinks continually in his heart that he is near the Creator, and that Hashem is surrounding him at all times. One should be so experientially con-

nected to this concept that he does not need to be constantly reminded of this truth, for he 'sees' with his inner eye Hashem's presence and that Hashem is the 'Space of the World'. Since Hashem was present before the creation of the world, the entire world is founded upon and is within the Creator, may He be blessed. Most people see the world first, and through Nature they may see Hashem. But when one places Hashem before himself always, he is able to see Hashem first, and through the Creator see Creation."

[*Likutei Yekarim*, p.3.
Baal Shem Tov al haTorah, Ekev, 42]

When your life is lived consciously, in the perpetual presence of Hashem, and you are seeing the guiding Hand of the Creator in every detail of your life, you are also aware of being seen by the Creator of the world.

In the words of the Baal Shem:

"This is a deep level (of living) in which he continually sees the Creator may His name be blessed with his inner eye, as if he is looking at another person. And he shall think to himself that the Creator too is looking at him, in the same way that another person can look at him and observe his thoughts in action."

[*Tzavaas haRiVaSh*, p. 15a.
Baal Shem Tov al haTorah, Ekev, 37]

"A person shall always be in a joyous state and he shall think and believe (sense) with complete faith (clarity) that the Shechinah (Divine Immanence) is always with him protecting him, and that he is looking at the Creator and the Creator is looking at him."

[*Tzavaas haRiVaSh*, p. 15b. *Baal Shem Tov al haTorah*, Ekev, 38]

Although these teachings use visual metaphors, it is the same for hearing Hashem's presence and being heard by Hashem. Essentially, they are describing an overwhelming sense of being cared for, empowered and understood. This generates the reassuring sensation that all of your life is of great value. Your life is being recorded for eternity, not for judgmental reasons, but because every moment of it is eternally precious!

'Living in the presence of the Ultimate Listener' is another way to describe *Kabbalas Ol Malchus Shamayim* / accepting upon yourself the yoke of Heaven. This awareness charges a person with a sense of heightened purpose, alacrity and alertness. In the powerful words of the Tanya: "And indeed, Hashem is standing over him, and the whole earth is full of His glory, and He searches his mind and heart, if he is serving Him as is fitting "[*Tanya*, 41].

This type of consciousness is the ultimate motivator to live a deeper, higher, holier, more meaningful life. If we can truly believe and feel this, not conceptually, but experientially, then we almost have no choice but to live an exemplary life. We feel alert and ready. How can we 'sleep' away our lives if our lives are so important? This is the ultimate orientation of one who has accepted the Kabbalas Ol Shamayim. They are charged with purpose and ready to act with consciousness, creativity and compassion.

The sense of being watched and heard awakens your awareness with a sense of urgency, empowering you to sense that every detail of your life has extreme importance and tremendous value. We each have a mission. We are all imbued with a deep purpose. We are soldiers of peace with strong marching orders. Every one of us is entrusted to be a channel of the Master of the Universe and a co-creator in making this world a kinder, holier place for all. This is an almost overwhelming sense of the majesty of the human spirit and the magnitude of our abilities. This is an awesome and awe-inspiring sense of being alive.

If you ponder this idea well, you will be awe-struck, and this is the sensation that we are supposed to feel on Rosh Hashanah, the Day of Judgment and our collective birthday. This is the 'awe' in the Days of Awe. It is not the shallow fear of being judged that makes these days so awesome. Rather, it is the existential urgency and the awesome responsibility that inspires us. We can truly impact and alter reality with our thoughts, speech and actions. How can we live with this awareness and not be overwhelmed?

The truth is, we are being judged every day and even every moment [*Rosh Hashanah*, 16a]. Similarly, we are being born and reborn every moment. And with every moment, we are being entrusted anew with this awesome mission. This is not a judgmental judgment, it is an acknowledgment of your total worth. A birthday is a day in which Hashem says, 'I need you.' Every day that we wake up is our birthday. Every moment we are alive is a cause for celebration. Each and every moment Hashem is saying, 'I really need you.' The whole world is saying, 'You are necessary.' All of Creation is saying, 'Without you, all of life would be different.' On the other hand, it is easy to feel overwhelmed with the sense of urgency and responsibility when you recognize that every single moment of history led up to this very instant in time, and that the future is waiting for you, right here and now, to make the right choices and thus further Hashem's presence in the world for now and forever.

Just considering this awakens one to the 'yoke of heaven', to our sense of responsibility, and to the seriousness of this and every moment. Here is another important teaching by the Baal Shem Tov:

> "Too much (false) humility causes one to distance
> himself from the path of serving Hashem (which, by
> extension, is serving humanity and benefiting one's
> soul as well). On account of his humility he does
> not believe that his actions, whether Torah, prayer
> or acts of loving kindness, cause a *Shefa* / flow to all

the worlds. But the truth is that even angels receive nourishment from his actions. And if he would truly believe in this (power and magnitude of his actions), he would serve Hashem with joy and awe. How careful and scrupulous he would be with every word (he says) and every slight movement (he makes), if he would really ponder this and put his heart to the matter. Certainly, who is the person who would not be gripped by trembling and sweat when considering how the Great and Awesome King is keeping watch on his lowly lips (observing what will come out of his mouth).... The same person should open his heart and say, 'I am a ladder that is firmly planted on the ground, but the upper part of the ladder reaches Heaven. All my movements, words and actions create an imprint in the upper worlds.' As a result of this awareness, he will be scrupulous that everything he does and speaks will be for the purpose of Heaven (to further the revelation of Hashem's presence in this world). However, if he thinks, 'Who am I? How can I possibly affect any change or make any difference above or below?' This will cause him to be lax in his behavior and do as his (ego) pleases with no sense of consequence...."

[*Toldos Yaakov Yoseph*, Ekev. *Baal Shem Tov al haTorah*, Amud haTefilah, 137. See also *Zohar Chai* (Komarna) Yisro, p.80b]

Indeed, who is the person who will not be gripped by trembling and sweat at the very thought that the Great and Awesome King is keeping watch on him? The Nochechus of Hashem is palpable, awesome and overwhelming.

//

Be still and focus your attention on your breath.

If other thoughts arise, observe them,
and let them go.

Return to your focal point, your breath.

This will gradually quiet the mind.

Now begin thinking about your role
and responsibility in life.
Say to yourself: *'My life really matters.'*
'I am instrumental to the welfare
of the entire world.'
'Hashem believes in me.'
'Hashem is watching over me and waiting for me.'
'The whole world needs me.'

Allow yourself to feel the urgency
of this very moment.

This sense of Nochechus of Hashem brings a
person automatically into a state of *Yirah* /awe,
which is the next step in the
Baal Shem Tov's path of prayer.

STAGE TWO

··

YIRAH
FEAR AND AWE

Yirah is an easily misunderstood concept. 'Fear' is not something that most people have a positive relationship with. But that is strictly speaking about the lowest levels of fear. These types of fear are often associated with one's sense of physical or ego survival. There is also a concept of holy fear or Yirah. This is a positive, spiritual form of fear that is more akin to awe. There is also the idea of a kind of holy terror in the presence of the tremendum of the Ultimate Infinite One. It is a sense of our paradoxical importance and insignificance within the world and in the light of the Infinite One.

It is known that Yirah is the gateway to all Divine service, personal transformation, and rectification [*Shabbos*, 31b]. But what is Yirah?

There are people who pray with a certain *Far-kvetsh-keit* / a feeling of smallness, 'meekness' and melancholy, and they assume that this is a holy or deep way of praying. But this is nothing more than a form of spiritual depression, and certainly not a commendable or desirable emotion [*Likutei Yekarim*, p.3. *Baal Shem Tov al haTorah*, Amud haTefilah, 59].

Other people think of *Yirah* as 'fear of Heaven', translating this into their lives as a fear of being judged. They are afraid of being caught doing the wrong thing and being 'punished'. Such fear, no matter the behavioral benefits, is ego-based. The ego is afraid of rebuke or punishment. Any threat to the ego's authority is unacceptable and thus a cause for anxiety on its part. This is actually referred to as *Yiras Onesh* / fear of punishment. But this aspect of Yirah, as the Ramchal writes [*Mesilas Yesharim*, 24], "is only for the lowly (immature, unintelligent, or unsophisticated). This is not the Yirah of the wise and the mindful."

As mentioned above, *Yirah* is normally translated as 'fear', and fear is generally seen as an inferior emotion. All fears are rooted in the ego, whether they are real or illusionary. An example of real fear is fearing a drunk driver on the road. An example of an illusionary fear is the fear of darkness, or of public speaking. Either way, the root of all these fears is the ego's instinctual avoidance of pain and insecurity.

Ultimately, the ego fears its annihilation and termination. From the greatest fears to the slightest, all fears are based on an avoidance of partial or total extinction, whether that be physical or psychological. Ranging from the fear of being physically hurt to being punished or crushed mentally, all fears are a manifestation of the core fear of losing the ego. When thus triggered, the ego has many cunning schemes available to secure survival and self-perpetuation, from methods of fleeing and avoiding, to fighting and outsmarting. Anything or anyone that threatens survival is worthy of fear and defense.

Yet, despite all of this, the deeper you understand and embrace your fears, the more they are transformed into awe. Untransformed fear is holding on to the ego-self. Awe is letting go of the ego-self within the majesty of Creation and the Creator. This is the experience of losing yourself within something larger than yourself.

Recognize that the root of your fears is the fear of letting go of assumed control. Ask yourself: 'Do I really have full control over the circumstances of my life?' Our responses to what life throws at us are in the domain of our control. But we cannot control everything — we cannot control the weather or other people. Ultimately, we cannot even control whether we make or keep our money, or whether we have children or not. None of these basic turns in life are fully up to us.

The illusory thought that somehow we can control every situation we encounter is the root of our fears. And this very thought is the fruit of the ego's twisted root. Control belongs to Hashem, the Master and Guide of the Universe. The deeper we see our fear for what it is, the more it dissolves into awe, surrender, and loss of self within the Divine guidance. This is *Yirah Ila'ah* / higher Yirah. In the words of the Maharal [*Nesivos Olam*, Nesiv Yiras Hashem, 1]: "Yirah means to make oneself as if he did not exist." Yirah is the sensation of the total collapse of the I, the ego. Awe descends at the one moment one surrenders the self. This is an *awe-ha* moment. At the moment of awe, there is very little self, or self- awareness.

One can experience this higher awe in the face of nature, beauty, human heroism, or the Creator, the ultimate source of awe. Yet, sometimes the only way to access Yirah Ila'ah is through *Yirah Tata'ah* / lower Yirah, the fear of losing control of the self. When you experience fear, it is altogether possible that this lower Yirah is a gate to the higher Yirah. Once you move through and transform your sense of lower Yirah, meeting it head on and penetrating to its root, you are able to access the Higher Yirah, a total overwhelming of self, which is a gift bestowed from Above.

In the words of the Baal Shem Tov:

> "There are those who pray with sadness because they are depressed, and (yet) they think they are praying with great Yirah…. True Yirah is a Yirah that is bestowed upon one (i.e., it falls upon him spontaneously), not the Yirah that he himself awakens. The latter Yirah is considered 'feminine waters' (inspiration that comes from below, from oneself). True Yirah falls upon one from Above, causing him to tremble and quiver. And because of this great fright, he has no idea where he is. As a result, his mind (thoughts) become clear and tears begin to flow involuntarily from his eyes."
>
> [*Likutei Yekarim*, p.3. *Baal Shem Tov al haTorah*, Amud haTefilah, 59]

The steps to receiving the Higher Yirah are as follows: Perhaps you start from the fear of punishment, or better yet, the egoic fear of losing control. By sitting with this fear and following it to its root, you are able to tap into a higher Yirah. You realize that there is an Ultimate Controller of the world beyond you, and you are then able to 'let go and let G-d'. Your fear then transforms into awe. Finally, the highest Yirah descends upon you from Above, completely washing your sense of separate self-consciousness away in the presence of the Infinite One. Here is a relevant teaching of the Baal Shem Tov:

"Commenting on the verse [*Koheles*, 3:14], 'Hashem has made it that men shall (be in) fear before Him,' the Sages say [*Berachos*, 59a]: 'Thunder was created only to straighten out the crookedness of the heart.' Hashem desired that all of Israel have true Yirah of Hashem. One who is smart will achieve Yirah by thinking (to himself): 'Hashem is the master of the world and the source of all reality, and if the Divine animating force would leave Creation for one moment, all of Creation would disappear.' Because of this focused thought (about the majesty and absoluteness of the Creator) he will attain awe of Hashem until all the limbs of his body tremble.... It is not like the ignorant people who say that Yirah is depression....

"This (thought process) works only for people who have *Seichel* / proper intellect. Only they can contemplate Creation and initiate an internal state of Yirah for themselves. For one who does not possess Seichel, and yet Hashem also desires that he too should have Yirah, Hashem gives him reason to be in fear according to his small intelligence — for instance, through the sound of thunder, as explained above. In such a case, the Divine intention is for him to move from this lower form of Yirah to the higher Yirah. He should think to himself, 'This thunder is merely one expression of the mighty Creator, and if I am scared of it, then certainly I should have Yirah

of the Creator, who created the thunder.'
(Here is the main point that is relevant to our discussion:)
"And the same is true for all externally generated fears, such as the fear of the government, or the fear of (G-d forbid) losing a child. The reason Hashem created these types of fear is so that we can move from this lower Yirah to the higher Yirah."

[*Meor Einayim, Yisro.*
Baal Shem Tov al haTorah, Ekev, 26]

What the Baal Shem Tov is teaching above, is that when we do not have the proper Seichel to initiate our own sense of holy fear, we need to think about all of our lower fears in order to inspire us. We can move deeper into any given lower fear, and find the primary fear at the basis of that fear. For instance, if we look closely at a fear of losing a specific job, there may be a deeper fear within it of losing our property and money. Within that fear, there may be a fear of lacking basic control over our lives. As we gradually go deeper into each fear, we will be able to recognize that although we actually have very little control over our lives, there is a Controller, and that is Hashem. This realization both alleviates and elevates our fears, transforming them to awe.

In order for this process to be effective, we really need to consider our own smallness and insignificance in the face of the magnitude of the entire cosmos. Once we realize how

small we really are and how little control we really have, we
are able to release our egoic grip on reality and let go into
Hashem's hands. This feeling of letting go is 'awe'. When
we let go of our limited anxieties, tears of joy, longing and
amazement can start falling from our eyes.

We can see clearly from these teachings of the Baal Shem
Tov that true Yirah has nothing to do with depression or
sadness. On the contrary, there is even a sense of joy, desire
and *Deveikus* / cleaving that is present in the higher levels
of Yirah. True Yirah is the bridge to *Ahavah* / love.

For this reason, the Baal Shem Tov taught that Yirah,
prayer, and joy, are all meant to be joined together.
To quote:

> "Prayer that is uttered with joy is more readily
> accepted on high, much more than a prayer that is
> said with sadness or a sense of defeat. This is similar
> to a poor man who comes in front of a king (or a
> wealthy person) and pleads with cries and tears for
> the their help. In such a case, the king only gives
> him a small amount (just to get rid of him). How-
> ever, when the king's minister speaks lovingly and
> with joy to the king, and then requests of the king
> a favor, then certainly the king gives a lot more, as
> befitting to a minister."

[*Tzavaas haRiVaSh*, p. 13a.
Baal Shem Tov al haTorah, Amud haTefilah, 60]

In the higher state of Yirah, we feel deep joy and pleasure. It is not 'fear'; it is the opposite of fear. Yirah is the relinquishing of the egoic illusion of control. It is the surrender of the self into a state of *Bitul* / self-nullification. Here are two short meditations that may help a person achieve some form of Yirah:

MEDITATION 1

Quiet the mind and Meditate on the following:

Have you ever felt like you were losing control?

Think of a situation in your past where life seemed beyond your control.

How did it make you feel?
Small? Powerless? Afraid?

Feel the fear. Sit with it.
Acknowledge it in your body.
Recognize that most of life is simply beyond your control.

Recognize that there is a Controller and that is Hashem, the One Above.
Relinquish your egoic need to control and simply let go.

How does it feel to let go?
Allow any tears to flow.
Feel awe washing over your entire body.

MEDITATION 2

Quiet the mind and meditate on the following:

Imagine that you are in an airport with many people.

You feel small in the presence of so many people.

Visualize yourself boarding the plane.

The plane is taking off and climbing into the sky. You are flying higher and higher.

Everything down below is getting smaller and smaller.
Look out the window of the plane into the wide-open expanse of the sky.

Think about the inconceivable vastness of the cosmos.
Consider the fact that it would take 100,000 light years to travel across just our galaxy.

Let it sink in that we know of close to 200,000 billion galaxies.

Feel your smallness and insignificance.
Relinquish control, let go, and let Hashem in.

STAGE THREE

....

AHAVAH

LOVE

While Yirah is a *Tenuah* / movement of contraction, stepping back, and being humbled in the presence of the Omnipresent, *Ahavah* / love is a movement forward, an expansion, a coming closer.

Yirah is a feeling of existential isolation. To be in the place of Yirah you need to be alone. As Rashi writes, speaking of the *Kohen Gadol* / High Priest [*Yumah*, 4b]: "He would separate himself from other people so that awe could rest upon him." Being alone allows you to enter a state of awe. Ahavah, on the other hand, is a shared experience that opens us up to others and to deeper aspects of ourselves. In Yirah, we contract and even cease moving, both outwardly and inwardly. In love, we open up and move outwards and upwards.

Ultimately, love flows from awe. In our state of Yirah we yearn to open up and to connect with that which is outside of ourselves. We want to feel closer to Hashem and to others. This requires us to move upward and out of our narrow self. Although, at this point we are still gripped by higher 'fear' and frozen in awe. But as we said, this state of isolated wonder in which one feels so small and insignificant is the catalyst for more expansive connection that is Ahavah.

One begins this journey of transforming fear into love by first entering the gate of Yirah and thinking to oneself: "I now desire to connect myself, in a revealed way, with the Creator of all life and all worlds." This desire is further aided by meditating on the greatness and awesomeness of the Creator [*Tzavaas haRiVaSh*, p. 7b. *Baal Shem Tov al haTorah*, Amud haTefilah, 58]. And since, "Yirah is the gate to Ahavah" [*Likutei Yekarim*, p.3. *Ibid*, 59], these thoughts and the arousal of these emotions bring one to love. That is, the cultivation of awe brings one to love.*

---

* The Rambam writes, on the other hand, that Ahavah comes first, then Yirah [*Hilchos Yesodei haTorah*, 3:1]. The Baal Shem Tov is speaking about a higher Yirah. So, with this all in mind, the progression is from a lower Ahavah to a lower Yirah and from a higher Yirah to a higher Ahavah. Indeed, Ahavah is the higher level [*Tana D'vei Eliyahu Rabah*, 28. See also: *Sotah*, 31a. *Sifri*, VaEschanan, 7. Yirah is the gateway that leads to Ahavah. *Akeidas Yitzchak*, Ekev. *Avodas HaKodesh*, 1:25]. Thus a positive Mitzvah — rooted in Ahavah — pushes aside a negative Mitzvah that is rooted in Yirah [*Ramban*, Shemos, 20:8].

Love is a gift that follows awe. We slip into love after feeling completely overwhelmed and over-awed. We learn from this that we need to work on Yirah, and Ahavah will come on its own. [See *Keser Shem Tov*, 2, 17d. *Bnei Yissachar*, Tishrei 4:14. *Derech Pikudecha*, Hakdamah 7]. You can't force love. It is a gift from Hashem that follows naturally from the attainment of true Yirah.

In truth, love is difficult to describe, define or quantify [*Keser Shem Tov*, 2, 24:1. *Baal Shem Tov al haTorah*, Vaeschanan, 51]. Suffice it to say that when we are talking about 'love of Hashem' we are not talking about the kind of love one feels when they say they love ice cream, for example. To love ice cream just means you enjoy the taste and texture. You do not really love the ice cream itself. You just like what the ice cream does for you.

Even when a person loves another person, for the most part, it is a contingent and dependent form of love [Rebbe Rashab, *Sefer haMa'amarim 5666* ("Samach Vav"), Ki Nahar Yisrael]. In this way, love between humans is also often self-serving. You love what the other person does for you, or how the other person makes you feel. Love between people is really most often a kind of self-love. Most relationships are founded on what each participant can obtain from the other; one gives in order to get. This is a conditional love — if it can even be called that. Such a relationship will last as long as both parties are getting what they want from the other. For example, an employer may appreciate, or even 'love', an employee for what he does for the company. The moment, however, the employee ceases to produce the desired results, the employer will cease to experience such warm feelings for the employee.

Other human relationships are rooted in a higher reality. For example, many spousal couples that stay connected across many seasons and through many ups and downs are not limited to this give-and-take modality. Their interactions express a higher measure of unconditional love. They may never even consider the question, 'What has s/he done for me lately?' as both partners might be focused only on fulfilling the other person's desire or will. Yet most spousal relationships, even long lasting ones, also begin with a conditional love — their origin and foundation being initially contingent on physical, emotional, social or intellectual attractions. In the end, these loves are also conditional.

The closest thing to the love for Hashem that we can experience in our daily life is our love for our children. A parent's love for their children is intuitive and instinctual, because a child is actually in a very real way a part of the parent. A parent's love is intrinsic and unconditional, and is not founded in physical sensations, emotions or intellectual constructs.

Imagine you are a parent and you instruct your child to clean his room. The instruction is for the child's own benefit — to teach responsibility — but for whatever reason, the child does not listen. The room remains uncleaned, and your will has been disobeyed. Your initial reaction is frustration. You might punish the child, again intended for the child's own benefit, seeking to teach him that his actions or non-actions are significant and are attached to consequences. Although tearful and hurt, the child instinctually turns to you and reaches out for a comforting embrace. Suddenly, you are in touch with a place deep within yourself where your love for your child is more powerful than your desire to be obeyed, or even to teach the child a lesson. This natural, instinctive love is the true essence of the relationship between children and parents, parents and children.

After contemplating the awesomeness and Infinite power of the Creator of this vast and magnificent universe, we are filled with a profound type of love as we recognize that despite such inconceivable vastness, we are nevertheless intimately bound to the Creator, as the Creator is to us.

Just to put all this in perspective, let's consider some statistical facts. Light travels at a constant, finite speed of 186,000 miles per second. If you were traveling at the speed of light you would circumnavigate the equator of the earth approximately 7.5 times in a single second. Now imagine 60 times this distance, and that would only be one light minute. Now imagine 60 times that distance; one light-hour. And 24 times that distance would be a light-day. And 360 times that distance would be one light year. Now, imagine

100,000 years of travel at the speed of light. This is the approximate diameter of our galaxy. The vastness of our galaxy is obviously beyond human imagination and comprehension. And now imagine that there are not just two, three or even 100 or 1,000 or even 1,000,000 other galaxies, but there are billions, in fact over 200 billion known galaxies.

Now try to integrate the deep truth that despite this incomprehensibly huge universe, and despite the fact that our entire planet is but a speck in the orbit of our galaxy, and despite the fact that we are just one tiny living organism among millions on earth, still, you can sense that Hashem makes room for you, cares about you, chooses you, and is in fact within you. Hashem entrusts you with the mission of revealing and manifesting the entire purpose of Creation. This paradoxical and miraculous realization arouses a very deep feeling of unconditional love.

When this cosmic love and connection is awakened, all a person wants and desires is to become closer to the Beloved. A person who is truly in love wants only to please their beloved one. Love is not about consuming, as in eating the ice cream, nor is it about self-centered gratification, such as how the beloved makes you feel. Rather, true love is all about the beloved.

When our love for Hashem is fully awakened, all we can think about is Hashem. And all we desire is to live our lives in such a way that we truly are a *Kidush Hashem* / sanctification of Hashem's name.

In the words of the Baal Shem Tov:

> "There are those who pray and think they are praying with love when in truth they are just in a good mood (i.e., they are feeling good about themselves and their life, so they think this is what it means to love Hashem.) The truth is that when a person is really in love with Hashem, a great humility falls upon him. All he wants to do is beautify the name of Hashem (to live his life as a Kiddush Hashem), and all he desires is to overcome his negative (ego-based) inclinations. When he experiences this, then he knows that he is experiencing true love."
>
> [*Likutei Yekarim*, p.3.
> *Baal Shem Tov al haTorah*, Amud haTefilah, 59]

According to these teachings of the Baal Shem tov, there seems to be a psycho-spiritual pattern of development. One state follows the last. First one attains awe, and then one is granted love. Gradually, as we progress deeper on the path of prayer, these two emotions vacillate continuously. We are constantly moving in and out of Yirah and Ahavah. This is a form of running and returning, as well as expansion and contraction. Throughout the process of a single prayer session as well, we alternatingly experience feelings of love while we are close and intimate with Hashem, and then awe and trepidation in the awareness of our distance and desire to come close to and approach the Utterly Transcendent One.

For the most part, at least initially, love follows awe. At the beginning of a prayer or the path of prayer, a person may feel dramatically overwhelmed by what they must undertake and experience — standing with humility and awareness in the Presence of the Infinite One. This humbling sensation inspires a person to feel their own lowliness, smallness and existential distance from Hashem. But as one ascends the ladder of prayer, traveling deeper and higher, he begins to feel closer and closer. This generates, circulates and reciprocates more love and feelings of connection and belonging. The trajectory of psycho-spiritual maturation generally travels in the direction from Yirah to Ahavah. But in a healthy spiritual process it will also vacillate from Ahavah back to a Yirah, and then from Yirah to Ahavah, ad infinitum. This is the spiral nature of spiritual development. The path is not purely linear, which would imply that we are moving ever-forward in a straight line of progression. Nor is it only cyclical, which would mean that we keep coming back to the same place in the same way over and over again. But the nature of Creation seems to organize itself in a series of spiral dynamics. We continue to come back to the same root of reality and identity, but from a different, deeper level and perspective.

To illustrate this process of vacillation, we need go no further than the standard six-word blessing formula. In the structure of a traditional blessing, we begin with *Baruch Atah*, "Blessed (or 'The Source of blessing') are You", which is in the second person. This is a very direct address — "You". But then, we continue and refer to G-d in the third person, "Hashem". This is a more formal and less intimate address. According to this linguistic formula, we start by feeling close and intimate, as if being cradled by Hashem. When we say "You", we mean literally You, as if we were speaking to a loved one or a dear friend. Hashem, the Creator, in our prayers becomes a You — a subject. From this perspective, G-d is no longer an abstract object or idea, but a living presence in our life — a real 'You', with whom we feel close and intimate.

But then a deeper, higher awareness sets in and we begin to feel distant again. Every level we attain through love, opens up to a more expansive conception of Divinity and to a more pronounced awareness of our own smallness within that immensity. A dreadful, overwhelming sense of the Holy Transcendent Other sets in and we feel far, small, alienated and distant. With what little strength we have left, we say, "Hashem" [*Noam Elimelech*, Bechukosai]. And from this state of awe, suddenly a breakthrough occurs and once again we feel close, embraced, cradled and loved. From this place of love, we are able to say, *Elokeinu* / our G-d. Then, a deeper realization sets in and we once again feel distant. We experience this back and forth, running and returning, moving deeper into and out of love/closeness and awe/distance throughout these six words, as well as throughout the prayers in general and our spiritual path in general. And in fact, we need both of these modes of awareness, to feel love and connection and to feel distance and awe, so that our relationship with Hashem does not become one of callousness [*Yalkut Shimoni,* Iyov, 1:891]. This vacillation continues throughout the process of our prayers until we reach the Throne of Unity, the highest level, where both feelings of closeness and distance, love and reverence, exist simultaneously as one.

Through this dynamic of feeling first close and then distant, first loving and then reverent, we are able to sense the transcendence of the Holy Other and become overwhelmed by the mystery and majesty of the Creator and of all Creation. And we are able to sense as well the immanence, closeness and familiarity of Hashem, as if we were being held in a Divine Embrace. We are perpetually moving into and out of both of these perceptions. They are in fact two poles of a greater emotional spectrum, and each one strengthens and sensitizes us to its opposite.

As a reflection of these oscillating realizations, our physical bodies respond in kind. At times during the prayers we Shuckel from right to left, and at times, almost involuntarily, we Shuckel from front to back. Moving from front to back is a movement of awe — as we bow the head forward in reverence and then move backward. Moving from right to left, side to side, is a movement of affection and love as we feel ourselves 'cradled' by Hashem.

On a deeper level, these are not two separate movements. Rather, these movements and their attendant emotions are aroused and awakened simultaneously within the context of prayer. It is taught in the name of the Ramban: "Although it is impossible for these two attributes (Ahavah and Yirah) to coexist in general, it is possible for these two emotions to exist simultaneously in the context of Divine service." [Baal Shem Tov in the name of the Ramban, *Ben Poras Yoseph*, 45:3. See also *Toldos Yaakov Yoseph*, Mishpatim].

In other words, with regards to serving Hashem we can concurrently experience two seemingly conflicting and opposing emotions. Outside of contact with the Divine, this is not possible: "There is no Ahavah in the same place as Yirah, or Yirah in the same place as Ahavah. This only occurs with Divine attributes." [*Sifri*, Parshas Ekev. *Reishis Chochmah*, "Sha'ar Ahavah", 1. "Within my joy I fear, and my joy is within my fear (awe)." *Tana D'vei Eliyahu Rabbah*, 3].

Yirah and *Ahavah* are each spelled with four letters. When you place the word *Yirah* above the word *Ahavah*, the word *Yirah* can be spelled with the first two letters of *Yirah* and the first two letters of *Ahavah*. Similarly, *Ahavah* can be

spelled with the final two letters of *Yirah* and the final two
letters of *Ahavah*:

אה	יר
בה	אה

What does this mean? How can Ahavah and Yirah come
together? When you are in awe, and certainly if you are
fearful, there is no room for real love. And conversely, when
you are reaching out in love there is no room for contracting in fear. They are antithetical. And yet in prayer, these
conflicting emotions can be maintained simultaneously.

The reason for this is, first of all, they are both connected
within the Infinite One, and in a state of *Ayin* / nothing-
ness or nullification within the Infinite, all opposites are
reconciled [*Magid Devarav leYaakov*, 7. *Ohr Torah*, Vayera 27-28].
Secondly, there is something paradoxical in the way the
world was created and within the nature of the relationship
between the Creator and Creation. Let us use the body and
soul as an example. On one hand, the body is part of Creation; it was created and formed at a particular time and
will return back to the elements after the age of 120 years.
On the other hand, we possess a spark of the Creator, which
makes us eternal and therefore connected to a world beyond Creation, beyond space and time. And so, maintaining
both of these perspectives at once, we relate to Hashem as

our Creator; and paradoxically, as our own deepest essence.

Hashem is both the 'distant' Creator as well as the 'intimate' Emanator of Creation. We are both 'far' and small, and also 'close' and big in the eyes of Hashem.

In a worldly relationship, when you are feeling strong love and connection, your separative boundaries are eliminated and you can experience a genuine sense of intimacy. You are able to fully enter into the other person's 'space' and they in turn are able to fully enter into yours. Yet, when you are feeling this type of intense love there is no room for Yirah, trepidation or reservation. By contrast, when you are feeling overwhelmed by the other person's presence, and sensing their majesty and grandeur, you feel hesitant to move closer, out of a sense of humility and smallness. When the Ahavah inevitably wells up in response to the distance and you do move closer, then there is less Yirah.

This is all true in the context of earthly, human love, because the love you are experiencing in such a case is a 'created' love; it is not innate, it has a beginning and potentially an end. Additionally, it is a love that is trying to bridge a gap, implying that there is a distinction between you and your beloved. Here love is needed to draw you closer. This is in contrast to a parent-child love, in which there is a sense of inseparability.

To an even greater degree than parent-child love, love for Hashem is a) innate, and b) is not trying to fill a gap; rather, it is more akin to an experience of revelation or realization of what is already present. Our love for Hashem is revealed when we begin to feel the innate connection we have with Hashem. We are endowed with a connection that is deeper than that of Creator-to-Creation. This is because we are actually a part of Hashem.

And yet, despite this essential inseparability, it is equally true that Hashem created us, and the Creator is unique and apart from us. Thus, the experience of Yirah awakens and reveals this aspect of 'relationship' with Hashem, as a creature approaching his or her Creator. Sensing an existential distance between Creator and Creation is necessary in order to cultivate the reverence and yearning for connection that will ultimately pull us closer than ever, closer than if we were to never feel any distance.

Ahavah represents the experience of Hashem's immanence and accessibility, while *Yirah* represents our experience of Hashem's transcendence and grandeur. On one hand, we sense Hashem as being completely beyond us and the world, and yet we also recognize that Hashem is immeasurably close and deep within us. Hashem is both Infinite and Incomprehensible, and also Immediate and more Real than any observable reality. In fact, both immanence and transcendence are definitions and manifestations, whereas

Hashem, who is beyond infinity, is expressed through all manifestations, no matter how seemingly contradictory to our normative binary logic. Every-thing and no-thing are all present and connected within Hashem. In this way, these two emotions can be experienced simultaneously.

All of the above reflects the general mindset and emotions that are required to put us in the right state of mind, and connect us overtly with the Source of All Life, so that we can pray with openness and authenticity. Now, the next step is the particular *Kavanah* / intention that we should meditate on in relation to the actual words we are about to utter in prayer.

STAGE 4

....

KAVANAH
THOUGHT-INTENTION

Once we establish a strong sense of *Nochechus* / being present with and within the Divine — and once our emotions of reverence, awe, love and yearning are aroused and inspired — we can begin to actually pray.

There is an original idea suggested by the Baal Shem Tov related to the use of Kavanah during the act of prayer that we will discuss below. But first, let us take a moment to explore the issue of intention more generally.

All agree that prayer without intention is "like a body without a soul" [*Chovos haLevavos,* Sha'ar Cheshbon haNefesh, 3:9. *Sefer haYashar,* Sha'ar 13, p. 124]. 'Mindless' prayer has also been described as "bringing a fork and knife to the table without serving the food,"[Chidah, *Chomas Anecha.* Yeshayahu, Chap. 29] or, like going through the mechanical motions of chopping wood [Rambam, *Morah Nevuchim,* 3:51]. Moreover, without any general intention there is no real *Metziyus* / existence of prayer at all [*Chidushei Reb Chayim,* Rambam, Hilchos Tefilah, 4:1]. The solution to this issue offered by the Arizal was the practice of *Kavanos* / formulaic intentions and *Yichudim* / formulas of unification. It was strongly suggested by the Holy Ari that one should establish and maintain these formulas of intention within their mind during the recitation of one's prayers.

The *Chidush* / novelty of the Baal Shem Tov's teaching, which contrasts slightly but significantly with the prescription of the Arizal, is that he strongly encourages that we focus on the Kavanah right before we recite the words of prayer, but that when we are vocalizing the words we should drop the formula and just be present in the words themselves [*Toldos Yitzchak,* Noach. *Baal Shem Tov al haTorah,* Amud haTefilah, 20]. In this approach, we fuse our mental and emotional energy in the themes of the prayers and what they mean, right before we speak them. But once we begin reciting the words we need to just be present in their sounds and vibrations and not be distracted by any mental gymnastics or even any thoughts beyond the words themselves. Just be present within the sonic field of the words as you recite them in prayer. This practice of radical presence is not as simple as it sounds, considering the fact that our minds are constantly grasping for, or devising, semantic boxes to stuff our feelings and experiences into.

In general, the principle of 'thinking before you speak' is appropriate and greatly valued, even in casual conversation. Prior to opening your mouth to saying something, it is commonly agreed that it is a sign of compassion, consideration and mindfulness to think about what you want to say, and even to think about whether or not you should even say it. Someone who speaks without *Machshavah* / thought is like someone 'spilling his seed' [*Likutei Yekarim*, p. 4b. *Baal Shem Tov al haTorah*, Amud haTefilah, 44]. He is taking his vital energy and most Divine-like human quality, the ability to communicate and create, and wasting it. As a result, he squanders his *Chayus* / life energy on triviality and empties himself and his energy into a veritable vacuum with no purpose and direction.

In the teaching of the Baal Shem Tov, this idea of Machshavah and Kavanah before *Dibbur* / speech means literally thinking of the actual words — not just the ideas — you are about to say (in prayer) before saying them. Only after you have thought about the actual words of prayer do you say them with full presence, completely absorbed in their vibrational qualities. This practice entails more than just a general thought or quick review of the words and ideas you are about to say, rather it implies a detailed thinking about and even visualizing of the actual words before saying them. For example, if in prayer you are about to say the four let-ter-word *Baruch* (Beis, Reish, Vav, Chaf), before vocalizing the word imagine seeing these four letters standing separate from each other, and then using your power of imagination draw these four letters together, internalize what the word *Baruch* / bless really means, and then say the word [R. Ze'ev Wolf of Zhitomir, *Ohr haMeir*, Shoftim]. This practice is similar if you are saying three words at a time, as suggested by nu-merous teachers. For example, *Baruch Atah Hashem* / You are the Source of all blessings, Hashem. Take a moment to collect all the letters from these three words, read them in your mind's eye, or in the Siddur, think about what they mean, then stop thinking and say them with a clear mind and all the strength of your being.

An earlier source for this practice can be found in the writ-ings of the Ramban. There is a well-known letter that he sent to his son, Nachman. At that point in time, the Ram-ban was living in Israel, in the city of Akko (Acre), as he needed to escape his birth-land of Spain following a series of contentious theological debates. His son was living in Catalonia, Spain. The letter was meant to strengthen and inspire the character trait of humility within his son. He instructed his son to read the letter at least once a week.

In fact, he assured his son that every day that he read this letter, Heaven would answer his heart's desires. This letter became publicly known after being printed in Mantua, Italy in 1623, and over time it has become quite famous. It is a letter that is recited and studied regularly by many people throughout the world on a daily or weekly basis.

In the letter, the Ramban urges his son to "think about your words before you let them out of your mouth." If we read this carefully, we can see that it is referring to more than just 'thinking before you speak', which everyone understands to be a considerate way to live. The letter is saying something more specific. It is suggesting that you should think clearly about *the actual words* you are about to say, and only then should you say them.

In the teachings of the Baal Shem Tov, the quality of thought that you should apply to your words before you speak them goes beyond merely formulating them in your head before you say them. Rather, it is suggesting that you put all your attention and intention into what you are about to say. See the words with your mind's eye, let them sink into your psyche. And then, when you finally recite words of prayer, do so free of thought. Allow yourself to move out from the purely semantic definition of the words into the deeper sonic aspect of the prayers.

SPEECH WITHOUT KAVANAH

When we recite the letters, words and sounds of prayer, our minds should not be occupied with their intricate meanings and interpretations, no matter how lofty these Kavanos are. Rather, we should be simply and fully present with their actual sounds, and the sensations of these vibrations.

We should enter into and relate to the words that we utter in prayer as "letters without any interpretation" [*Degel Machaneh Ephrayim*, Eikev. *Baal Shem Tov al haTorah*, Amud haTefilah, 23]. In fact, if you are thinking about the meanings of the words of prayer at all while you are uttering them, you are 'limiting' their inherent power. Whatever meaning you construct in your limited understanding pales in comparison to what truly lies within these holy words. If you are thinking about a particular Kavanah while reciting them, you are limiting their true capacity. If, however, you are simply saying these words of prayer without a personal, subjective understanding of what they mean, then the words retain their maximum potential.

In the words of the Baal Shem:

"One who holds a particular intention (that is known to him) while Davening or performing a Mitzvah, only has access to the intentions that are known to him. However, if you are saying the words (of prayer) with deep connection to their *sounds*, then all the Kavanos are automatically included within them. Every letter is an entire world. Thus, when a person recites the words of prayer with deep connection, the corresponding upper (inner) worlds are aroused and caused to create shifts and impacts within the world below."

[*Tzavaas haRiVaSh*, p. 14b.
Baal Shem Tov al haTorah, Amud haTefilah, 26]

SWEETENING DIN / JUDGMENT THROUGH VOCALIZING THE WORDS

This is the power of the sounds and vibrations of the words in the prayers. Words create reality, as will shortly be explored. Yet, this is only true once the words are spoken, once the letters are combined and verbalized in prayer. [Accordingly, a merely visual reading is not enough: *Shulchan Aruch*, Orach Chayim, 47:4 (note, *Biur haGra*, ad loc). Alter Rebbe, ibid, 47:2]. Until then, the letters on the page are considered 'dead'. Without a sentient consciousness to vocalize the letters on the page, they amount to nothing more than ink on paper. They need to be animated, enlivened, sounded, felt, heard. These letters and words become energetically charged by means of our emotional arousal, and they become charged with mindfulness via our consciousness and *Kavanah* / intention. In this way, they become 'living words', and can make waves in the world.

For this reason, when a scribe writes a Sefer Torah / Torah Scroll it is considered more scrupulous to actually vocalize every word he is about to write before he writes it, even if he is looking into another Torah when writing [*Menachos*, 30, *Tosefos*. *Mordechai*, 957. *Tur*, Orach Chayim, 32]. The reason for this stringency, in the language of the *Bach* (Rabbi Yoel Sirkis, 1561 – 1640), is so that the Kedusha / sanctity that emanates from his breath shall be drawn into the letters of each word he is writing on the parchment.

Letters on a page are inanimate and lifeless. Letters are a form of concealment, although their actual purpose is to reveal. This is true in varying degrees for both written and spoken language. Yet, a distinction must be made between the written and spoken word, as they do function different-ly. With speech, there is a higher degree of instantaneous revelation. As the word is spoken, it is also heard. Of course, there still remains some element of concealment in the spo-ken word as one can never fully express what one truly feels and experiences. As such, the spoken word is simultaneous-ly a revelation (of experience) and concealment (of under-standing).

In regards to the written word, the situation is a bit differ-ent. First, the author commits the ideas to paper, which is 'book number one', as it were. Only after the fact can the reader read these words and thus create 'book number two'. [Pirush HaGra, *Sifrei deTzniusa*, Chap. 1]. In writing, there can be no instantaneous revelation. It is in fact a medium defined by a process of delayed revelation. In this way, writing suggests a double concealment in both the reception of the revelation as well as the understanding of the words themselves. Until the reader reads the words (and understands them) on the paper, they are utterly lacking of vitality, and are like 'dead'. It is only through the act of reading, chanting, singing, and understanding their meaning that these letters of *Din* / concealment become 'sweetened' and assume meaning, purpose, and life. Words become 'alive' and animated by the mere act of reading them, but they become infused with meaning and intention only when understood. This is true even according to Halachah: a printed word of Torah (not a written word), is not yet considered holy until a human being reads it. Until then, the writing can actually be discarded. Only once a human being has read from a text does the printed word become holy and need to be treated with the respect of a sacred item. Only through the reading and vocalizing of the words do the letters become alive and thus 'sweetened' of their inherent quality of Din.

One of the interesting features of Chasidic thought as expressed in the teachings of the holy Baal Shem Tov is that previously abstract and metaphysical concepts of Kabbalah and spiritual cosmology became 'psychologized'. Mystical ideas and structures that were previously used to map out and understand the nature of the universe were transformed and appropriated as means and mediums through which to understand the inner workings of the human psyche and soul.

Malchus, the final Sefirah of the Kabbalistic Tree of Life, is classically understood as a Sefirah that has "no life (substance) of its own". Malchus is the ultimate 'receiver' of the Ten Sefiros. Malchus represents the Feminine Aspect of the Divine and is also referred to as 'Daughter'. Binah, the upper Sefirah, is also a 'feminine' Sefirah, and is considered the 'Mother', the one that births the lower eight Sefiros. Inwardly, says the Baal Shem, Malchus represents the areas in our lives, whether within us or around us, that have "no life of their own". They are essentially lifeless without any influx to activate them. They have potential for purpose and impact, but without the right 'fuel', they will not give off any light. Binah represents our mindful consciousness; the aspect of awareness that has the power to animate and energize dormant potential, if channeled properly. When we join our Binah with our Malchus, we inject vitality into the areas of our life that seem lifeless and full of concealment. "The root of prayer is to sweeten the *Din* / judgment of Malchus by connecting it to its source, which is Binah," says the Baal Shem [*Ben Poras Yoseph*, p. 116b. Amud haTefilah, 77].

What this means is as follows: When a person is sick, G-d forbid, or for that matter whenever there is anything amiss in a person's life, it is considered *Din*, a concealment, an aspect of Malchus. When we pray for healing or for whatever is lacking in our lives with intention and mindfulness (an aspect of Binah) by reciting and giving life to the 'dead' letters on the page, we are *Mamtik haDin* / sweetening the Din. The act of praying itself is an act of sweetening the Din. By giving our Binah to the letters of Malchus, we are stimulating a sweetening of any Din in our lives.

This is the power of connecting our Binah with our Malchus — our deeper understanding and intentionality — with our words and actions. Indeed, this theme of connecting 'mind' with speech and action is a critical credo in the Baal Shem Tov's teachings [*Keser Shem Tov*, p. 4]. Mindfulness is integral to living a holy and meaningful life.

The Baal Shem Tov, as well as many other sources, teach us that everything we experience in the outside world is merely a projection that is filtered through our internal subjective prism. Our *Machshavah* / thought creates our reality. Prior to the interplay between observed object and observing subject, the object itself does not really exist; at least not in the form it exists when observed. Not only does observation create a transformation of *context*, but it can create a transformation of *content*. We gave an example of this above: the act of reading a printed word renders the page sacred. On a quantum level, a particle's behavior will change depending on whether or not there is an observer. Observation is creative. Reality does not exist until it is measured, at least on the atomic scale. Spiritually, this means that our Machshavah is the most integral part of our existence, and in fact it creates our existence. We therefore need to ensure that we have the most beneficial form of attention, intention and interpretation. Everything that we experience is dependent on our thoughts. If we have good, healthy and holy thoughts, our lives will be experienced, felt and enacted in a good, healthy, holy way.

MACHSHAVAH / THOUGHTS AND DA'AS / AWARENESS

From another perspective, Machshavah is a *Levush* / a garment on top of a preexisting form or 'content'. Prior to the manifestation of Machshavah is a process of Chochmah, Binah and Da'as. Our Da'as is linked to our *Keser* / Crown which is our inner world of Atzilus. Even beyond these exceedingly subtle levels of consciousness is our access to the higher emptiness of all forms of existence: our inner *Ayin* / No-thingness.

Let us explore, for a moment, our higher Da'as. There is a tradition that a great ambition of the holy Baal Shem Tov was to teach people how to untangle themselves from their emotions and even their bodily sensations so that they could be fully present and mindful. Only by untangling these are people able to experience a real *Yishuv haDa'as* / settling of the mind. How is this practically cultivated? How do we go beyond merely attempting to force the mind to be present, and actually step into full presence?

The part of you that is observing your experience right now is called *Da'as*. The word *Da'as* contains the letters *Eyd* / witness. It is the part of the self that is always observing and witnessing life. Wherever there is a duality, such as 'being present' versus 'not being present', there is a third option that reconciles the two opposites by transcending and including them both. Da'as is a good general term for the experience of 'the third path, which reconciles the two'. Da'as experientially transcends the objects that are known, yet also includes and unifies them. By including both the state of presence and the state of distraction, Da'as is the impartial and unaffected common ground for both. Yet it is of a totally different order as well. It is off the map, so to speak, as it is not part of the spiritual struggle or game.

This aspect of higher Da'as is the best tool to attain true presence. The effort exerted in trying to avoid or banish distraction, and the effort of trying to directly strengthen presence, both merely intensify the swing between the opposite states. In other words, every time you powerfully assert presence, distraction comes swinging back with equal power. The only way off this pendulum is by going off the analytic and affective map and settling into Da'as, the knowing witness, the higher context of consciousness that embraces and allows both presence and distraction to emerge and exist. The end result of this embrace is authentic, lasting presence.

So, whenever you feel that you are not being present, or lacking Kavanah, stop and take notice. Ask yourself: Who is the you that is looking at the distracted 'you'? The answer is *Da'as*, your knowingness, your ability to notice. Consciously knowing your non-presence is the only real way to become truly present. Be the *Eyd*, the 'witness' beyond the opposite manifestations of distraction and focus. This 'practice' is not something you need to believe in. You can experience it and verify it for yourself.

Kavanah and Machshavah are essential and pertinent in all areas of life and in prayer. Yet, on the path of the Baal Shem Tov, it is important to remember that our attention to Kavanah needs to be secured prior to reciting the words of prayer. When we then recite the words, we enter into their actual sounds and vibrations. When you chant the sacred words of prayer do not *think about* their meaning, rather, experience them viscerally through your senses, through their sounds and inner vibrations.

///////////////////////////////////////

STAGE 5

....

DIBBUR

SPEECH

As above, when we speak words of prayer, we should let go of their semantic definitions and simply be present within the sonic vibrations of the words themselves. In the story of the Great Flood, *Noach* / Noah is told to construct and then "enter into" a *Teivah* / Ark. Commenting on this passage, the Baal Shem Tov teaches that the word *Teivah* also means 'word'. Thus Noach was being told, and we too are being told every day, that in order to protect ourselves from the floods and turbulent waters of the world, we need to enter fully into the words of Torah and *Tefillah* / prayer.

These 'revealed' words are designed to create a sanctuary of meaning and purpose amid the raging flood-waters of life. But to allow them to have the maximum effect, we need to "enter into" them. What does this mean and how can we put it into practice?

Every word we utter in prayer should be invested with the full involvement of our mind, body and spirit. "Know that every word is an entire *Partzuf* / structure. A person needs to put his entire strength into each word, otherwise it will be missing a limb" [*Tzavaas haRiVaSh*, p. 4b. *Baal Shem Tov al ha-Torah*, Amud haTefilah, 25]. If we are not fully present in every single word and letter that we utter, we will be missing a part of the whole structure. Our mind is involved through the preparatory Kavanah. Our body is involved through the physical vibrations and movements of energy generated by the sounds of the words themselves. Our spirit is involved through the breath, as it initiates and carries the words of prayer out into the world.

All the strength of your being participates when you "enter into the word." Say them slowly if it comes naturally, or say them quickly, if this is more effortless and flowing. Feel their vibrations penetrating and permeating your entire being. Ride the sound waves as they rise and fall, swell and recede, run and return.

Allow yourself to simply be present with every sound, movement, and vibration. Let the light and energy of the letters fill and infuse your entire body. Let go of trying to think about the meaning of the words, just like you did when you were beginning to speak. Experience the entirety of their sound with the entirety of your senses.

One way to practice this profound yet simple method of prayer is to utilize the natural rhythm of your breath. Before you are about to recite a word or short phrase, inhale and reflect on the meaning of the words you are about to say. Gently hold and retain your breath. Then, as you are exhaling, recite the words with your full presence.

You may even wish to try to do this with each letter and sound you recite. For example, before you say the word *Baruch*, as you are inhaling pause a moment and think about the word and concept of blessing. Then, slowly exhale the first syllable: *Baaa....* Take another inhale, pause and exhale the rest of the word: *Ruuuch....* Again, contemplating the word's meaning transpires before the actual speaking, and in the act of speaking, there is no thinking, just the intimate experience of sounds and supersonic vibrations.

If you find it difficult or too time-consuming to pause at each letter or even at each word, then pause before reciting every two or three words. There are sources that suggest we should never utter more than three words in one breath during prayer [*Yesod Shoresh haAvodah*, Shar 5:1]. Between every two to three words pause for a brief moment, inhale and reflect on the meaning of the next two to three words, and then recite them. Pause, inhale, reflect, and then recite another two-three words. What is unique about this path is that when you recite the two or three words, letting go of the mental activity and meaning-making, the words truly speak for themselves — not merely to your mind, but to the deeper strata of your being.

All of this is especially important before reciting a blessing. Before reciting *Baruch Atah Hashem* / You, G-d are the Source of Blessings, pause, inhale, and think deeply about what these words mean. Hold that meaning in your mind and inhale it into your body. Then with one powerful exhale, say the words *Baruch Atah Hashem*, entering their sounds fully and riding their vibration out into the world.

Sometimes it would even be appropriate and beneficial to say the entire blessing in one powerful and extended exhale — especially if one is struggling with extraneous thoughts that are distracting your focus. [A suggestion by many Tzadikim from the last 500 years. *Totzaos Chayim*, 36. *Ohr Tzadikim*, 5:15. *Ohr haGanuz*, Bechukosai. *Siddur R. Shabtai*, Seder haLimud]. Whether you say one letter, one word, or many words in one exhale depends on your level of concentration and focus, as well as what comes more naturally and effortlessly. In fact, this detail can change from day to day, from prayer to prayer, and even within a single prayer session, page, paragraph or sentence. Sometimes you may feel that taking a pause before every syllable is appropriate and natural, while at other times you may feel like you can hold your concentration on a longer passage, and then let the whole passage come tumbling out of your mouth in an onrush of sound [*Tzavaas haRiVaSh*, p. 4b]. The point is to always check in with yourself beforehand to know what is appropriate. Do you currently have an expansive or constrictive state of mind? Do you feel like moving quickly or slowly?

Whereas it is much easier to place our full self into the sounds and words of prayer when we are praying out loud, such as in the earlier stages of *Shacharis* / the Morning Service, it becomes more challenging to enter the sounds and vibrations during the *Amidah* / silent Standing Prayer. The recitation of the Amidah is not actually completely silent, rather it is in a very low voice, just loud enough to be heard by the person uttering the words. Thus, riding the vibrations of this prayer necessitates sensitizing yourself to hear subtler sounds.

ELEVATING THE ENTIRE WORLD
THROUGH THE WORDS OF PRAYER

Let us look a little deeper at the impact of vocalized prayer. Besides clarifying the mind and heart of the individual, the act of vocalized prayer elevates the entire world. According to the path of the Baal Shem Tov, we are able to 'elevate sparks', and the world itself, by using *Osyos* / letters and sounds.

To quote:

> "A person should have in mind that through his prayer he is arousing the Osyos and sounds that created the entire world, including both the upper and lower worlds. As such, when he recites his prayers and sings Hashem's praises, he is doing so together with all the worlds and all the creatures. Since he aroused the Osyos and the Osyos are the life force of all of Creation, everyone and everything is praying with him, and helping to elevate his prayer. Additionally, he is also elevating all of Creation with his prayers and intentions."
>
> [*Darchei Tzedek*, 39.
> *Baal Shem Tov al haTorah*, Amud haTefilah, 80]

On one level, we are connecting with the entire world and the entire world is praying with us. On an even deeper level, we are actually elevating the whole world through our prayers.

The whole world is filled with and made up of Divine letters. The letters and sounds of Divine speech that say, "Let there be light," for example, are the metaphysical vibrations that trigger corresponding physical vibrations that manifest as energy and eventually matter, as explored earlier. The existence of light is a physical manifestation of the Divine word Light being spoken into being.

Everything in our universe has a unique structure, sound and rhythm. Everything has a distinct vibration. The multiple things we observe with our senses are physical manifestations of their respective spiritual frequencies. The Hebrew word for 'thing' is *Devar*, which also literally means 'word' or 'utterance'. Every 'thing' is essentially a product and physical manifestation of a unique Divine 'word' or vibration.

When we gather sacred words of prayer or blessing, we are gathering the sounds and letters that make up the world. When we speak them with Ahavah and Yirah — which the Zohar calls our "wings" — we fly up with our prayers, as it were, and elevate the world. We are interconnected with all of Creation: "A human being is an *Olam Katan* / small world." The entire world is also called "one big human being". Everything in Creation reflects within everything else. This is why what happens in a microcosm affects the entire macrocosm, and visa versa.

The Divine *Dibbur* / speech that fills the world yearns to reconnect to its Source Above. Through the act of prayer we elevate everything in the world to its Source and reconnect it. In the words of R. Avraham *haMalach* / the Angel (the son of the Maggid of Mezritch, the great student of the Baal Shem):

> "This is why the verse says, 'I long, I yearn for the court of Hashem' [*Tehilim*, 84:3]. Speech desires to rise upwards to its Root. What is the root of speech?

Speech is rooted in the *Maskilim* / the primal cause of awareness, the Divine level of *Chochmah* / wisdom and *Binah* / understanding.... This is what it says regarding Noach: 'Make yourself a *Teivah* / ark (or word)...with lower, middle and upper decks.' Meaning, with regards to speech there are three levels. The lower level is foul and negative speech. In the ark the lower level was for animal dung. The middle level of speech is ordinary everyday conversation. This corresponds to the dwelling of the animals themselves. The third level of speech is holy speech, such as prayer and Torah, spoken with love and awe of Hashem. Through this level of speech all of Creation is elevated back to its Source. This level corresponds to the third deck in the ark, which was for the dwelling of the humans...."

[*Chesed leAvraham*, Noach]

The whole world, and every creature in it, yearns to be elevated. The letters, sounds and vibrations within each being long to return to their Source in holiness, which is the song of the Unity of Hashem, the *Ma'amar Echad*, and the Aleph of *Anochi Hashem*. When we speak or sing holy words in prayer, for example, we are gathering and elevating all of Creation to vibrate with the sound of Hashem's presence.

This is the way we practice *Hala'as haNitzutzos* / the Elevation of the Sparks that have fallen through the devastating cosmic *Sheviras haKelim* / Shattering of the Vessels. This initial shattering occurred due to the intensity of the Divine Infinite Light. The initial vessels of Creation could not contain this light, and so they imploded, scattering sparks of holiness throughout Creation.

Throughout the world there are broken, exiled and fallen sparks of Divinity that originated in the pristine sound of the Aleph of *Anochi*. Currently, these sparks are in a state of exile, and thus give off alienated vibrations of despair, death, sin, estrangement, and indifference. Through our prayers and holy words, we are able to elevate and return the Sparks to their Source. In this way, all of the broken sounds of the universe are recalibrated and reconfigured into a redemptive prayer, singing the song of Hashem's Oneness.

Our vocalized prayers gather all of the broken sounds of the world, whether it is the screams of sin and negativity or the whimpers of despair and lifelessness, and transform them into the song of life, holiness, and goodness. By virtue of our interconnection with all of Creation, and through the power of our positive speech, we have to ability to elevate the world in order to sing the song of the Creator.

When we positively or prayerfully utter the sound of a *Beis* / 'b' or *Gimel* / 'g', for example, all the Beises and Gimels of the world are transformed and uplifted. Even the letters of other languages, insofar as they are the 'back side' of the original sounds in Lashon Kodesh, are elevated and healed. For example, the vibrational energies of the 'b' in the word/concept of 'bad', is uplifted when we say the words *Baruch Atah* / Blessed are You. The 'g' sound in the word/concept of 'glutton' is healed when we pronounce *Gadol Hashem* / Great is Hashem. Once articulated in prayer, the *Chayus* / energy of the 'b' and 'g' sounds are metaphysically tied to holier words and loftier concepts, causing the roots of the negative qualities of 'badness' or 'gluttony' to be weakened and eventually to wither away.

RIDING THE WAVES OF PRAYER

In prayer, we gather all the fallen sparks, letters, words, sounds, vibrations, and expressions of the world and elevate them. By following the prayer-path of the Baal Shem Tov, which directs us to let go of all thought and intellection, no matter how lofty, in the moment of articulation, we are able to enter fully into the sounds and vibrations of these sacred words and letters. Once we have intoned the prayers, the sounds ripple out and fly 'upward'. As the sounds move upward, so can we. We can ride the waves of sound, as it were, higher and deeper inwardly.

Within the sonic field of our prayers are gathered all the sounds of the universe. Each of these sounds is then equipped with the two wings of love and awe as transmitted through our vocalization. With these wings, the sounds surge upward, and we ride these waves. Although this is a metaphor for a metaphysical process, there is actually a visceral sensation of movement when we pronounce words. Sound waves are physical phenomena and we can become more and more aware of them, along with their metaphysical impact, even in our silent Amidah prayers. By investing ourselves in them completely we *Bo El haTeivah* / enter into the words of prayer, as into a vehicle. In this vehicle we can ride with these spiritually charged sounds all the way up to the place where they are rooted. Through sound we can tap into the inner world of *Beriah* / creation, and even deeper than that, we can reach the silence before all sound, the Aleph of *Anochi*, and the world of *Atzilus* / Nearness or Total Unity.

Here is another teaching-infusion from the Baal Shem:
"In prayer, one must place all his strength in the words he is praying. In this manner, he shall move (via his chanting and reciting the letters) from letter to letter until he forgets (releases the grip of attention on) his corporeality, which will allow him to notice how the letters are combining with each other (becoming words), and this (unification of sounds) arouses a degree of pleasure. [As the individual syllables of each letter are combined to form words, harmonious sounds are produced by these combinations, which produces an experience of aesthetic pleasure for one sensitive enough to appreciate it.] And just as the combinations of certain sounds, in

a nice song or tune for instance, can arouse a sense of physical pleasure, how much more must this be so on an emotional level. This is the world of Yetzirah, the realm of the emotions. [First the sounds are physically pleasurable to our ears, and then they register deeper within our hearts as they arouse an emotional response.]

And then (as one continues to pray and senses the physical and emotional pleasantness of the sounds and tunes he is producing) he comes to (experience) "letters of thought", in which he no longer hears what he is praying (or chanting). This is the world of Beriah, the world of the intellect and mindfulness. [He thus moves from the external world of sound, to the world of aroused emotions, to a subtle world of quietness in which he is still vocalizing the prayers, just in a much more quiet and relaxed manner.]

After all this he will come (automatically) to the level of *Ayin* / no-thingness, where he will (experientially) lose all of his physical potentials (his body will go limp and he will enter into a trance-like state with no movement, not even speaking.) This is (experientially) the world of Atzilus, the level of *Chochmah* / pure consciousnes'."

[*Keser Shem Tov*, 2:17b.
Baal Shem Tov al haTorah, Amud haTefilah, 16]

This technique, from gathering of individual letters together to form words of prayer, to entering the silence of pure consciousness, is a form of *Hispashtus haGashmiyus* / divestment of entanglement with physicality.

The more we enter into the letters, vibrations and sounds of the prayers, the more the 'rational' content of the words recedes. The words, in effect, become a background noise. We slowly lose ourselves within the vibrations of the letters as the sounds morph into words, and the words into a kind of musical chorus endlessly resonating and reverberating. In this way, we are able to move from the world of Asiyah, the physical dimension, where every letter is distinct and separate, into the inner dimension of our emotions, the world of Yetzirah, where letters are forming words. There, our emotions are aroused by the stringing together of the various sounds of the letters and words, and our heart opens to their Source.

What began as a single letter-sound becomes a word; and then many words and many sounds. There is a subtle inner joy and pleasure generated by gently moving from one sound into the next, like playing consecutive chords of music. This is the inner experience of Yetzirah. From this moving experience of having our emotions aroused by the music of the letters we are able to move deeper into ourselves as we become more sensitized to the contemplative introspection of the world of Beriah, the dimension of mindfulness.

The aroused emotions become subtler and subtler and so too does our chanting of the prayers. Similarly, during the Shacharis service, we move from singing the 'verses of praise' loudly, to a quieter, more tranquil state, when we sit down and recite the Shema and its adjacent blessings.

Finally, there is a complete collapse of all sound and noise, both external and internal. The mind is cleared of all thoughts, feelings and sensations, and we arrive at a motionless state of total oneness, and connect with the Light of the Ein Sof within the letters. This is the inner world of Atzilus.

Letters are likened to horses; they are a mode of transportation. If you have an idea in your mind that you want to communicate to another person, you need letters and words. The words of prayer, uttered with love and awe, fly and rise upwards, like dancing flames or billowing smoke upward [Ohr HaMeir, Shir Hashirim]. We are able to ride on these heaven-bound horses, these waves of sound, these clouds of glory, as they fly upward.

Through this method of prayer, not only are we able to experience the rush of emotions of Yetzirah, the subtleness and tranquility of Beriah, and the stillness and no-thingness of Atzilus, but we are actually able to enter into these realms themselves. The letters (the horses) are created via our vocal utterances in the world of Asiyah. From here they move upward (and inward) all the way to Atzilus (and beyond). By entering deeply into them we are able to catch a ride and move along with them from the world of Asiyah until the world of Atzilus [Rabbi Yaakov Yoseph of Ostro (1738-1791), *Sefer Rav Yeivi*, Tehilim, 45]. In prayer, we are moving through the inner upper worlds and pulling along all of Creation with us, elevating everything back to its Source.

Sometimes the *Machshavos Zaros* / distracting thoughts that pop into our mind during prayer also want to catch a ride [*Tzavaas haRiVaSh*, p. 8a]. The issue of intruding thoughts would require a lengthy discussion and many possible suggestions. In brief, however, these suggestions would include pausing and letting the thought pass, clapping the hands or shifting the body to disentangle from these thoughts, and more technical methods of elevating the actual kernel of the thought back to its root. It is important to mention here that according to the Baal Shem Tov, sometimes negative thoughts, in the form of letters and vibrations, enter a person's mind because they too wish to be freed from their exile and return to their root in the upper worlds [*Ben Poras Yoseph*, p. 50b-c. *Divrei Moshe*, Lech Lecha]. Thus they seek to hook into our consciousness and catch a ride upwards through our prayers.

WORDS OF PRAYER CREATE REALITY

A major Halachic component of prayer is *Bakashas Tz'ra-chav* / requesting what is needed. This is rooted in our human desire to reach out for help, as it were. Hashem in fact puts us into difficult situations and circumstances so that we pray. From this perspective, we do not pray to get out of trouble. Rather, the reverse is true, trouble and difficulty were created so that we would pray.

But what about everything we spoke about until now? What about all the presence, awe, love, and divesting from the physical in order to experience *Deveikus* / cleaving to Hashem? How does all of the above, the real idea of Tefilah fit with the Bakashah aspect of prayer? Tefilah seems to be about Deveikus, while 'requests' seem to be self-centered. [Although, from Chazal it seems that indeed Tefilah and requests are two separate ideas. *Avodah Zarah,* 7b]. And what does sound and vibration have to do with the effects of our prayers, and with whether or how they are answered?

In the teachings of the Baal Shem Tov on prayer, much is dedicated to the mechanics of prayer. How does it actually work? What is Bakasha? And how are prayers actually answered? Here too, many great *Chidushim* / novel ideas are revealed.

Besides the elevation of the entire world, including yourself, via the sounds of the prayers, the actual recitation of these specific sounds creates their corresponding reality. In other words, in an almost reverse process, besides the fact that the words and sounds of our prayers are moving 'upward' and 'inward', they are also moving 'downward' and 'outward' as they manifest in the manifest world. When we say that the words of prayer 'heal' us, for example, it is because we have created new patterns of vibrational energy, and drawn them downward until a new, 'healed' reality has been brought into manifestation.

Reality is created through our prayers. Normally, prayer is understood as a paradigm in which people beseech the Creator 'Above' to grant all of their heart's desires, requesting that their needs may be fulfilled in the most immediate and befitting way. The Baal Shem Tov revealed that the answers to one's prayers arrive and materialize in the very manner in which the prayer is formulated. When we say 'heal us,' and say so with Deveikus, we are co-creating healing energy. When we say 'bless us,' we are co-creating blessing in our lives.

Divine speech creates reality. "G-d said, 'Let there be light', and there was light." Human speech is a limited reflection of the unlimited potential of Divine speech. Although we do not have the power to 'create' reality in the way that Hashem does, we can shape and influence our reality through our speech. In this way, we are co-creators of our life and world along with Hashem. The Creator creates 'context', while our words create 'content'.

Another way of phrasing this dichotomy is that our communication is dialogic in its very nature. Human speech only began to exist in the context of an 'other'; it did not exist before the appearance of a paradigm of 'addressing' another. It is only once human communication and dialogue began to break down that 'monologue' appeared. Divine language, on the other hand, is inherently monological: "Hashem said, 'let there be light', and there was light." Divine monologue itself creates the 'other', and with it the potential for dialogue.

This is one distinction between human and Divine language. However, sometimes, e.g. in a state of *Deveikus* / cleaving and connection with the Creator, our words and expressions have a Divine-like quality to them. They are, as it were, imbued with the power to create.

This power is vested within us when we pray with full presence, awe and love, which are the wings that allow us to fly 'upwards'. With Deveikus we become one with the Source of all Life, as it were, and our speech and prayers become an instrument through which Divine resonance vibrates. Not that we personally have the power to create reality — rather the converse. Only when we empty ourselves of ego is it possible that the Divine speech speaks through us and creates new realities. As the prophet says, "And I placed My words into your mouth, and with the shadow of My hand I covered you, to plant the heavens and to establish the earth" [*Yeshayahu*, 51:16]. This means that when a person is in a state of *Bitul* / 'self-nullification' and Deveikus, they have the power to "plant heaven and establish earth".

Sefer Yetzirah correlates the *Bris Milah* / the covenant of circumcision with the *Bris haLashon* / the covenant of the tongue [1:3]. The verse, "Death and life are in the power of the tongue" [*Mishlei*, 18:21], can be understood metaphorically, as in our words have the power to hurt or heal, and also literally. Just as the covenant of circumcision (the procreative organ) creates new life, the same is true with our mouth and power of speech. Our words can create new realities.

In a state of Deveikus, our words have 'procreative' power. The well-known magical idiom *Ab'ra keDab'ra* is a Talmudic-like phrase meaning "I will create (*a-Bara*) as I speak (*ke-Dab'ra*)." Our Sages tell us [*Sanhedrin*, 65b] that *Rava Bara Gavra* / the great sage Rava created a man — a being referred to as a *Golem*. The classic commentator Rashi writes that Rava did this by employing the techniques of Sefer Yetzirah and the art of letter combinations. [See also *Maharshal* ad loc. *Sefer haBahir*, 196]. While in a state of Deveikus, the sage Rava was able to use his power of speech to transform an inanimate lump of clay into an animate, living being. It is important to note that a golem is not a real human being. It is a being with limited faculties; it has a Nefesh, the lowest level of animating soul, but does not have a Ruach or Neshama, and thus it does not have the power of speech or free-will. [See R. Meir Ben Gabbai *Avodas HaKodesh*, 2:28].

Such is the power of speech when in a state of Deveikus. This indeed is the highest form of prayer. In this trance-like state the words of prayer simply come tumbling out of our mouth, almost automatically, and these divinely inspired and invested words create new realities. This is the 'answer' to (or 'in') our prayers. In the terms of the Baal Shem Tov: *Shelach Dibburcha* / Send forth your words, *veYa'ase Shelichus'cha* / and they will do (create) your message (request). In other words, the speaking of the words of prayer in a state of Deveikus is itself the answer to prayer.

From this perspective, when a person prays in a state of Deveikus, his prayers are always immediately 'answered'; new divinely inspired vibrations are created and drawn into the world. In other words, once spoken, these words have a creative vitality, and their vibrations give rise to new realities in the very moment of their articulation.

This is the deeper reason why we need to be very specific regarding what we pray for, because our words, when said in Deveikus, have the power to influence and even create the very realities we vocalize in our prayers. For this reason, it behooves us to be mindful of our words, especially while in deep prayer or Deveikus. We must insure that we have the appropriate *Machshavah* / thought before the *Dibbur* / speech, because the yearnings which we give voice to in prayer will be the realities we will have to live with.

The Medrash speaks of a person who was trudging along in the desert. When his legs began to tire, he prayed, "Please G-d, if only I had a donkey." A moment later, he noticed a Roman officer standing nearby. The officer had stopped traveling as his she-donkey had gone into labor. The Roman noticed the man and ordered him to carry the colt on his shoulders. The man sighed, "I asked for a donkey, but did not ask correctly" [*Medrash Rabbah*, Esther, 7:24. *Ohr HaChayim*, Devarim, 3:23]. The man prayed for a donkey in the hopes that it would carry him, but he did not specify that, and received a donkey that he had to carry.

"Hashem sends forth His messages unto earth, the word arrives with alacrity" [*Tehilim*, 147:15]. Perfected speech, such as that of the Creator's, arrives swiftly and simultaneously creates that which is spoken. The words' Divine vibrations instantaneously manifest and alter reality. When we redeem and align our own potential of speech with the Ultimate Speech of the Creator, meaning when we pray in a state of Deveikus, our words are vested with this creative power. And when we pray in a state of *Bitul* / nullification of self and verbalize the word *heal*, healing must descend into the world. It is important to keep in mind, however, that the new reality revealed through your prayer may manifest in a more general sense, and not impact you personally in any demonstrable way [*Ben Poras Yoseph*, the end. *Baal Shem Tov al haTorah*, Amud haTefilah, 127]. For instance, through your prayers, healing energy is drawn into the world. Yet, it may be drawn down in a more general manner than you imagined, perhaps inspiring medical breakthroughs or more general healings across the globe, or even a healing for another person, just not for you specifically.

All of the above applies when you are praying according to the general *Nusach haTefilah* / the codified structure of set prayers. Now let us explore a few dynamics from the perspective of individual spontaneous prayer. Assuming there is a *Gezar Din* / a heavenly decree against a certain person, we have the power when praying in a state of Deveikus to connect to the Light beyond the letters (the world of Atzlius) and thus transform this presently harsh energy into something healing. Any heavenly decree, whether positive or seemingly negative, is revealed through the letters, sounds, and vibrations of Divine Speech. Say the Divine sound/vibration manifests in someone's life as a stream of three letters — Tzadik, Reish, Hei, which spell the word *Tzarah* / hardship. A righteous person praying with pure presence and intention for this person's Tzarah to be eliminated [*Kesones Pasim*, p. 47b. *Baal Shem Tov al haTorah*, Amud haTe-filah, 159] connects with the source of the letters, the Light, and thus can take these very same three letters and rear-range them to read (in his mind's eye) as *Ratzah* / desired. By rearranging the letters of creation while in a state of Deveikus, the previously harsh decree was transformed into something beneficial, and even pleasurable [*Toldas Yaakov Yo-seph*, Noach, 15d].

Normally, we are not privy to the power to completely eliminate a specific flow of Divine energy that is coming down into the world. What we can do, however, is alter the frequency and trajectory of the Divine flow from neg-ative to positive. Imagine this in terms of a current that is streaming from Above to below. Divine influx begins as an unformed flow of infinite energy rushing down towards a person. That unformed flow will eventually take shape as a specific transmission according to a person's moral state or spiritual station. What has a person put out into the world lately? Are they acting with integrity and transparency? If a person has deviated from his inner nature and distanced himself from the Infinite One, the form in which this flow will funnel towards him will be in the letter/sound/vibra-tion sequence of *Tzarah* / hardship. In such a case, the per-son himself can change, thus re-aligning himself in relation to the Source of the Flow, which elicits a corresponding shift in Divine Speech. Or, the form of the flow itself can be altered through another person praying in complete Deveikus. When the latter occurs, the person to whom the prayers were directed experiences a positive influx of energy, rather than the previously decreed negative one. The original unformed flow eventually and inevitably reaches the person, but instead of receiving that influx through a form of hardship and suffering, he received it through a 'desired' form.

The point of all this is that our words, certainly those said in Deveikus, are vested with the power to create distinct vibrations and frequencies, which manifest particular realities. This process is analogous to the story of the *Mon* / manna in the Desert. The Mon in its root is pure potential. It could literally taste like anything a person wanted. Yet, according to the Medrash, in order to imbue the Mon with a particular flavor, a person would say, 'If only I could taste this or that food,' and instantaneously a miracle occurred and the Mon tasted just as he wished. [See *Medrash Rabbah*, Shemos, 25:3. Although, another opinion in the Medrash is that all he needed to do is to 'think' about the particular flavor and it would manifest (Osyos of Machshava). See also *Yumah*, 75a].

In prayer, we connect and align ourselves with the Source of all life and potential. This is the root of the *Shefa* / Divine flow that animates the world; this is the Light beyond the letters. Once we have tapped into this infinite wellspring while in a state of Deveikus, our 'premeditated' words come pouring forth from our mouths almost involuntarily. They create vessels to receive and channel all the blessings that are needed, for us and for the entire world.

Clearly, it is true that once a person has entered into a state of Bitul and Deveikus, they are no longer are thinking only about themselves. They are, in such a state, beyond their own personal needs, wants, desires or even hardships, and thus the requests of the Amidah are for the collective: *Refa'einu* / Heal *us..*, *Bar'cheinu* / Bless *us...*. Yet, because this person began praying with a specific intention in mind and secured that Machshavah and Kavanah before articulating his prayers, the blessings that manifest more generally on account of his prayers will also impact him as well. This is true even if he is not thinking specifically about himself in the moment of saying the prayers.

Similarly, if a person began their prayers focused on a particular healing for one of their relatives, and then slipped into a state of Deveikus, and while in the state of Deveikus they were no longer thinking about that particular person in need of healing, but about Creation in general — their prayers will still draw down healing for that person, along with a more general influx of healing energy. When the word *Refa'einu* is uttered in a state of Deveikus, a flow of Divine energy is initiated to funnel down into the world for all those who need an extra dose of healing energy.

CREATING A YICHUD IN THE
WAY OF THE BAAL SHEM TOV:
WORLDS, SOULS & DIVINITY

As above, in order for our words to have a truly creative potential, they need to be uttered in a state of Deveikus. Presence, *Yirah* / awe and *Ahavah* / love are the wings to bring
us to a place of Deveikus. Additionally, in order to attain a
measure of Deveikus we must experience, intellectually and
then existentially, a degree of unity and integration with the
actual world around us. We accomplish this by perceiving
and acknowledging the Divinity that is being expressed in
the world at all times and in all spaces.

There is a celebrated epistle of the Baal Shem Tov that
he wrote to his brother-in-law. In the letter, he writes the
following: "On Rosh Hashanah of the year 5507 (1746), I
made an oath and elevated my soul in the manner known
to you. I saw wondrous things in a vision, the likes of which
I had never witnessed since the day my mind first began
to awaken.... I ascended from level to level until I entered
the Palace of the Moshiach.... I asked Moshiach: "When
will you come, Master?" And he replied, "By this you shall
know: I will arrive at a time when your teachings have
been publicized and revealed to the world, when your wellsprings have overflowed to the outside, [when] that which I
have taught you, and that which you have perceived by your
own efforts, become known so that others too will be able

to perform mystical *Yichudim* / unifications and ascents of the soul like you." I was amazed by this response and greatly troubled, since a long time must pass for this to be possible.... Yet this I can tell you...whenever you pray or study, and in fact with every utterance of your lips, *intend* to bring about the unification of a Divine Name. For every letter contains *Olamos* / worlds, *Neshamos* / souls, and *Elokus* / Divinity.... These are the words of your brother-in-law who longs to see you face-to-face, who prays that length of days be granted to you and your wife and children, and who wishes you peace...."

It is known that one of the ways for a person to create wonderful *Yichudim* / unifications as the holy Baal Shem Tov revealed is through the animation of, and unification with these three dimensions. In another place it is recorded, "In every word there are *Olamos* / worlds, *Neshamos* / souls, and *Elokus* / Divinity... and a person needs to integrate his soul with each of these levels. All worlds will then be unified and they will ascend (with the person). This effects immense joy and delight in both the upper and lower worlds." [*Tzavaas haRiVaSh*, 75. *Baal Shem Tov al haTorah*, Amud haTefilah, 15. In the language of the Arizal, these very same three dimensions are called *Malachim* / angels, *Neshamos* / souls and *Shechinah* / Divine Presence. See *Zohar Chai*, Parshas Tetzaveh, 139d].

What this means is as follows: Every word, which essentially means every 'thing' and every aspect of this and of all worlds, has three dimensions:

1) The 'letter' or the object itself. This is its dimension of *Olamos*, also called the *Kli* / vessel or body.

2) The particular quality and distinct vibration of the entity. This is its *Neshamah*, the soul of the object. It is also the Divine Spark or Word that gives life and animates that word or object.

3) The highest level of meaning associated with the entity, even when not yet practically manifest. This is the *Elokus*, the Divinity within the object, and its inner dimension which reveals that there is nothing else besides Hashem, literally. As the whole world is ultimately part of Elokus, this is the dimension of the entity that is one with all other entities.

What do the words of the Baal Shem mean: "A person needs to integrate his soul with each (of these three) levels; all worlds will then be unified and ascend (with the person)"? And in what sense would this be a *Yichud* / unification?

There are three progressive stages of integration and unification that a person can experience with objects in the outside world:
1) Unification with the *Olamos* — connection with all creatures, animals, elements, life forms and indeed all objects.

This is the simple sensation that everything and ourselves are all part of one vast ecosystem; all life is intimately interconnected.

2) Unification with the *Neshamos* — by connecting your contemplative awareness with the Divine Spark present within every inch and aspect of Creation, you ascend and thereby cause a corresponding ascension of the *Olamos* dimension. This is the more evolved spiritual sensation that you and every entity are expressions of specific Divine vibrations. It is the awareness that every person and object in our lives is interconnected with our own soul journey. Each of our particular employers, co-workers, neighbors, community and family members, are connected with our Neshamah's path of Tikkun. In this recognition of soul-connection, we create a Yichud between ourselves and everything around us on this vibrational level, like notes that make up a great harmonic symphony.

3) Unification with the *Elokus* — by connecting with the Infinite One, the Divinity within everything, you integrate yourself and all the worlds together with the highest sphere, the Crown and Root of every 'word', every 'thing'. When you attach yourself to the Creative Root of all creations, you reach the highest and broadest level of *Deveikus* / unity. This is the complete recognition that everything is Elokus. Practically speaking, whether you are praying in a field or encompassed by brick and mortar, open yourself to sense

and connect to your surroundings. Become aware of the particular tree or table you are standing next to, integrate it within your own mental space. Recognize the interconnectedness between you and everything around you. Indeed, on a molecular level all organisms are composed of the same material, and there is one biosphere that integrates all of life on earth. This is the first level of awareness, *Olamos*. Nothing happens in a vacuum. Just consider the 'butterfly effect', whereby even the slightest beat of a butterfly's wing can influence the trajectory of a hurricane across the world. Everything in Creation is connected to and affects everything else. The first level of Yichud and integration occurs through the awareness that all of Creation is interconnected. The interconnectivity within Olamos is a fact whether or not we are aware of it. Thus, on this level of Yichud we are opening ourselves to the awareness, the sensation and experience of what is already the case.

Now, go deeper and open yourself up to the *Neshamah*, the 'soul' of the tree or table. Hear and feel the tree 'tree-ing', the table 'table-ing'. On this level, you are not only connecting yourself to the physical existence and interconnectivity of everything around you, rather, you are connecting consciously to the Neshamah of each creation. Everything that we own, and everything that exists in our sphere of sight and hearing, is connected and bound with our own soul. This, too, is also always the case.

There is a deep soul connection between yourself and the objects in your life [*Keser Shem Tov*, 218, 194. *Tzavaas haRiVaSh*, 109. *Magid Devarav leYaakov* 101d. *Meor Einayim*, Likutim, p. 166. See Chulin, 91a]. It is as if our soul expands beyond our body and permeates everything in our sphere and all that we possess [*Ohev Yisrael*, Matos], and thus our Sages tell us, "One who steals a penny from his friend, it is as if he robbed his soul" [*Baba Metziya*, 112a]. This interconnectivity on the world of Neshamos exists with everything in our lives, including whatever we see, hear, touch, smell or taste. Even if you are praying standing next to a particular person, or sitting on a specific chair, holding a unique *Siddur* / prayer book, it means that your soul gravitated toward this exact situation, because you are connected on a soul level. Their vibration, their distinct spark is connected with yours, in some way. Their narrative, as it is projected to you, the recipient of the situation, is specifically meant for you, and on a deeper level it is part of you, an extension of your own soul, your own narrative.

Thus, step two, the Yichud with Neshamos, is to open yourself to truly sensing the inner nature and Divine Spark with the world around you. Feel the 'soul', the rhythm and vibration of the inner life of each thing. Sense the consciousness of everything around you, and notice how that is included within your own consciousness; everything is truly 'part of you'. Things do not happen 'to' you, they are part 'of' you.

This second level of Yichud and integration occurs through an awareness that things are an expression of their deeper soul-consciousness, their subtle root vibration, their inner song.

Now go even deeper. Connect to the level of *Elokus* / Divinity within yourself and within the world around you. Integrate yourself within the highest sphere of existence, even beyond Creation itself. This is the ultimate Source of every word, vibration, movement, object and aspect, around and within you. On this level, you are acknowledging the G-dly presence within each and every thing in this world, and that *Ein Od Mil'vado* / there is nothing else besides Hashem.

On the level of Olamos, you connect on the physical and vibrational level with all of Creation. On the level of Neshamos, you connect with all on the level of consciousness and spirituality. But on each of these first two levels, you are still connecting as an individual with other individual entities or aspects. On the level of Elokus, you are connecting to that aspect of yourself and of each creation that is truly from the upper worlds, beyond individuality. The level of Elokus is the level on which all independent existences lose their ego-based sense of separation, as this is the wellspring of unlimited and unformed potential from which all things emanate and flow.

Another way of thinking about this is as follows: everything in this world is a reflection of, and is animated by, the vibration of a particular Divine Sefirah or Divine energy. Understood very broadly, we could say that a lion reflects *Gevurah* / power and might. Rainfall is also Gevurah. Dew, on the other hand, reflects *Chesed* / kindness and giving, as does a white sheep. Everything in this world can be traced via its physical or spiritual qualities back to its Sefirah. This is its share of Divinity, which defines its inner life force, and connects it to the upper worlds of limitless potential. This is the wellspring of Divinity that irrigates and enlivens each quality, energy, object and word.

This goes beyond the Yichud with Olamos in which one perceives the interconnectivity of everything in the world, and the Yichud with Neshamos in which one unifies with the sense of soul deep within each creation. Here, again, one unifies and integrates himself with the Divine Creative Potential within the world, until he reaches the highest, deepest level of *Deveikus* / unity with Elokus, and the insight that there was never anything else.

Once you have created a Yichud on all three levels, you have effectively elevated all objects or words to their Root, thereby returning all into the cosmic Inhale, into Deveikus. Once this has all been accomplished you have the power, as it were, to reverse the order and draw energy back down into the world from the Divine Exhale through the descending stages of Divinity, Souls and Worlds, and thus enhance the very fabric of reality.

Earlier, we explored the idea of securing your Kavanah during the inhale and then saying the words of prayer with strength and presence in the exhale. Now, based on this teaching of the Baal Shem Tov, you can add a new dimension. In addition to whatever specific Kanavos you are cultivating during the inhale, you could also use that time prior to speaking (and in general the period of time before you begin a prayer session) to perform a Yichud on the levels of Olamos, Neshamos and Elokus.

As you are inhaling and breathing in, in addition to any specific Kavanah you are building, you can gather in, integrate and create a Yichud with yourself and everything around you. You are breathing in the world around you. The interconnectivity is already there, but you are internalizing it as you breathe it in and unify with the *Neshamos* / souls of everything around you. On a deeper level, you are connecting to and unifying with the Divinity that is being expressed in the world around you.

This inward breathing exercise transforms the mere conceptual understanding of the intrinsic unity that exists between creation and Creator into a visceral sensation of oneness and Deveikus. With every contemplative inhale, you integrate and assimilate the Olamos, Neshamos and Elokus all around and within you. There is no longer any separation between the 'interior self' and the 'exterior reality'. You are one with all of Creation and one with the Source of all life. Thus you "elevate" yourself and the world, the Olam around you, to the level of Neshamah and to the Elokus within. You are lifting the entire Creation to Elokus. And once you have thus gained some level of Deveikus with the Source of All Life during your inhale, the words and prayers that you express with your exhale will be infused and empowered with a Divine-like creative potency.

This breath and Yichud-based practice can be done before praying or throughout your prayers, whether before reciting each word, every two to three words, or before every Berachah. It is even possible to perform one of each of these three Yichudim during the inhale before reciting the first three blessings of the Amidah. For instance, during your inhale before reciting the first Berachah you would focus your intention on connecting with and elevating the level of Olamos. During your inhale right before reciting the second Beracha you would focus your intention on the world of Neshamos, and so on. By the time you began the *Bakashos* / requests section of the Amidah you would have made a Yichud on and with all three levels of Olamos, Neshamos and Elokus, deeply empowering your requests.

Throughout this process we have cultivated experiential states of genuine presence, holy Yirah and Ahavah; we have connected with our breath and prepared ourselves for prayer by performing a series of *Yichudim* / Unifications between ourselves and the three levels of Olamos, Neshamos and Elokus; and we have striven to achieve some level of *Deveikus* / connection, cleaving and unifying with the Source of all Life. And yet, this has all been merely a preparation for the final stage of the Baal Shem Tov's path of prayer: letting all of these concepts and contents go and just surrendering. This is the final step in this process, which is paradoxically the simplest and the most difficult.

/////////////////////////////////////

STAGE 6

....

SURRENDER

Once we have done all that we could to prepare, once we have invested our entire being into our prayers, next we simply let go of all expectations and just be present in the moment. We should certainly not allow ourselves to become anxious anticipating the results of our prayers. In the words of the Baal Shem:

"A window/light you shall make for the Ark, and finish it one cubit from the top (upwards)" [*Bereishis*, 6:16].

This literally means that Noach was asked to build an Ark and to place a window or a glowing stone one cubit from the roof of the Ark, and make the Ark a peak on the top. And this teaches us that as soon as a word emerges from your mouth, do not dwell on it, just move on. Do not remain looking on High..."

[*Tzavaas haRiVaSh*, p. 8b.
Baal Shem Tov al haTorah, Amud haTefilah, 15]

This letting go, especially after all the hard work that has gone into your prayers, is an act of *Bitul* / nullification of the ego. A full cup cannot be filled. We need to experience being *Ayin* / no-thing so that a new *Yesh* / some-thing, the new reality co-created through our prayers, has a fertile space to manifest within. Essentially, we need to get out of the way. In the context of prayer that specifically means letting go of our expectations. This detachment from the outcome of our prayers also allows us to enter more deeply into the present moment. It is only in the present moment that we can truly sink into the vibrations of the *Lashon ha-Kodesh* / the sacred sound of our prayers. From this place of sonic immersion, it is then possible to ride or 'surf' those sound waves all the way back to their Source, to the One Who Spoke the World Into Being.

///

OTHER BOOKS BY THE AUTHOR

RECLAIMING THE SELF
The Way of Teshuvah

Teshuvah is one of the great gifts of life. It speaks of a hope for a better today and empowers us to choose a brighter tomorrow. But what exactly is Teshuvah? How does it work? How can we undo our past and how do we deal with guilt? And what is healthy regret without eroding our self-esteem? In this fascinating and empowering book, the path for genuine transformation and a way to include all of our past in the powerful moment of the now, is explored and demonstrated.

THE MYSTERY OF KADDISH
Understanding the Mourner's Kaddish

The Mystery of Kaddish is an in-depth exploration into the Mourner's Prayer. Throughout Jewish history, there have been many rites and rituals associated with loss and mourning, yet none have prevailed quite like the Mourner's Kaddish Prayer, which has become the definitive ritual of mourning. The book explores the source of this prayer and deconstructs the meaning to better understand the grieving process and how the Kaddish prayer supports and uplifts the bereaved through their own personal journey to healing.

UPSHERNISH: The First Haircut
Exploring the Laws, Customs & Meanings
of a Boy's First Haircut

What is the meaning of Upsherin, the traditional celebration of a boy's first haircut at the age of three? Why is a boy's hair allowed to grow freely for his first three years? What is the deeper import of hair in all its lengths and varieties? What is the meaning of hair coverings? Includes a guide to conducting an Upsherin ceremony.

————————

A BOND FOR ETERNITY
Understanding the Bris Milah

What is the Bris Milah – the covenant of circumcision? What does it represent, symbolize and signify? This book provides an in depth and sensitive review of this fundamental Mitzvah. In this little masterpiece of wisdom – profound yet accessible —the deeper meaning of this essential rite of passage and its eternal link to the Jewish people, is revealed and explored.

————————

REINCARNATION AND JUDAISM
The Journey of the Soul

A fascinating analysis of the concept of Gilgul / Reincarnation. Dipping into the fountain of ancient wisdom and modern understanding, this book addresses and answers such basic questions as: What is reincarnation? Why does it occur? And how does it affect us personally?

INNER RHYTHMS
The Kabbalah of MUSIC

Exploring the inner dimension of sound and music, and particularly, how music permeates all aspects of life. The topics range from Deveikus/Unity and Yichudim/Unifications, to the more personal issues, such as Simcha/Happiness and Marirus/ sadness.

MEDITATION AND JUDAISM
Exploring the Jewish Meditative Paths

A comprehensive work encompassing the entire spectrum of Jewish thought, from the sages of the Talmud and the early Kabbalists to the modern philosophers and Chassidic masters. This book is both a scholarly, in-depth study of meditative practices, and a practical, easy to follow guide for any person interested in meditating the Jewish way.

TOWARD THE INFINITE

A book focusing exclusively on the Chassidic approach to

meditation known as Hisbonenus. Encompassing the entire meditative experience, it takes the reader on a comprehensive and engaging journey through this unique practice. The book explores the various states of consciousness that a person encounters in the course of the meditation, beginning at a level of extreme self-awareness and concluding with a state of total non-awareness.

THIRTY – TWO GATES OF WISDOM
Awakening through Kabbalah

Kabbalah holds the secrets to a path of conscious awareness. In this compact book, 32 key concepts of Kabbalah are explored and their value in opening the gates of perception are demonstrated.

THE PURIM READER
The Holiday of Purim Explored

With a Persian name, a masquerade dress code and a woman as the heroine, Purim is certainly unusual amongst the Jewish holidays. Most people are very familiar with the costumes, Megilah and revelry, but are mystified by their significance. This book offers a glimpse into the hidden world of Purim, uncovering these mysteries and offering a deeper understanding of this unique holiday.

EIGHT LIGHTS
8 Meditations for Chanukah

What is the meaning and message of Chanukah? What is the spiritual significance of the Lights of the Menorah? What are the Lights telling us? What is the deeper dimension of the Dreidel? Rav Pinson, with his trademark deep learning and spiritual sensitivity guides us through eight meditations relating to the Lights of the Menorah, the eight days of Chanukah, and a fascinating exploration of the symbolism and structure of the Dreidel. Includes a detailed how-to guide for lighting the Chanukah Menorah.

THE IYYUN HAGADAH
An Introduction to the Haggadah

In this beautifully written introduction to Passover and the Haggadah, we are guided through the major themes of Passover and the Seder night. This slim text, addresses the important questions, such as: What is the big deal of Chametz? What are we trying to achieve through conducting a Seder? What's with all that stuff on the Seder Plate? And most importantly, how is this all related to freedom?

PASSPORT TO KABBALAH
A Journey of Inner Transformation

Life is a journey full of ups and downs, inside-outs, and un-expected detours. There are times when we think we know exactly where we want to be headed, and other times when we are so lost we don't even know where we are. This slim book provides readers with a passport of sorts to help them through any obstacles along their path of self-refinement, reflection, and self-transformation.

THE FOUR SPECIES
The Symbolism of the Lulav & Esrog

The Four Species have inspired countless commentaries and traditions and intrigued scholars and mystics alike. In this little masterpiece of wisdom both profound and practical - the deep symbolic roots and nature of the Four Species are explored. The Na'anuim, or ritual of the Lulav movement, is meticulously detailed and Kavanos,, are offered for use with the practice. Includes an illustrated guide to the Lulav Movements.

THE BOOK OF LIFE AFTER LIFE

What is a soul? What happens to us after we physically die?
What is consciousness, and can it survive without a physi-cal brain?
Can we remember our past lives?
Do near-death experiences prove immortality?

What is Gan Eden? Resurrection?
Exploring the possibility of surviving death, the near-death
experience and a glimpse into what awaits us after this life.
*(This book is an updated and expanded version of the book;
Jewish Wisdom of the Afterlife)*

———————

THE GARDEN OF PARADOX:
The Essence of Non - Dual Kabbalah

This book is a Primer on the Essential Philosophy of Kabbalah presented as a series of 3 conversations, revealing the mysteries of Creator, Creation and Consciousness. With three representational students, embodying respectively, the philosopher, the activist and the mystic, the book, tackles the larger questions of life. Who is G-d? Who am I? Why do I exist? What is my purpose in this life? Written in clear and concise prose, the text, gently guides the reader towards making sense of life's paradoxes and living meaningfully.

BREATHING & QUIETING THE MIND

Achieving a sense of self-mastery and inner freedom demands that we gain a measure of hegemony over our thoughts. We learn to choose out thoughts so that we are not at the mercy of whatever belches up to the mind. Through quieting the mind and conscious breathing we can slow the onrush of anxious, scattered thinking and come to a deeper awareness of the interconnectedness of all of life. Source texts are included in translation, with how-to-guides for the various practices.

———————

VISUALIZATION AND IMAGERY:
Harnessing the Power of our Mind's Eye

We assume that what we see with our eyes is absolute. Yet, beyond our ability to choose what we see, we have the ability to choose how we see. This directly translates into how we experience life. In a world saturated with visual imagery, our senses are continuously assaulted with Kelipa/empty/fantasy imagery that we would not necessarily choose. These images can negatively affect our relationship with ourselves, with the world around us, and with the Divine. This volume seeks to show us how we can alter that which we observe through harnessing the power of our mind's eye, the inner sanctum of our imagination. We thus create a new way to see and experience the world. This book teaches us how to utilize visualization and imagery as a way to develop our spiritual sensitivity and higher intuition, and ultimately achieve Deveikus/Unity with Hashem.

———————

THE POWER OF CHOICE:
A Practical Guide to Conscious Living

It is the essential premise of this book that we hold the key to unlock many of the gates that seem closed to us and keep us from living our fullest life. That key we all hold is the power to choose. The Power of Choice is the primary tool that we have at our disposal to impact the world and effect change within our own lives. We often give up this power to outside forces such as the market, media, politicians or peer pressure; or to internal forces that often function beyond our conscious control such as ego, anger, lust, greed or jealousy. Making conscious, compassionate and creative decisions is the cornerstone of living a mature and meaningful life.

MYSTIC TALES FROM THE EMEK HAMELECH

Mystic Tales of the Emek HaMelech, is a wondrous and inspiring collection of stories culled from the Emek HaMelech. Emek HaMelech, from which these stories have been taken, (as well as its author) is a bit of a mystery. But like all good mysteries, it is one worth investigating. In this spirit the present volume is being offered to the general public in the merit and memory of its saintly author, as well as in the hopes of introducing a vital voice of deeper Torah teaching and tradition to a contemporary English speaking audience

INNER WORLDS OF JEWISH PRAYER
A Guide to Develop and Deepen the Prayer Experience

While much attention has been paid to the poetry, history, theology and contextual meaning of the prayers, the intention of this work is to provide a guide to finding meaning and effecting transformation through the prayer experience itself.

Explore: *What happens when we pray? *How do we enter the mind-state of prayer? *Learning to incorporate the body into the prayers. *Discover techniques to enhance and deepen prayer and make it a transformative experience.

This empowering and inspiring text, demonstrates how through proper mindset, preparation and dedication, the experience of prayer can be deeply transformative and ultimately, life-altering.

WRAPPED IN MAJESTY
Tefillin - Exploring the Mystery

Tefillin, the black boxes and leather straps that are worn during prayer, are curiously powerful and mysterious. Within the inky black boxes lie untold secrets. In this profound, passionate and thought-provoking text, the multi-dimensional perspectives of Tefillin are explored and revealed.

Magically weaving together all levels of Torah including the Peshat (literal observation), to Remez (allegorical), to Derush, (homiletic), to Sod (hidden) into one beautiful tapestry. Inspirational and instructive, Wrapped in Majesty: Tefillin, will make putting on the Tefillin more meaningful and inspiring.

THE SPIRAL OF TIME:
A 12 Part Series on the Months of the Year.

Now Available!

THE SPIRAL OF TIME:
Unraveling the Yearly Cycle

Many centuries ago, the Sages of Israel were the foremost authority in the fields of both astronomical calculation and astrological wisdom, including the deeper interpretations of the cycles and seasons. Over time, this wisdom became hidden within the esoteric teachings of the Torah, and as a result was known only to students and scholars of the deepest depths of the tradition. More recently, the great teachers, from R. Yitzchak Luria (the Arizal) to the Baal Shem Tov, taught that as the world approaches the Era of Redemption, it is a Mitzvah / spiritual obligation to broadly reveal this wisdom.

"The Spiral of Time" is volume 1 is a series of 12 books, and serves as an introductory book to the basic concepts and nature of the Hebrew calendar and explores the special day of Rosh Chodesh.

THE MONTH OF SHEVAT: ELEVATING EATING
& The Holiday of Tu b'Shevat

Each month of the year radiates with a distinct Divine energy and thus unique opportunities for growth, *Tikkun* and illumination. According to the deeper teachings of the Torah, all of these distinct qualities, opportunities and natural phenomena correspond to a certain data set. That is, the nature of each month is elucidated by a specific letter of the Aleph Beis, a tribe, verse, human sense, and so forth. The month of Shevat is particularly connected to food and our relationship to bodily intake. During this month we celebrate Tu b'Shevat, the New Year of the Tree, and aspire to create a proper and physically/emotionally/spiritually healthy relationship with food.

THE MONTH OF IYYAR: EVOLVING THE SELF
& The Holiday of LAG B'OMER

The month of IYYAR is the second month of the spring, a month that connects the Redemption from Egypt in Nissan with the Revelation of Torah in Sivan. The Chai/ Eighteenth day of the Month is the day we celebrate the Rashbi (Rabbi Shimon Bar Yochai) and the revealing of the hidden aspects of the Torah. This is the 'Holiday' of Lag b'Omer.

The book explores the unique quality of this special month, a month that has a Mitzvah of counting the Omer every day. In addition, the book explores the roots and significance of the mystical 'holiday' of Lag b'Omer. Including the customs & Practices of Lag b'Omer, such as, bonfires, bows & arrows, parades, Upsherin, and more.

_____

THE MONTHS OF TAMUZ/AV:
Embracing Brokenness, Transforming Darkness
The Three Weeks: From the 17th of Tamuz until the 9th of Av & Tu b'Av

Each month and season of the year, radiates with distinct Divine qualities and unique opportunities for growth and Tikkun. The summer month of Tamuz and Av contain the longest and hottest days of the year. The raised temperature is indicative of a corresponding spiritual heat, a time of harsher judgement and potential destruction, such as the destruction of the first and second Beis HaMikdash, which began on the 17th of Tamuz and culminated on the 9th & 10th of Av. A few days later, on Tu b'Av, the darkness is transformed and reveals the greatest light and possibility for new life. During these summer months of Tamuz and Av we embrace our brokenness so that we can heal and transform darkness into light.

_____

THE MONTH OF TEVES:

Refining Relationships: Elevating the Body

Each month of the year radiates with a distinct Divine qualities and unique opportunities for growth. The nature of each month is elucidated by a specific letter of the Aleph Beis, a tribe, verse, human sense, and so forth. Teves begins the harsh, cold months of the year, and thus the month of Teves is particularly connected to the physical body and intimate relationships. During this month we also fast on the tenth of the month, Asara b'Teves, a time we mourn and reflect on the beginnings of our collective exiles, and we learn to create a Tikkun

---

NEW!

THE SECRET OF THE MIKVAH

Waters of Transformation

A Mikvah is a pool of water used for the purpose of ritual immersion; a place where one moves from a state of Tumah / impurity, blockage and 'death', to a place of Teharah/ purity, fluidity and life.

This text delves into the depths of wisdom to reveal the secret transformative power of the Mikvah and water. Exploring the nature of Mikvah from multi-dimensional perspectives, from the Peshat (literal observation and Halacha), to the Remez (allegorical), the Derush, (homiletical and philosophical), to the Sod (hidden, Kabbalah and Chassidus). This empowering, insightful and inspirational text, demonstrates how the Mikvah experience can be truly transformative and life-altering.

The text also includes various particle Kavanos / intentions that can be used when immersing in the Mikvah.

www.ingramcontent.com/pod-product-compliance
Lightning Source LLC
Chambersburg PA
CBHW070403100426
42812CB00005B/1620